Paul Weller and Popular Music

Using research, analysis and a range of historical sources, *Paul Weller and Popular Music* immerses the reader in the excitement of Paul Weller's unique creative journey, covering topics such as the artist's position within his field; his creative processes; the contexts in which the music was made; the artist as collaborator; signifiers that mark the trajectory of the music; and formative influences. Focusing on over 40 years of recorded work from 'In the City' to 'Fat Pop (Volume One)', this study explores why Paul Weller's music is widely considered both timeless and of its time, and with reference to a wide range of interviews, reviews and texts, it offers an in-depth critical analysis of Paul Weller's music. It will be of particular interest to scholars and researchers of popular music, popular culture, performance studies and music production.

Andrew West is a Professor and Head of Postgraduate Studies at Leeds Conservatoire, UK.

Ashgate Popular and Folk Music Series

Series Editors:

Lori Burns, Professor, University of Ottawa, Canada

Justin Williams, Associate Professor of Music, University of Bristol, UK

Popular musicology embraces the field of musicological study that engages with popular forms of music, especially music associated with commerce, entertainment and leisure activities. The Ashgate Popular and Folk Music Series aims to present the best research in this field. Authors are concerned with criticism and analysis of the music itself, as well as locating musical practices, values and meanings in cultural context. The focus of the series is on popular music of the twentieth and twenty-first centuries, with a remit to encompass the entirety of the world's popular music.

Critical and analytical tools employed in the study of popular music are being continually developed and refined in the twenty-first century. Perspectives on the transcultural and intercultural uses of popular music have enriched understanding of social context, reception and subject position. Popular genres as distinct as reggae, township, bhangra, and flamenco are features of a shrinking, transnational world. The series recognizes and addresses the emergence of mixed genres and new global fusions, and utilizes a wide range of theoretical models drawn from anthropology, sociology, psychoanalysis, media studies, semiotics, postcolonial studies, feminism, gender studies and queer studies.

One-Track Mind: Capitalism, Technology, and the Art of the Pop Song
Edited by Asif Siddiqi

The British Folk Revival: Second Edition
Michael Brocken

Community-Based Traditional Music in Scotland: A Pedagogy of Participation
Josephine L. Miller

Paul Weller and Popular Music: Identity, Idiolect and Image
Andrew West

For more information about this series, please visit: www.routledge.com/music/series/APFM

Paul Weller and Popular Music

Identity, Idiolect and Image

Andrew West

Routledge
Taylor & Francis Group
LONDON AND NEW YORK

Cover image: © Maaike Ronhaar

First published 2023
by Routledge
4 Park Square, Milton Park, Abingdon, Oxon OX14 4RN

and by Routledge

605 Third Avenue, New York, NY 10158

Routledge is an imprint of the Taylor & Francis Group, an informa business

British Library Cataloguing-in-Publication Data
A catalogue record for this book is available from the British Library

Library of Congress Cataloging-in-Publication Data
A catalog record has been requested for this book

ISBN: 978-0-367-24323-4 (hbk)
ISBN: 978-1-032-36475-9 (pbk)
ISBN: 978-0-429-28173-0 (ebk)

DOI: 10.4324/9780429281730

Typeset in Times New Roman
by KnowledgeWorks Global Ltd.

Contents

Introduction

A singular, evolutionary voice who embodies influence and individuality, since 1977 Paul Weller has moved with and against the times, frequently inspiring and confounding his audiences. In retrospect, the musician and the music are frequently considered both timeless and of their time. As musicologist Stan Hawkins writes, Weller is 'a figure of our age, post-modern and confrontational, he is a veteran of sophistry who makes everything he performs a novelty' (2009: 188). The son of Ann, a part-time cleaner, and John, a taxi driver and builder, Paul was born in Sheerwater, a suburb of the Borough of Woking in 1958. Married twice, firstly to Dee C. Lee and currently to Hannah Andrews, Weller is father to eight children by three separate partners.

Paul was bought a guitar by his parents in his early teens and, from the outset, his father John took on the role of managing his career. Like two of his avowed heroes Ray Davies and John Lennon, much preferring the fantastic to the formal, Paul's teenage years were characterised by uneven moods and problems at school. A self-taught musician, or autodidact, Weller formed his first band, The Jam, in 1972. The Jam served a lengthy apprenticeship, playing at pubs and clubs in their local area, and following the punk boom, Weller, bassist Bruce Foxton and drummer Rick Buckler were signed to a recording contract by the London-based record label Polydor in 1977.

As Spicer notes 'for many artists (The Beatles being probably the most obvious example) it is impossible to categorise them within the boundaries of one particular style; indeed, stylistic eclecticism becomes the defining feature of their music' (2010: 124). Over the past six decades, Paul Weller's words and music have sustained a sense of constant adventure, traversing so many textural iterations that it is impossible to classify him as anything other than a popular music artist. On the achievement of Marcel Proust's 'Remembrance of Things Past', Conrad writes of how Proust was able to convey the notion of a prismatic identity (1998: 66). A stylistic shapeshifter, Weller has acquired a multi-faceted persona.

Particularly in the United Kingdom, but also to lesser degrees in Japan, Europe and America, his music has brought him great success and fame. In his sleeve notes for Weller's 2010 release 'Wake Up the Nation', the novelist

DOI: 10.4324/9780429281730-1

and playwright Irvine Welsh writes that Weller is 'probably the solitary artist from this era to indisputably move into the pantheon of British rock n' roll greats, encompassing Jagger, Richards, Lennon, McCartney, Townshend and Davies, his sixties antecedents, and Bowie, who emerged earlier in the seventies'. Indebted to numerous influences yet immediately identifiable, he is, as his friend and occasional collaborator Robert Wyatt describes him, 'new furniture seasoned from old wood' (Ingham, 1998: 39). In a 2016 interview with Barry Cain, Weller describes his childhood:

> When we lived in Stanley Road, we had no hot water, no bathroom and no central heating, just a coal fire and an outside toilet.... It was a tin bath in front of the fire on a Sunday night.... With everyone bathing in the same water. It was grey by the time I got in but we didn't give it a second thought because that's the way it was. When people started moving out of the slums into decent council estates, the world changed. People became more aspirational.... Working class people would compensate for having nothing by trying to dress up to the nines when we went out.
> (2016: 434)

Speaking in the mid-nineties, Weller describes the predominantly suburban town of Woking as 'the area where I used to play as a kid, the woods around there, the rural side' (Heatley, 1996: 7). In a posthumous thesis, the socio-cultural theorist Lev Vygotsky discusses the significance of childhood experience in facilitating our ability to adapt to what is around us as adults, writing 'When I recall the house where I spent my childhood or the distant lands I have visited in the past, I retrieve impressions that I formed early in my childhood ... my actions do not create anything new, but rather are based on a more or less accurate repetition of something that already exists' (2004: 8). In Weller's music over the years, the bucolic aspects of his childhood environment have similarly facilitated a profoundly deep capacity for using memory to fire exploration.

Occupying a rarefied commercial level with contemporaries Madness and The Police, between 1979 and 1982 The Jam regularly made records that sold over 100,000 copies in the United Kingdom alone. Despite this success, increasingly agitated with fame, Weller's accounts of his time in The Jam portray a steadily increasing lack of fulfilment. Writing in the NME in 1978, journalist John Hamblett describes Weller as 'Chain-smoking, introspective, anxious to communicate.... Charged with something less tangible than physical energy' (1978: 31). As The Jam became more successful, the expectations placed by critics and audiences on Weller's de facto role as 'spokesman for a generation' (Hawkins, 2009: 187) ultimately created what Weller later described as a conveyor belt he 'needed to jump off' (Cain, 2016: 422). Weller's decision to split the band in 1982 was, however, widely unanticipated. Not drawn to nostalgia, Weller has no wish to reform The Jam, reasoning 'I don't want to do the same things in life. I don't want to play the same sort of music all the time. I want to change, I need to change and find something different along the way' (Heatley, 1996: 95).

Among their followers, The Jam left a lasting legacy. In the 2015 film 'About the Young Idea' the consensus held by guest narrators including actor Martin Freeman, is that The Jam had a profound influence, not only on their musical tastes but also on their attitudes towards life. In a typical testimony, Freeman says 'I know every inch of those records, I know every lyric of those records, I know every beat. It is a huge part of who I am'. The following year Weller reflected 'When I speak to old Jam fans from that time, I get to the feeling it meant so much more to them than just a good record; there was a true cultural connection.... We caught the mood of the times, I guess, the zeitgeist or whatever you want to call it' (Cain, 2016: 420). Snowball and Deabill's vivid, democratic account forefronts the fans, who variously explain how 'The Jam certainly helped to create a social, political and psychological foundation.... They were that one special band in mine and a generation's psyche.... They gave me the strength, belief and confidence to feel like I was somebody' (2012: 109, 125, 128). During a social period in the United Kingdom defined by cold war neurosis, domestic poverty and unrest, The Jam sought to turn a desolate mood into a positive one, channelling the hopes of disaffected youths whose outlook appeared bleak.

Initially comprising just Weller and keyboardist Mick Talbot, and marking a significant change of musical and aesthetic direction, The Style Council was formed in early 1983. The first Style Council live appearance, a benefit for CND, was characterised by mud throwing, problems with backstage security and heckling by angry Jam fans. Early recordings were well received, however, and in the Christmas edition of the New Musical Express, Weller declared the year his 'favourite year for years.... I was sick of being judged constantly by everyone.... I have exorcised most of my demons and I am happier for that' (NME, 1983: 27). Noting the intuitive way in which Weller assembled his live band, Ian Munn's book 'Mr. Cool's Dream' chronicles how bass guitarist Anthony Harty 'got the gig by writing to Paul' and how singer Dee C Lee had never heard of The Jam or Weller when she joined. As drummer Steve White, recruited at age 17 reflects: 'I think it was a really inspired move to bring in musicians that were largely unaware of his past because we weren't intimidated' (Munn, 2016: 15, 26, 48–49, 71). Expanding on the theme in 2020, Steve remembers:

> When we set out to tour, we had a female vocalist and a male vocalist. Our female vocalist was a black woman, which doesn't make any difference to me, but back in 1983/1984 it did. Half the band were girls. You do forget how much we've come on in terms of integration and progression. We felt it was a really, really good theme and it was really fresh having a nice mix of cultures and backgrounds and different genders. I think Paul did that deliberately to countenance quite a lot of the testosterone fuel of the The Jam, because that was a very blokey band.

Early Style Council releases were eclectic, with big hits sitting alongside instrumentals and political material co-existing with love songs. Released in 1985, the peak Style Council recording is considered by many to be the LP 'Our Favourite Shop'. In a contemporary interview Weller described the album as:

> Britain today, all that we see around us. There are songs about families breaking up, who have to find work in new areas, new towns where only a façade of real community exists, the disgusting waste of life through heroin. Songs of despair, hope, total realism, luck, selfishness and love.
>
> (Munn, 2016: 102)

Writing in Munn's introduction, Weller's recollection of his time in the band is warm:

> The Style Council for me represents a wonderful time in my life. I was still a young man, still discovering myself as a musician and as a person. I've only got good memories, really.... For me the Style Council will always represent youth, vitality, sunshine, friendships made that have pretty much endured. I loved it.
>
> (ibid.: 10)

Upset at having been released from his record deal by Polydor in 1989, Weller stayed at home to look after his son Nathaniel for a couple of years (Ingham, 1998: 40). In 1991, with no record deal, Weller embarked upon what he later described as a frustrating, but exciting phase spent re-establishing his career. Although an audience of only 240 attended an early solo show at Newport Leisure Centre, by performing incendiary live shows and making increasingly fine records, Weller gradually rebuilt his audience. Integrating the free spirit of The Style Council and the intense focus of The Jam, Weller's music as a solo artist has sustained high quality. As Eccleston notes, 'The change in Weller over recent years, from the fierce, slightly awkward guardian of what felt like a fairly narrow band of musical wavelengths, into a man comfortable discussing Pierre Schaeffer and willing to ponder the depth of 'our ancient roots' is marked' (2020:75). Since 2010 Weller has performed live with the same band line-up, yet conversely his studio recordings typically involve numerous friends and collaborators. As music critic Pete Paphides (2021: 18) writes, 'if Weller likes your new record, you will know it, because he will soon be inviting you to play on one of his'.

1 Identity

1.1 Modernist

Remarkably few high-profile popular music artists in the present century have aligned themselves to modernism, a temporal yet influential movement with its origins in the twentieth century that has crossed continents and evolved through numerous iterations. A notable exception is Paul Weller, who often refers to himself as a modernist in interviews, and is regularly called a modernist by music critics. In his discussion of identity in popular music, Frith observes how 'Identity is not a thing but a process' (Hall and Du Gay, 1996: 110) and in Paul Weller's case, the process of making and sharing music over the past five decades has led him to shape a fluid and progressive modernist identity.

Reviewing one of Weller's live performances for the San Diego Reader, writer Robert Duffy (2015) seems particularly struck by the behaviour of the audience, who appear more interested in his older material. 'Shame' concludes Duffy, 'some of the newer songs were superb. Weller acknowledges that he isn't a tribute act to his past; he's a modernist with a capital M'. In this context, modernism seems to apply to the habit of selecting new over old; present over past. There is a permanence though, as Weller explains:

> My roots are strong, and it's important to remember where you came from. These things define who I am, my background, my upbringing. The whole mod thing helped define who I am, and I guess a lot of it has never really gone for me, and the rules still apply and I still believe in those things.
>
> (Hewitt, 2006: Intro)

In his warmly reflective foreword to Paolo Hewitt's book 'The Soul Stylists: Six Decades of Modernism – From Mods to Casuals', Weller looks back fondly on his late arrival and ultimately pivotal involvement in a distinctly London centric, popular music influenced strand of modernism. As previously noted, aesthetic qualities and principles associated with the terms 'modernist' and 'modernism' move elliptically across time, between

DOI: 10.4324/9780429281730-2

the arts. Whilst it shares a number of key attributes with prior modernist phases, Weller's scene is not to be confused with earlier ones. Uniquely, over the past five decades, Weller's music and style seem somehow to have come to *embody* the term; over time, in a popular music context he has become the modernist around whom other modernists orbit.

Weller defines modernism in terms of a specific look and attitude, his chosen descriptors including: Precision, neatness, streamline, clean; hard, expressive, improvised, rebellious, creative, fresh and fast-changing (Hewitt, 2006: 11–13). In his book on The Who, Cohn (1969: 175–176) characterises Mod as a 'strictly male world and you would see them mooching around in big tribes, their girls trailing forgotten behind them.... And they would dance all by themselves, sunk deep in narcissistic dreams. They didn't smile'. Like Daltrey, Townshend, Entwhistle and Moon, Weller's modernism belongs to a post-war working-class culture 'made for the kids by the kids involved' (ibid.).

Reflecting the divisive nature of subcultural activity as explored by Brake (1985: 8) and further outlined by Chambers in his overview of the numerous factions involved in the shaping of 50s and 60s mod culture – British vs. foreign, modernist vs. non-modernist, functionalist vs. baroque – there is a vivid sense of a malleable 'us and them' dynamic (Chambers, 2002: 50). Significantly, within this polarised dynamic there is fluidity; borne of self-determination, as Weller is keen to stress, modernism is not beholden to money, rather to an autonomous form of aspiration. A modernist is one who acquires energy from progress, who strives to move forward without specific aim or end goal, as Weller concludes:

> It's all made an everlasting impression on me. I took it very seriously and I always will because in a cultural way it has been a huge influence on me. It helped me to find and think of different worlds, different possibilities, different ways that life can be. And it's in that sense that I feel it is a faith. A true one.
>
> (Hewitt, 2006: intro)

Modernism arose as a rebellious movement throughout Europe between 1900 and 1930; one that rejected the moral codes of society and broadly sought to undermine the establishment. Like the popular music modernists of the late sixties who Osborne (2015) describes as preoccupied with onward progress, originality and technological experimentation, modernists of the early twentieth century saw conformity as a means of exerting control over the human spirit. Energised by the sense of freedom created by the innovations of the day, the original modernists sought to embrace an individuality unencumbered by the past. Modernists refused to commit to any one systemic doctrine, but instead lived in constant anticipation of new situations and fresh opportunities. Ultimately, Schleifer (2011) explains, despite having lent its features to hybrid forms under different names dependent upon its surroundings, the essence of modernist philosophy has held through time.

Referring to the movement as it was in the years before Weller became cognisant of it, author Richard Weight (2013) describes the late 50s London modernist aesthetic as a cosmopolitan, affluent and uniquely British melting pot of American, European and Caribbean music and fashion. Proud of the island that brought these influences together, post war, pre-Beatles modernism rebuked the colonial prejudices held by older, more entrenched Britons. Patrick Uden, a London resident at the time, recalls how modernism was essentially eclectic, interweaving such disparate elements as music, car design, fashion and food (Hewitt, 2006: 86). As a British modernist, from a definitive position as a member of an identifiable community, one could be free to explore an unlimited field of interests. At the core of the movement, Weight (ibid.) explains, was a keen sense of ambition borne of a desire to escape from the estates, pits and factories of post war Britain. Chiming with Weller's own definition of the movement, Weight describes modernism as a frame of mind, an immediately recognisable and inclusive club of aspirational, forward-thinking individuals.

In numerous contexts, this inclination to favour one element over another, to curate whatever is on offer by judging it either good or bad without recourse to middle ground, seems key to the modernist way of thinking. Emphasising his own predilection for the definitive, Weller's acknowledgement of artists who emerged as influences during his youth is similarly binary. Bowie, for instance, is namechecked regularly, but not Bolan. Despite the intense interest in black American music shown by such apparently kindred spirits as Eric Clapton and the Rolling Stones, those artists are notable by their absence from Weller's mythology; rather he tends to claim kinship to the streamlined and intense compositional stylings of the Beatles and the Kinks. In modernist circles the role of the curator is central, and as evidenced in the book of quotes edited by Heatley (1996), in terms of Weller's musical tastes, bands and artists are frequently favoured and dismissed at whim.

Like the contemporary New York jazz modernist scene, the initial cultural emphasis in the United Kingdom was on urban living, with scenes developing in the bars and cafes around London's Leicester Square. Interviewed by The Independent, original London modernist and renowned tailor John Simons considers the sartorial element of the UK modernism of the late 1950s to have been a catalyst for a new, previously inaccessible egalitarian tradition (Burrell, 2015). Viewing modernism as inclusive, Simons shares Weller's idea of modernism as membership of a club that never expires; that excludes no one, yet requires adherence to a set of codes; a culture that never changes made of people who seek endless change. Immediately following the seismic intervention of guitar driven popular music, Shuker (2017: 165, 216) recalls that the London modernist subculture circa 1963 comprised mainly of working-class individuals influenced by the urban fashions of young American blacks, and who wore expensive, tailored clothes. Noting the significance of extra musical influences, Shuker (ibid.) identifies a range of distinctive types of mod, some of whom were drawn to the music of The Who and Tamla Motown, while others identified by Anderson (2013) inhabited a scene that revolved around pills and violence.

Reflecting Wellers' creative modus operandi, Little (2014: 98) argues that the key attribute linking all strands of modernism in the arts is the embrace of experimental art. Offering a perspective that resonates with Weller's contemporary modifications of American Soul, Acid Jazz and Krautrock, in his writing on the American popular music of the 1930s, Schleifer (2011: 2, 13, 20, 32) frames modernism as the re-contextualisation of received conventions in an inclusive urban setting. The best popular music of the early twentieth century, argues Schleifer, invented other realities by realising cliché 'so that shared commonplaces can come to seem to be real in a new way'. With urbanity at the core of its identity, the performances of early modernist jazz singers like Billie Holiday made commercial music that somehow refracted the mundanities of everyday life, transforming it into music of social relevance. Where Cole Porter was able to refract and make poetic social issues of the day for American audiences with songs like 'Love for Sale' and 'Anything Goes', Weller was similarly able to do so for UK audiences in the eighties with 'Going Underground' and 'Town Called Malice'. As Rutherford Johnson (2017: 103) writes, 'contemporary composers upset the stability of their musical materials, either to highlight modern anxieties about identity and responsibility or simply to surf the currents that get stirred up'. Elsewhere, in his inventive observational lyric for 'That's Entertainment', Weller's sensory observations of incidents common to the urban English landscape – babies wailing, stray dogs howling, lovers missing the tranquillity of solitude – succeed in turning the commonplace into the rare.

With its connotations of unfettered free expression, improvisation, another of Weller's selected impressions of modernism, might at first appear to sit uneasily with the simultaneously favoured aesthetic of precision. Loosely constructed songs that break away from formal pop structure such as 'Set the House Ablaze' and 'Study in Blue' are, however carefully arranged to *appear* improvised. Here, the listener is invited to perceive the absence of calculation; the sound of expression free of constraint. Elsewhere in Weller's catalogue, concisely structured and arranged songs such as 'Start!' and 'Attic' adhere more closely to the established modernist aesthetic of neatness and precision. Reviewed in tandem, this combination of controlled and uncontrolled expression reflects the culture of calibrated excess earlier identified as typical of sixties modernism by Simons and Anderson.

Focussing on the art of one of Weller's fellow Londoners, Stratton (Bennett and Stratton, 2011: 50) notes how, by 1966, The Kinks' Ray Davies was writing classic songs of social observation and commentary like 'Dedicated Follower of Fashion' and' Sunny Afternoon'. On those song recordings, Stratton observes, Davies theatrically adopts an exaggerated fictitious vocal persona. These linguistic variations, which partially remove the singer from the character, gave Davies the leeway to make overt social commentaries in a manner later used by Randy Newman, who, with his update of 'Old Kentucky Home' adopted a caricature role to lacerate an identified villain of contemporary American society. In contrast, Weller's approach to his performing style is never exaggerated; instead, he sings in his own voice as 'Billy Hunt', as himself to the fictional protagonist 'Mr. Clean' and as himself observing 'The Man in The Corner Shop'. Where the imaginative approaches of Ray Davies and Randy Newman are playful and use embodiment to acquire satirical punch, true to his own modernist code, Weller's approach emphatically adheres to his own persona.

Much of Weller's musical identity is rooted in the way he fuses his uniquely urban, observational lyric writing with other, often recognisable stylistic modes. As told to David Simpson of the Guardian in 2014, Roger McGuinn and David Crosby's accounts of how 'Eight Miles High' was written, acknowledge how the basis for the composition came from a combination of influences provided by Ravi Shankar and John Coltrane, whose tapes had been playing on The Byrds bus during a tour of America. Initially, McGuinn recalls using his Rickenbacker guitar to create a recurring phrase in response to Coltrane's track 'India'; this motif can be heard within the hypnotic structure of the recording, which fuses west coast guitar pop and Jazz to develop a distinctive folk psychedelia. Drawn from the past, these unlikely external influences were the building blocks upon which the lived experiences of McGuinn, Crosby and fellow bandmate Gene Clark (involving among other things aeroplane travel, and being caught in rainstorms) were able to create an artefact that seemed at the time to be startlingly unique. Whilst listeners heard an expression bordering on the futuristic, for the authors of 'Eight Miles High' the process involved no perceptible attempt to leap towards originality, rather it reflected a coherently realised process involving the amalgamation of a series of unrelated yet juxta-positionally effective external and internal felt experiences. As such, the song's unique power, the aspect of its creation that links it to Weller's best work, is rooted in the skilful judgement of those involved in selecting and sifting the chance encounters that come together to form a single encounter.

Coincidentally, the music that inspired much of Weller's early work with The Jam was made at the same time as the music that informs many of the textures used on his post 2006 solo work. Stockhausen's 'Hymnen', a contemporary of the Beatles' 'Strawberry Fields Forever', for example, is identified by Holmes (2002: 279) as influential upon Can and Tangerine Dream; Krautrock pioneers whose synthesisers, grooves and tonal dis-colourations stylistically embellish later period Weller songs like 'Moonshine' and 'Woo Se Mama'. Again, the modernist impulse to curate is at play. Confident in the knowledge that these borrowed sounds and textures have never met *these* songs or the voice of *this* author before, they are selected to reimagine what has already been.

Like the original modernists described by Little (2014), Weller's modernism has always sought to be forward looking. Writing at the outset of the modernist era in 1913, Italian Futurist painter and author of the book on musical aesthetics 'The Art of Noises', Luigi Russolo argued that the parameters of Greek music theory and Gregorian chant were fast becoming obsolete as a means of capturing the sounds familiar to the public as inhabitants of the natural world; that the traditional instruments of the time were incapable of reflecting the multiplicity of noises being generated by industrial development. With his exhortations to overthrow all music that can be anticipated, Russolo comes across as a kindred spirit to Weller, whose musical directions and live sets remain notoriously hard to anticipate.

In his constant quest to distil and update the essence of his own individual sound, Weller seems to have been driven to expand the palette of sounds available to him during each of the three phases of his recording career. On The Jam's valedictory album 'The Gift', horns were added to accentuate the trio line-up; multiple voices were drafted into the Style Council's final live sets at the Royal Albert Hall; and from '22 Dreams' onwards programmed sounds that defy instrumental categorisation inhabit the musical spectrum. For the modernist, endless movement is essential; as Reynolds advises in his polemic on the subject of noise: 'forget subversion. The point is self-subversion, overthrowing the power structure in your own head' (2005: 57).

Reflecting the impermanence of these multiple shifts of sound and aesthetic, in her article 'Modernism vs. Classicism: Paul Weller Interviewed', Valerie Siebert (2014) asks the reader:

> Which is your favourite Paul Weller? The extremely serious teen thrashing away on a Rickenbacker? The mop-haired rocking modfather? The earthy, pastoral psychedelic? The Arty soul singer? The angry luddite? Well, it doesn't matter really, because in case you hadn't noticed, those Paul Wellers are all dead and gone.... His work, like his attitude, is a constantly shifting thing, never made to order.

Discussing the work of Sara Cohen, whose 1991 ethnographic study of Liverpool musicians focuses on the value of popular music as a local resource, Bennett (2000: 56–57) identifies the writing of songs as 'the product of local knowledges and sensibilities and a form of independent cultural territory'. Songs simultaneously capture the temporal atmospheric of the place in which they were made while refracting that mood through the unknowable natures of those who make them. Writing half a century earlier for the New York Times in his polemic 'A Modernist Defends Modern Music' (1949), the composer Aaron Copland explains how Modernist compositions are at once recognisable yet strange and different:

> A composer writes music to express and communicate and put down in permanent form certain thoughts, emotions and states of being.

> These thoughts and emotions are gradually formed by the contact of the composer's personality with the world in which he lives. He expresses these thoughts ... in the musical language of his own time. The resultant work of art should speak to the men and women of the artist's own time with a directness and immediacy of communicative power that no previous art expression can give.... My love of the music of Chopin and Mozart is as strong as that of the next fellow, but it does me little good when I sit down to write my own, because their world is not mine and their language not mine.

Perhaps in terms of their quest to capture something of the essence of their immediate environment, Copland and Weller have some equivalence of intent. However, unlike his American predecessor, who upholds the modernist ideal of not looking back to move forwards, threads of Weller's music often transparently hark back to earlier times. For Weller, looking back is useful as a means of rediscovering roots, of curating moments to convey temporal moods. The sources are often an amalgamation of recognisable threads, but the shaping of those materials draws them into the here and now.

Like the Beatles, who appropriated elements of Nina Simone's 'My Baby Just Cares for Me' and Howlin' Wolf's 'Killing Floor' into 'Penny Lane' and 'Lady Madonna' respectively, Weller sees the black urban American musical backdrop, with its subliminal promise of escape, as an ideal setting for narratives on modern English modernity. As Shank (Frith, Straw and Street, 2001: 256) explains, white fascination with black music goes back a long way beyond Elvis, and Weller's formative influences are immediately obvious; early covers pay homage to black American soul icons Larry Williams, Martha Reeves and Wilson Pickett. Symptomatic of what Chambers (2002: 50) calls the unfailing presence of transatlantic inspiration in UK male subculture, at the time of recording in the late seventies, from Weller's perspective those early covers perhaps express a dimension of his identity better than one of his own songs could. By dealing with subjects of love and leisure difficult to make authentic in the youthful white English tongue, they act as a counterpoint to more introspective original songs about identity and conflict. Ultimately, they help to paint a more complete picture by resolving a perceived deficit. This effect recurred later, as Paphides writes of the Style Council era: 'When Weller wanted to find a means of providing spiritual uplift with gospel directness, he had to borrow songs by other singers – 'Move on Up', 'Promised Land' – to do it' (2021: 18).

Discussing the reintroduction of music hall stylings into the popular music scene of the late sixties, Stratton (Bennett and Stratton, 2011: 46, 48) observes how, as a means of contextualising and adding value to rock n' roll, music hall variety styles increasingly pervaded rock performances. One example of this is 'Something Happened to Me Yesterday' on the Rolling Stones (1967) album 'Between the Buttons'; here the Rolling Stones go back in musical time as they celebrate pharmaceutical effects. Stratton notes how, at around the same time, the Beatles looked for a way forward by writing and recording the fondly nostalgic 'When I'm Sixty-Four'(ibid.) and soon after, The Kinks released 'Village Green Preservation Society', a pop album laced with references to iconic English nostalgia. A working-class English pop obsessive familiar with music hall as a component of his surrounding culture, Weller occasionally leans towards the style, latterly on 'Equanimity' but particularly and perhaps most poignantly in his early work. Unlike his predecessors, who use music hall variety to frame lyrics that evoke a quaint English nostalgia, where similar musical stylings intermittently occur in Weller's music, the lyric theme is invariably darker and more concerned with endings. On the string quartet arrangement of 'Smithers Jones', at the end of his working life the lead figure in the song faces the bleak prospect of redundancy, whilst on 'Little Boy Soldiers' the plaintive waltz-time middle section offsets a lyric that confronts the deathly harsh realities of colonialism. Where the Beatles, The Rolling Stones and The Kinks seek comfort in going back, Weller seems to caution against it.

Participants in a psychological study by Kawakami et al. (2013) found that listeners to sad music perceived the tragedy in the music, but that it tended to make them feel positive in response. Perhaps this helps to explain why there are so many popular music songs with lyrics that focus on heartbreak; as a community of listeners, we are, it seems attracted to the sound of turmoil. Expanding on this duality, Russell (1997: 139, 140) writes about the escapism sought by thousands of working-class people who were happy to be entertained by the music hall songs of the late nineteenth and early twentieth century, many of which, like Weller's songs, sugar coated grim realities. UK popular music audiences, it seems, have a long tradition of volunteering to view social turmoil through the allegorical prism of music, a tradition that extends in a variety of ways through Weller compositions such as 'Just Who Is The 5 O' Clock Hero', 'Money Go-Round' and '7 and 3 is the Striker's Name'.

Huron (2006: 33) identifies a number of musical devices used to evoke a humorous reaction; these include material that is incongruous; oddly mixed; drifting; disruptive and implausible. Like the Beatles elegiac and troubled yet ultimately optimistic 'You Never Give Me Your Money', a feature of Weller's (2010) song 'Trees' is that it possesses all of the attributes cited by Huron yet at the same time it embodies a unique compositional identity to circle and confront the reality of loss. A curatorial pick and mix that alternates haphazardly between rock and music hall, 'Trees' is a meditation on death inspired by the passing of his father John. Fiercely modernist in its freewheeling introspection, subversion of form and ambition to confound expectation, it stands among the truly great songs in Weller's catalogue. Writing at the time of its release, Weller describes 'Trees' as:

> Written as a poem after visiting my father in a rest/respite for people waiting for God, or whatever you believe comes next. I tried to imagine

> the old people's lives, when they were young and fit and active, making love, having babies. I wanted to believe they were all just waiting to be replanted back into earth where, once again, they would stand tall and be at peace.
>
> (2010: 186)

Modernists, claims Hewitt (2006: 87), 'had no problem mixing other cultures into their own.... One of their credos was simple; if it's good – take it, wherever it's from'. Weller's music, always on the move, ever seeking new pastures, is anchored by the permanence of his self-identification as a modernist; the sole constant feature. His writing and recording career can be viewed as having moved from streamlined to diverse twice; from the punchy and lean early Jam compositions to the sprawling, searching late Style Council and then again from the streamlined guitar band arrangements of early solo Weller to the multi-layered and exploratory later solo works. Essentially, neither trajectory observes, or could have the capacity to observe *all* of Weller's self-prescribed codes of modernism, rather his entire output moves across the modernist dial, allowing him to indulge the particular elements of modernism that apply to his life at any particular time. To cite Frith's essay on Music and Identity, 'Making music isn't a way of expressing ideas; it is a way of living them' (Hall and Du Gay, 1996: 111). By this means the music is invariably authentic, always true to its originator's core identity as it spins unpredictably across the multiple facets of modernism.

1.2 Londoner

> In 1993, London's gross domestic product was around 18% of the national GDP ... greater, in fact, than the national output of all but the world's 20 richest countries. A city with the capacity to generate wealth on such a scale does not need to endure overfilled railway carriages, understocked classrooms, decaying social services, underfunded libraries, neglected housing estates or families living in firetrap bed-and-breakfast accommodation. These things are a matter of choice, not necessity.
>
> (Inwood, 1998: 937)

Inwood's quote speaks to the heart of Weller's London, a city of inexhaustible impetus in a country described in the sixth century by the monk and historian Gildas as 'stiff with icy cold'; 'involved in the thick darkness of black night'; a country in which 'the landscape is always black' (Ackroyd, 2004: 39). By way of contrast, in the mid-nineties, Weller said of the London of his youth: 'It was where it was happening. London was a special day out; you'd only go couple of times a year which made it even more magical' (Du Noyer, 1995: 26). This sense of wonder has stayed with him; in the 2010 Julien Temple film 'Find the Torch' Weller surveys the central London district of St. James, alerting the camera to places where The Beatles and The Rolling Stones would gather to socialise. Clearly, for him such places are hallowed ground. According to Chiswick label owner Ted Carroll, because they were out of town boys at the time of their emergence on the capital scene, The Jam were seen by Londoners as yokels (Wilson, 2018: 79). Concurrently, London society was experiencing a feminist revival alongside struggles to assert rights of minorities, especially gays and blacks; in the fabric of the capital to which Weller was so in thrall, a series of social reckonings were in play (White, 2008: 345).

Physically and thematically, the identity of many of Weller's recordings is steeped in London. In the late seventies, 'In the City' and 'This is The Modern World' were recorded just off Oxford Street in Central London; 'All Mod Cons' at Eden in Chiswick, 'Setting Sons' and 'Sound Affects' at Townhouse in Shepherds Bush and 'The Gift' at George Martin's Air Studios. The Style Council recorded at Weller's Solid Bond in Marble Arch, on the street where The Jam recorded their first two albums. The effect of recording in London is difficult to gauge, but an argument could be made for a link between the taut earlier recordings recorded 'on the clock' in the capital and the stylistic sprawl and textural variation of the later tracks made in the countryside with less heed to time. Since 1993, Weller has opted to record outside London, preferring the peace of mind and perspective afforded by studios in rural Oxfordshire, Somerset, Berkshire and for the past few albums at his own Black Barn studio in Ripley, Surrey.

Although born and raised 23 miles to the southeast of London's Charing Cross, Weller's identity as a London musician is imprinted through song and biography. His identity as a Londoner is inevitably tied to his singing accent, which is an unaffected extension of his speaking voice. Reflecting on the writing of 'You Really Got Me', Kinks lead singer Ray Davies recalls:

> When I wrote the song as a teenager, I thought I was writing something John Lee Hooker or Howlin' Wolf could record. I was just a honky from North London so what did I know? I always sought out a great riff, but I would put my own spin on it thereafter in order to retain some originality. I sang in my London accent, which in many ways separated my band from the rest.
>
> (2013: 19–20)

Similarly, Weller's recordings have musical and textural subtexts that evoke a panoply of settings, yet are drawn to a particular place of origin by Weller's voice. 'In the City', 'A Bomb in Wardour Street' and 'Strange Town' are immediately and unmistakeably set in London, and 'Down in the Tube Station at Midnight' is similarly impossible to relocate. Written and recorded decades later, 'Fast Car Slow Traffic' and 'The Cranes Are Back' are later period examples of urban impression and observation. Each of these songs differ in tempo, structure and lyric theme; there is no immediately obvious compositional code, linear perspective or 'London sound'. This is unsurprising since, in the popular music era alone, the variety of styles and identities of London bands is vast; Culture Club, Free, Motorhead, The Police, Status Quo, The Yardbirds; each immediately identifiable yet stylistically disparate. To identify Weller as a London musician is at one to locate his work and to place his music within a vast and ever evolving cultural panoply. As Bradley observes, the key is for London music is to *interact* with its environments, rather than exist as a hermetically sealed subculture (2013: 14). Reflecting the prevalent social conditions, popular music songs about London tell us something of the way its inhabitants have perceived it over time.

At the time of Weller's birth in Woking in 1958, London was long accustomed to insularity, discontent, the rich and the poor, the new and the old. Following the Abercrombie Plan of 1943, many Londoners had moved to growth points 30 or more miles from the centre of London and retained economic links to the centre. Ackroyd (2001: 757–758) explains how the greenbelt and the new towns, characterised by endless movement, caused Londoners to look inwards rather than outwards. There was a feeling of discontent, primarily with the post-war hierarchy and its inherent repression, but also with the perceived shabbiness and dreariness of London. Also noting the vivid contrasts of glamour and despair between inner and outer environs, reflecting on his childhood in Paddington in central London, Elvis Costello characterises his locale as 'Accommodation for a population passing through and out to the suburbs'. He writes:

> The street outside smelt of manure, there were Rag and bone men and milk deliveries by horse-drawn floats. By contrast In East Twickenham a neighbour is a glamorous woman with a blonde ponytail who drives a red sports car and there are nightmarish neighbours who give threats and abuse.
>
> (2016: 82–85)

White relates how, in the 1950's, the 2I's coffee bar in Old Compton Street, owned by Paul Lincoln, an Australian professional wrestler otherwise known as Doctor Death, was the first to give talented young working-class Londoners a stage that successfully projected them from Soho to the wider world. Tommy Steele, Cliff Richard, Adam Faith, Joe Brown and Johnny Kidd were among the artists whose skiffle and rock'n'roll were discovered and launched to a mass audience. Café Society and musical performance were closely interlinked in Soho culture, and in the 1960's an inexhaustible cast list of working-class talent was pitched into worldwide stardom. The emergence on the global stage of David Bailey, Terrence Donovan, Terence Stamp, Michael Caine, The Rolling Stones, The Kinks, Twiggy, The Pretty Things, Helen Shapiro and The Small Faces led to Time magazine proclaiming London as 'The swinging city' in 1966 (ibid: 340–342).

Many rising stars dissolved in the firmament, and a significant category of popular song portrays London as a cauldron, both welcoming and unwelcoming to inhabitants and strangers alike. With characteristic duality, Weller's 'Strange Town' conveys a warning and an invitation; I'm here but you shouldn't be. Perhaps counter intuitively, in a metropolis of ten million, in London, the feeling of not being at home is a common one. Porter (2000: 852) writes that between 1961 and 1966, almost as many incomers arrived in London from Ireland as from the rest of mainland Britain, with many settling in Kilburn, Willesden and Cricklewood. Gregarious in cultural outlook, the Irish brought dancehalls, pubs, clubs and festivals into London culture. Poles were initially considered by many Londoners to be a community of exiles, since unlike many Irish they tended to long to return to Poland. An influx of Greek Cypriots settled in Islington, Hackney and Camden, and by 1991 the London Cypriot population was equal to a fifth of the population of Cyprus. Starting with those who arrived on the SS Empire Windrush in 1948, a Jamaican community settled in Brixton and by 1961, there were 172,000 West Indian Londoners from Jamaica, Barbados, Trinidad and British Guiana. Many were skilled white-collar workers, forced into unskilled labour who faced discriminatory landlords and ended up scattered around poorer inner London suburbs.

Crime continued to rise in London in the 1960s and 1970s as teenage boys felt a sense of failure in a meritocratic and materialistic society which prized educational and career success and the accumulation of goods, and began to look for a way out (Porter, 2000: 863–864). Hooliganism against parental authority and middle-aged standards grew. Weller's invented character 'Billy Hunt' is an escapist of the fabulist kind, a dreamer of schemes that will one day see him rise up against authority. Elsewhere, in 'Going Underground', the narrator seeks to escape from the nightmare of braying sheep, lies and ammunition. Similarly agoraphobic and loved by the public in perpetuity, in The Kinks 'Waterloo Sunset' Ray Davies hides, happy to view the world from his window as evening approaches. In each instance the singer/narrator escapes into a trap of sorts. Similarly, for other songwriters, escape from the cauldron comes through intoxication. In 'Blessed' by Simon and Garfunkel, the singer blesses the meth drinkers, pot smokers, and illusion dwellers of Soho, a congregation of which he is a member. Set in East London's Manor Park, Small Faces 'Itchycoo Park' extols the virtues of pot smoking and admiring nature. In contrast, true to the sense of wonder in which he holds the capital, Weller's songs of escape never stray from clear-eyed agency.

By the time of Weller's arrival on the London scene as a musician, Ackroyd explains, 'The commercial infrastructure of the music business … was already in place. In all areas of this teenage revolt, in fact, the youths themselves were exploited by a vast commercial project. It was a very London undertaking' (2001: 759). White explains how, in the mid-1970s purpose adapted halls and upstairs rooms in Victorian pubs like The Hope and Anchor in Islington and the George Robey in Finsbury Park suited the more oppositional music of the punk era and its various offshoots. In 1976, Weller saw The Sex Pistols at the Lyceum, while The Jam played at venues including The Roxy in Covent Garden, the Red Cow in Hammersmith and the Nashville Rooms in West Kensington. By 1986, the London music fan could choose from 100 gigs on any Friday, Saturday and Sunday night, and too late for The Style Council, whose song 'Internationalists' lamented the sense of isolationism pervading English life in the eighties, the nineties saw the rediscovery of the United Kingdom as a global culture hub (White, 2008: 347, 350).

As Ackroyd (2001: 754–755, 763) writes, in the seventies London was becoming, in a demographic sense, once more a young city … a younger society in rebellion against the limitations and restrictions of the post-war capital. 40% of the population were under 25, a statistic that made its way into Weller's clarion call 'In the City'. Alongside this youth explosion, in the 1970s some of the old problems of London reasserted themselves, dock trade with the Commonwealth decreased and docks closed down, leading to a loss of trade and provoking a general sense of dismay and anxiety. London lost its vivacity and much of its energy. In an affirmation of London's egalitarian instincts, the Greater London Council funded new community projects, with the emphasis resting on the vulnerable and the marginalised. From Weller's perspective in the late seventies, the fate of the culture of the capital continued to be in play, the outcome of competing visible and palpable tensions unsettled.

Typically filmic in detail, Weller's early London songs are often about him as an individual out of place. He finds himself in claustrophobic, alienating and threatening circumstances; his narrators often somewhere they shouldn't be. In these songs, Weller rarely seeks to physically draw us *into* the action; rather he invites us to view him experiencing some kind of revelatory episode; we watch the outsider from the outside. Londoners themselves are invited to recognise the authenticity of the work as a reflection of their lived experience, while for those unfamiliar with London the songs are a series of evocative and visceral postcards. The task of the songwriter as communicator becomes complex; to convey personal, communal and narrative lines of meaning in ways that aim to transcend time and place. Many of Weller's songs about London were written and recorded at a time when, as Ackroyd reports:

> The age of the boutique and the discotheque was also the age of the tower block, of public vandalism and increased crime…. The tower blocks, and the property speculators, and the Garish factions, all contributed to the mood of an implicit and explicit aggression … the later waves of youthful protest, from the hippies and flower children of the late 1960s to the punks of the 1970s, manifested confusion and anxiety in a highly unsettled urban society.
>
> (2001: 759–761)

Fellow historian Porter chronicles the times with similarly bleak prose, explaining how derelict buildings in the Docklands were redeveloped, but the wealth created did not trickle down to the under-skilled, unqualified or London's black communities. Consequently, there were more futures in low paid service work. Violent riots in Brixton led to escalating racial tension, and meanwhile The National Front, British Movement and British National Party were active in the East End and Southall. Violent tension between Asians and skinheads led to a race relations crisis of multiple conflicting dimensions, exacerbated by mass employment, heavy and repeated reductions in social spending, and high-profile allegations of racial prejudice within the police force (2000: 911, 918, 921, 923).

1980's London saw a widening of the gap between entitled and disenfranchised in which the poor were blamed for a lack of economic recovery, a dynamic that provided much impetus for 'Our Favourite Shop'. With the establishment of the International Stock Exchange and Global Finance Centre came a boom-and-bust economy and the decade which saw the emergence of yuppies also saw the re-emergence of street beggars (Ackroyd, 2001: 763, 765, 767). Within this setting, three songs written by Shane Mac Gowan and recorded by The Pogues romanticise the capital, offering poetic glimpses of spectacular heights and deep, dark crevices. 'London Girl', 'Rainy Night in Soho' and 'London You're a Lady' are celebrations of earthly delights that find their narrator voluntarily interred within the scarred glories of the city. Key to their lasting authenticity, while romanticising the English capital, these songs are unflinching in their portrayal of London as an uneven and unforgiving place.

Linton Kwesi Johnson's part-spoken, part sung 'New Crass Massahkah' is a raw meditation on racially motivated arson in 1981 that took the lives of 13 young black people. Written from a third person perspective, as outsiders we are drawn into the tragedy by the authors insistence that it could happen to any of *us*. Similarly positioning the listener at close quarters, 'Guns of Brixton' by The Clash asks the listener what they will do when their front door is kicked in. While 'New Crass Massahkah' surveys its theme in the past tense and 'Guns of Brixton' threatens the portent of trouble in the future, Weller's 'A Bomb in Wardour Street' conveys a stricken sense of immediacy in the present tense. Similarly set in the here and now, The Clash's 'London's Burning' and 'London Calling' are vivid tales of apocalyptic reportage from the frontline. Differing in perspective to encompass anger, mournfulness, dread, immediacy and warning, each song provides an authentic snapshot of the turmoil of life in London in the late seventies and early eighties.

Some songwriters seek to portray London in idyllic, warm tones. 'Mario's Café' by St. Etienne finds warmth in the cauldron of the capital, as does John and Beverley Martin's unblemished 'Primrose Hill'. In his autobiography of David Bowie, Trynka writes of how the young Bowie would spend afternoons walking around Fitzrovia and other quiet elegant Georgian streets around Manchester Square; magpie trips from which he would return with books (2010: 76). Similarly, in his autobiography Mike Scott of The Waterboys portrays a magical evocation of Notting Hill, of long afternoons spent imbibing history and writing songs surrounded by iconic imagery (2012: 67). Conversely, when it comes to portraying the capital in song, many other songwriters cast London as a scene of alienation. The Clash's 'White Man in Hammersmith Palais' sets the narrator as a lone individual in an overwhelming expanse, a theme that echoes Nick Drake's earlier bleak mediation on the loneliness of the city, 'Parasite'. By contrast, Weller's London is typically portrayed in song as a place of violent and nervous electricity.

Written and recorded in the early eighties, The Pogues 'The Dark Streets of London' and 'Old Main Drag' are written from the perspective of their downtrodden and impoverished narrator, who initially recalls happier times and contrasts this reverie with the harsh reality of the present time in which his good looks are ruined, and among other ailments, he is 'buggered to damnation'. Maudlin and melancholic, the imagery is infused with nostalgia, a quality that sets it aside from Weller's London songs, which tend to be framed in the here and now. Verse one of Weller's evocative 'Down in the Tube Station at Midnight' sets the scene, a tube station cold and uninviting, littered with papers and wrappers, a place most people pass through on their way to somewhere else. The sharpness of the observed detail confirms that he, the narrator is there; the drama is unfolding in real time, in the present tense. The story of 'Down in the Tube Station at Midnight' unfolds chronologically across verses two and three, the action unfolding with an increasing sense of terror, leading to its violent denouement. As a portrait of London, its message is clear; don't come close.

A London band for the entire duration of their recording career, in 1967, The Beatles used portraiture to capture a fleeting impression of London life with Paul McCartney's homage to a meter maid, 'Lovely Rita'. Originally intended as an anti-authority satire to encapsulate the contemporary public resentment of figures employed to give unwanted parking fines, the lyric to 'Lovely Rita' was redrafted when McCartney decided 'it would be better to love her' (Miles, 1997: 320). With a similar thematic duality, Lily Allen's celebration of pimps and crack whores 'LDN' observes the mugging of an elderly lady with upbeat music and gleeful humour. In both instances the light balances the shade, moments of bleakness are measured against moments of bliss. Contrastingly minor chordal and downtempo, Weller's portrait of the fictional commuter 'Mr. Clean' portrays an object of prosodic and myopic scorn, an emblem of cultural statis whose life of conformity Weller would like to violently disrupt. Unequivocal and free of subtext, the author's ire is palpable and direct.

In the 1980s, At the expense of historical sites including Printing House Square, Caledonian Market and St. Luke's Hospital, great fortunes were made in London by property developers building modern dwellings in London Wall, Centrepoint, Elephant and Castle. As Ackroyd describes it, in 'a deliberate act of erasure, the past had become a foreign country', with the Canary Wharf development exemplifying 'the aesthetic incoherence within which the city has flourished' (2001: 759, 760, 765). In a process of gentrification, many working-class properties were bought and improved, often with financial help, by entrepreneurs or middle-class owners. This led to an influx of wealthier citizens to the city, reversing the previous trend established in the 1950s, and displacing the working classes (Porter, 2000: 881). Written for 'The Gift' LP in 1982, Weller's 'The Planners Dream Goes Wrong' eviscerates the lunatics who left out human beings in their housing schemes. Here, screaming babies, the infirm elderly and the petty thieves who inhabit stinking hall-ways and broken-down lifts inherit the unwanted legacy of frivolous government plans. Sardonically, entwining the apocalyptic with the mirthful, the music has a calypso brightness that evokes carnival. Inspired by Canary Wharf, Radiohead's 'Fake Plastic Trees' surveys the exhaustion of living in a world of increasing artifice, the pervading dominance of pseudo over real. Adapting a forward-looking perspective to update 'The Planners Dream Goes Wrong' Weller's 'The Cranes Are Back' is a song of optimism, as he told John Lewis of Uncut magazine:

> It's a reaction to how the world is. In some cultures, when cranes – the birds – are back, it's a sign of good fortune. But I was also thinking about the mechanical cranes, when you see them back in the city, it normally means industry and business is starting up again. It's a song of hope, really.
>
> (2017: 65)

By the late eighties and early nineties, new generations of immigrants were resident in the capital; the 1991 consensus has London's non-white population as 1.3 million or 20% of the population. By 1989 about 70,000 were homeless. The collapse of manufacturing, high costs of renting, high labour turnover and a shortage of skilled labour added to the social flux, and the rise of tourism and the service economy brought an increased aura of transience. Office employment moved away from the city, and within this amorphous set of circumstances created by forces of unquantifiable, near invisible pervasive globalism, a sense of dilution made it increasingly difficult to identify or untangle issues (Porter, 2000: 882, 895, 902, 935). From the perspective of the songwriter, themes became harder to evaluate or elucidate with certainty.

As Mike Scott of The Waterboys writes of his return to London after a decade away:

> London itself changed. Everything seemed several degrees cruder, brasher and more loveless than I remembered. To my 1995 eyes, London looked insane. In the 10 years since I'd left, the city had morphed into a playground of beer bellied men with shirts hanging out and dyed blonde cropped hair in the style of troubled footballer Gazza, drinking in the

> open air and spilling across the street like tribes of boorish overgrown babies.... The cultural wars of the 50s and 60s were lost and the youth of the nation strode forth as identikit-clad money hungry business bastards.... London had sold its soul and its civic spaces to the marketing industry. Living in the heart of the metropolis was like walking through a giant promo display.
>
> (2012: 253)

As Ackroyd acknowledges, 'London has always been an ugly city. It is part of its identity. It has always been rebuilt, demolished and vandalised' (2001: 760). This formlessness is given expressive emphasis in 'Crushed Bones' by Why? which sets a bleak lyric portrait within an angular and awkward musical framework. In the London of 'Crushed Bones' it rains in July, sirens yelp like a helpless dog and the eyes of inhabitants are piss-holes in the snow. The rushed meter of the vocal evokes the frantic movement of inner London, and lacking any motific or lyric hook, the recording challenges the listener to keep up with it. Ultimately, the effect is of disorientation, of an inability to locate bearings. Conveying London as an unwieldy, improvised machine, Weller's 'Fast Car Slow Traffic' possesses a similar aesthetic.

Filmed in London in 2010, Julien Temple's film 'Find the Torch' follows Weller as he walks around London, imaginatively capturing the singer from distant cameras as he relays his thoughts on what he sees. Elsewhere in the film Weller's image is beamed onto walls in the capital, evoking a watchful presence over passers-by as they go about their daily lives.

Market stall owners and cabbies complain about post-recession conditions, inflation, congestion charges and the bilious bankers who populate the streets after working hours. Perhaps reflecting the good fortune of his trade, Weller tends to see wonderment where others see strife, admiring the modernist look of a storefront sign and observing how in London 'There's always history.... Something to see that you haven't seen before'. Ever the Beatle devotee, Weller recalls how his first flat in London was just off Baker Street, around the corner from Apple Boutique. Back then, he remembers London was full of filthy pubs and xenophobia but possessed a sense of community that no longer exists. Emphasising the contradictory nature of the capital, Weller observes how life has become quicker and more complicated, and how Londoners, have become nicer to each other while simultaneously becoming more suspicious of each other. An impression is made that Weller is acutely aware that London is, has been and always will be home to an infinite array of contradictions. Of the old and the new London, he concludes 'I think they can co-exist'. As Ackroyd (2001: 765) observes, 'Perhaps London's destiny is to represent the contradictions of the human condition, both as an example and as a warning'. In the words of historian Stephen Inwood (1998: 937):

> London is, as it always was, a city of spectacular contrasts. It is the richest and poorest city in the country. It is a town with innumerable

entertainments and pleasures ... (yet) also suffers from the prevailing social, economic and environmental maladies of its age on a colossal scale.... The challenge now, as ever, is to apply a share of London's vast economic and intellectual resources to solving its enormous social and environmental problems.

1.3 Activist

In shaping a metanarrative, or story to accompany musical activities, many popular musicians never declare an interest in activism. For many it is not an aspect of identity they wish to share, and for others it threatens to divide audiences. Activism in music has a long history, however, and remains prominent around the globe; contemporary examples include the 'Save the Palace' campaign focussed on preservation of music heritage in Melbourne (Bennett and Strong, 2018) and Beyonce, Kendrick Lamar and Kesha's politically aware, technology and social media driven interventions against the Trump administration's reactionary initiatives (King, 2019). Some contemporary activism is more sonic than social, for example The 1975's 2019 album 'Notes on a Conditional Form', which features a monologue by the Swedish environmental activist Greta Thunberg, and in the wake of protests against Hong Kong's extradition bill, Thomas dgx yhl's 'Glory to Hong Kong', a composition so influential it was described in the Hong Kong media as 'a new national anthem' (Westcott Grant, 2020).

In the digital era, the global reach of such forms of activism makes Bernie Rhodes' Situationists International slogans, repackaged for use by The Clash in 1977, seem relatively parochial. To Weller, however, The Clash lead singer Joe Strummer was an activist he could identify with, and in a 2013 interview with Daniel Rachel, Weller describes the emergence of The Clash as his generations 'wake-up call'. The Clash, he explained, were 'writing about society, about teenagers, being bored, just things you could relate to. I was really influenced by a lot of the things Joe Strummer sang; it was so different; no group had ever said it before' (Rachel, 2016: 21). Encouraged towards reactionary polemic by The Clash, in March 1977 Weller told the NME, that he would vote Tory at the next election. In hindsight, he would come to regret his actions, later reflecting 'I was 18, it was our first big interview. I really wanted the trendies to hate us and I succeeded. It was a mistake' (ibid: 348–349).

Cited by Solt (1989: 176), John Lennon asserts 'I think our society is run by insane people for insane objectives .... I think we're being run by maniacs for maniacal ends.... if it gets to destruction, you can count me out. But I'm not sure, you know, I'm human, and I'm liable to change depending on the situation'. In keeping with their efforts to present an ambiguous political front, in the summer of 1977 The Jam played pro Jubilee concerts and used a union jack backdrop (Poulsen, 2005: 176). Startled by the negative response of fans to the NME interview, Weller sought to steer clear of overtly political discussion in the print media until 1979, when the effusively political 'Eton Rifles' drew critical attention.

In 'About the Young Idea' (2015) Weller explains that 'Eton Rifles' is a parable based on Orwell's 'Animal Farm', a fiction based on Soviet politics. Weller's fiction is similarly modelled on a real dynamic, in this instance the Right to Work march in the late seventies. In storytelling terms, the similarity between 'Animal Farm' and 'Eton Rifles' lies in the ultimate conclusion that the revolution is doomed to fail. Speaking decades later, Weller explains:

> The unemployment march started out in Liverpool and passed Eton college. All the young chaps came out to cheer and take the piss. It was a mini class war being played out. It is supposed to be a funny song. It's not a political song in the sense of 10 Downing Street politics, but it's everyday politics .... It's the same old story, isn't it? Everybody's equal, but some are more equal than others.
>
> (Rachel, 2016: 350–351)

Drawing Weller's ire, in 2008, ex-Conservative Prime Minister and former Eton pupil David Cameron cited 'Eton Rifles' as his favourite song. Weller responded by telling The New Statesman 'Which part of it didn't he get'? (Wilson, 2008).

Reflecting the apocalyptic tone of the political age, Weller's 'Going Underground' (1980) addresses the nuclear threat in the wake of Russia's invasion of Afghanistan in 1979. Reflecting on the song in 2013, Weller views 'Going Underground' as 'a frustrated response to the old saying that the people get the government that it deserves – the public gets what the public wants' (Rachel, 2016: 347). At the time in the United Kingdom, war was a very real fear. Anthony Barnett outlines how, having been elected in 1979, the Conservative government of April 1982 sought to use arms rather than money, and to assert what he calls 'the ghosts of colonialism' to resolve the Falklands crisis. This was, Barnett argues, 'a worldview of the United Kingdom generated domestically, rather than a reality at any time'. Margaret Thatcher's subsequent classification of the Falklands war in June of 1983 as 'the biggest victory of all time' was denounced by Labour's Deputy leader Denis Healey as 'glorifying in slaughter', which in turn led to what Barnett calls a 'field day' for the right-wing press (2012: 1–2, 12–13, 161).

The inevitable failure of revolution as portrayed in 'Eton Rifles' was one possible narrative explored by Weller, who in the late seventies and early eighties repeatedly evoked the notion of revolutions of various types in lyrics and interviews. An impetus for change was at the root of his anger. Writing in 2012, Weller reflects 'I saw what the Thatcher gang were doing to the country and the working class and I thought, why do we have to fight each other when we could be fighting those fuckers'? (Snowball and Deabill, 2012: ix). A few years later, the 'us vs. them' dynamic is reasserted, with Weller telling Rachel 'In the Jam I didn't want to be part of any movement, but this was different, you couldn't sit on the fence, it was very black-and-white. We were trying to stir up a revolution of some kind' (Rachel, 2016: 382). Shifting in alignment, the key to Weller's political thinking during this era seems to have been a revolution of *some kind*.

In 'Just Who is the Five O' Clock Hero'? Weller's thoughts on the class system are projected with poetic clarity. As he told Mojo magazine's David Cavanagh in 2018:

> I would never, ever describe myself as middle class. That would be a big fucking insult for me. I'm still staunchly working class regardless of the money I've made and how I've got on in life. That's very, very important to me. That's my roots. My cultural roots.

In 'Just Who is the Five O' Clock Hero'? Weller writes and sings in the voice of a character who scrimps and saves just to get by, who wonders what right Prince Philip has to tell him to work harder, who watches the world pass from his window without the opportunity to affect it. The song eloquently voices a generation enduring 'the loss of individualism and the sense of having no control over our lives or our country, or our future….' (Rachel, 2013: 196). Having sung 'It's up to us to change' in the hit single 'Town Called Malice', Weller wrote in The Gift Tour Programme notes 'I hope this tour is a fucking shake-up. I hope it is the knife to slice through this increasing apathy…. Forget your prejudices forced on us by social conditioning. Forget them and find your own values'. In other words, we can't win, we must look inwards. In a gesture that mirrored Weller's impending departure from The Jam, the revolution was now down to the individual, not the collective.

By his own admission, Weller had a period of political awakening between 1982 and 1986, during which his perspectives on UK socio-political life acquired greater focus (Rachel, 2016: 348). As he explained:

> The Tories were trying to dismantle the communities of the working classes: attacks on the trade unions, small businesses disappearing, and so many aspects of English life being closed down to people. There was a phoney pretence that we could suddenly all be middle-class because we were allowed to buy our houses, get a mortgage, and be in debt for the rest of our lives.
>
> (ibid.: 352)

During this time, Weller developed a growing awareness of how politics and the media report and distort realities, the mechanisms of how the ruling classes manipulate the working classes, and the effects of these actions on working class lives. Touring the United Kingdom gave Weller an appreciation of regional inequalities and the resulting breakdown in communities caused by Thatcherite policies, particularly between those living in the north and the south (ibid.: 361). Weller's suspicion of the media was fuelled by the initial depiction of the miners as heroes and then villains (ibid.: 364). Problematically, for Weller in the early eighties an alternative to the Tories was lacking. Keen to adopt an activist role, as part of International Youth Year in 1985, along with actress Julie Walters, Weller accepted an offer to be President of the British Youth Council. Weller enjoyed this role, which involved regional work supporting arts-based projects and learning projects in schools, leisure and sports, and housing estates. Enabling conversations to take place, it echoed the camaraderie and in person communication he had enjoyed in the earlier years of The Jam. As he later reflected 'The grass-roots work was the real meat for me, working with drug rehabilitation centres and other local groups' (ibid.: 436).

Retrospectively identifying another potential vehicle for revolution, Weller told Rachel: 'there were only two alternatives; one was armed revolution and the other was the ballot box' (ibid.: 384). Later in 1985, Red Wedge, a collective of pop musicians formed with the aim of engaging young people in politics. In support of Labour with the aim of dislodging the Tories at the 1987 general election, the Red Wedge touring collective included a revolving cast of high profile left-wing popular musicians including The Communards, Billy Bragg, Kirsty McColl, Madness, The, Sade, The Smiths and The Style Council. Providing a further opportunity for the arts to be influential in effecting the political landscape, a comedy tour involving Ben Elton, Lenny Henry and Robbie Coltrane was also mobilised. With hindsight, Weller characterises the tour as an unrealistic attempt to use Red Wedge to act as a kind of pressure group within the Labour Party (ibid: 383).

A few months later, the UK election was lost, and after a briefly intense era of popular music activism led by Live Aid, and the Amnesty International 'Conspiracy of Hope' and 'Human Rights Now!' tours of 1986 and 1988, the era of political touring began to fade. Reminiscing a decade later, Weller's experience with Red Wedge had clearly left a sour taste: 'they were a bunch of wankers, looking back on it. It brought me full circle in how I feel about politics. It's a game. I've very little interest in it' (Du Noyer, 1995: 29). Speaking nearly twenty years later, his perspective had not shifted, telling Rachel: 'I think we were used, and it put me off politics' (Rachel, 2016: 502). Even at the time of Red Wedge and the Amnesty tours, attitudes towards popular music activism took on a questioning aspect. As Paul Carr writes in his book on Sting, the national press began to question the intervention of the wealthy celebrity into the struggles of those less financially privileged. Quite pointedly, it was noted how no new anthems were *written* to celebrate the cause by those involved in the 'Conspiracy of Hope' tour led by Sting and peter Gabriel (Carr, 2017: 155–160). It could also be noted that no new songs of activism were written specifically for Red Wedge, leaving the participation of those involved, rolling out the hits, open to question. As Simonelli observed 'New wave was an exciting change in rock music, but despite the commitment of musicians like Paul Weller … its power to move people to take social and political change seriously was non-existent'.

Writing on The Rolling Stones but with popular musicians of all stripes in mind, Simonelli concludes that 'At core, like almost any other popular musician, their political stance was more about show business than shaking down the cities' walls' (2013: 147, 246).

Ranging from the sublime to the ridiculous, in the mid-eighties, political songwriting in the United Kingdom encompassed many disparate styles and forms of expression. Accompanying Weller's erudite songwriting contributions on 'Our Favourite Shop', Elvis Costello's 'Shipbuilding', 'Russians' by Sting, 'The War Song' by Culture Club and Frankie Goes to Hollywood's 'Two Tribes' joined Billy Bragg's 'Between the Wars' and 'New England' at the commercial vanguard of the form. Perhaps as a consequence of The Style Council's predilection for mixing socio-political themes with love songs, comedic videos and a diverse and sometimes distracting multiplicity of aesthetic frameworks, as Weller acknowledges, the reception to 'Walls Come Tumbling Down' was relatively muted. 'We stood our ground', he later commented, 'but I don't think we were revered for it. People disliked us for it. I always say that the politics put people off more than me touching Mick's earlobe. What we did was divisive, but it was a divisive time' (Eccleston, 2020: 79).

Despite the uneven nature of his engagement with political organisations, the activism of the Style Council saw Weller's political vision evolve. Speaking in 2020, Style Council drummer Steve White reflects:

> When you talk about a band that was probably ahead of its time, I think we possibly were that band, especially politically. We get very discouraged from talking about music and politics, and with social media, anybody that expresses a political opinion, especially in this country at the moment, that is maybe left leaning, it can be battered quite relentlessly by the tropes of the hard right and the right wing that's pervaded this country. Well, this happened before. This happened in the '80s. They were not so populist in the way that our current government are. They were much more harder edge politicians, but they were no less class centric and no less brutal in their treatment of anything outside of the Westminster bubble. As a band, we stood up against that and we wrote songs in support of the miner's strike of 1985. We wrote songs which would be considered anthems of optimism. There's a particular song called 'Walls Come Tumbling Down', which is a very optimistic, some say very naïve rallying cry for socialism, for left-wing beliefs and for equality, basically. We did get hammered a lot for that. But in the retrospective that recently came out, people seem to have really appreciated it. I think one of the reviews said, 'Boy do we need a band like this now', which for me was quite an emotional thing to hear. It was quite lovely to hear that.

Weller's antipathy towards both organised political activism and the ruling classes remains undiminished. Whilst Simonelli (2013) observes how yesterday's rebels are today's establishment, he may also concede that Weller is an exception to the rule. Unlike two of his heroes Paul McCartney and Ray Davies, Weller is reputed to have turned down an honour, variously cited as a CBE or an OBE. Another of Weller's avowed heroes, John Lennon returned his MBE in November 1969, memorably citing British and American involvement in foreign affairs in Nigeria and Vietnam, and 'Cold Turkey' slipping down the charts. While Lennon invoked humour to turn down his honour, Weller's rejection was less amiable. He explained his thinking to Barry Cain:

> The bit about people should be doing something constructive is alright but the Royal family thing – nah, not at all. The aristocracy is bollocks. The Royal family is a fucking joke.... I've always hated the upper-class and anything to do with aristocracy. I saw how the other half lived from an early age because my mum used to go and clean their houses. I really didn't like the people she worked for – I suppose that was inverted snobbery. It was wrong in some ways, but I fucking hated them. I used to go with her sometimes and detested the way they spoke to her. Straight away they put my back up. They walked around like they had fucking sticks shoved up their arses. Horrible bastards.
>
> (2016: 434)

As evidenced by its subsequently lengthy absence as a theme from his music, Weller's disillusionment with politics has led to a consolidated perspective, one in which Weller freely acknowledge the limits of his, or any other artists' capacity to evoke change when it comes to activism. Politicians, he acknowledges, are the masters of appearing to do that, and he wants little to do with it. There remains, however, a sense that the itch to intervene in some capacity remains, and that activism is, in some contexts, more effective than writing songs. Speaking in 2016, he reflects:

> Things haven't changed too much (Since 1977). 'I knew fuck all about politics then and I know fuck all about politics now. I like Jeremy Corbyn.... It's all media led. I now regret doing the Red Wedge thing.... It made me cynical because I thought we were being used, exploited really. We weren't stupid enough to think it was possible to change the world, but after meeting some of the MPs on the road I realised they were just a bunch of fucking careerists and it put me off politics for life.... Really not my scene and not my people.
>
> (Cain, 2016: 440)

Now in his sixties, Weller retains a belief in activism as a mechanism of collective responsibility. He knows the authorities will not take care of society's most vulnerable and that individual action will always be needed. Occasionally drawn in by revolutionary ideas, he remains deeply suspicious of any attempt by the ruling classes to facilitate equality. Having written and recorded 'Eton Rifles', 'Going Underground', 'Homebreakers' and 'Walls Come Tumbling Down' in times of domestic and international turbulence, he has had multiple opportunities to evaluate the currency of activism. In the United Kingdom as in the United States, with Reagans' tone-deaf use of Springsteen's 'Born in the USA' and Trump's unsolicited use of 'You Can't Always Get What You Want', popular music activism has repeatedly been diluted, misunderstood and misused.

Weller's politically motivated songs reached an audience of millions, enlightened some and prompted others to re-evaluate their own perspectives; this in itself is a rare achievement. When one of his own songs strikes with the kind of directness and immediacy of communicative power alluded to by Aaron Copland in the sub-chapter on modernism, Weller feels no need to dilute the power of successful works by writing lesser iterations, reasoning:

> A lot of people ask me why I don't write the same kind of political songs that I used to write, but I'm better off just singing the same ones I wrote 30 years ago, as they're the same arguments and the same issues, really. For me to try and sit down and write a song like that, I'd find it really difficult. And I just be repeating myself – what I'd said years ago, or felt years ago.
>
> (Jones: 2015)

Angry that residents displaced by the Grenfell tragedy of 2017 had yet to be rehoused, in a 2018 interview with Mojo, Weller's current role as an activist is encapsulated when he speaks of going to Grenfell with his kids to donate some clothes: 'there was just everyone you could think of.... Rich, poor, all colours, all cultures, all races.... They organised themselves ... it's often painted by the media that we're divided but we're not. The media and the propagandists are not in touch with the people down there' (Cavanagh, 2018: 77). Sensing contemporary echoes of the precarity of global politics in the early eighties, Weller says: 'It's history repeating itself ... there are dark forces trying to drag us back to the old days, whether it's fascists or religions. It's almost like the first stirrings of World War 3. It's the most dangerous and dramatic time in my lifetime' (ibid.: 76). In conclusion, Mojo (ibid.: 80) reports how Weller took part in a fundraiser for then Labour party leader Jeremy Corbyn in Brighton in 2016. Weller, the article notes, considered Corbyn 'a good man' but was reluctant to commit to further involvement, reasoning that his involvement was based on his belief in a fairer system and the sharing of wealth: 'I don't think they're bad things. They're good things.... I don't want to be sucked into it. I'm not someone who joins a party. I'm in the Mod party and that's good enough for me'.

Ultimately, following phases of awakening and reawakening, Weller's activist philosophy has arrived full circle from the provocation in the 1982

Gift Tour programme for fans to looks *inside* themselves for the answer. Speaking to the Guardian in 2021, he muses:

> The real revolution could only come from within all of us…. To think outside of our egos and see that we're all part of one thing, of the earth, of the universe, and to submit our egos, to see that we're just part of this ongoing journey…. That would be the greatest thing we could to towards a real revolution.

1.4 Nonconformist

Speaking to Ted Kessler, Weller explained his spiritual philosophy: 'I'm not interested in any organised religion. Apparently on his deathbed Buddha said 'don't form a religion around me'. And what does everyone do? Shave their heads and wear fucking robes' (2006: 62).

Gioia (2019) notes how, since the time of Ancient Greece, musical innovation has come from those on society's margins, and in more recent times, focussing on the outsider identity of Steely Dan, Clements (2009) discusses the ambiguous socio-cultural and musical space they occupied in relation to American rock music in the 1970s. Nonconformists in the popular music arena might be classified as such for a variety of reasons; Bob Dylan for his capacity for reinvention; Kate Bush for the startling degree of compositional originality in her music; Prince in the nineties for his radical independence; Radiohead in the noughties for offering music for free. Variations on each of the above exist, and as such the positions of insiders and outsiders are often not polar opposites but exist as part of a continuum (Herndon, 1993: 66).

Merriam et. al (2001: 405–416), ask the salient question 'What does it mean to be a nonconformist'? Their conclusions indicate that across race, gender and religion certain complexities are inherent to insider/outsider status, and that, as Herndon infers, the boundaries between conformist and nonconformist positions are not clearly delineated. The notion of positionality rests on the assumption that a culture is more than a monolithic entity to which one belongs or not. Significantly, in Merriam's study nonconformists were often found to 'see things not evident to insiders, and render a more objective portrayal of the reality under study'. Thus, the outsider possesses a singular worldview of immediate value to the prevailing culture.

Writing on a nonconformist from an earlier time, Sheila Whiteley (2006: 85) explores Bob Dylan's disavowal of the acoustic fingerpicking style exemplified by his 1964 album 'Another Side of Bob Dylan', a move which opened up possibilities for greater artistic development. Dylan's set at the Isle of Wight in 1969 overlooked many of his most well-known songs, and sets on his never-ending tour which began in 1988 are ever changing, depending on his preference on the night. Similarly, as a solo performer, Weller is known for not playing 'hits' on stage; rather he curates his own back catalogue according to his own tastes. In taking this approach, among artists and bands who might be considered his contemporaries, who rose to prominence on a similar scale and at a similar time, he is alone. Madness, Elvis Costello and Squeeze for example are obliged to play hits, yet paradoxically, Weller's relative ambiguity towards what his audience might want to hear seems to have added to his relevance and longevity as an artist, bringing lasting depth to his status in popular music.

Modernism has its roots in anti-establishmentarianism, and from the outset of his career, the openly aspirational Weller has regularly sought to distance himself from those to whom he might be compared. Roads (2015: 334) observes how, throughout the history of music, provocative pieces have divided audiences into fans versus foes. From Verdi's 'La Traviata' through Stravinsky's 'Rite of Spring' and the combustible atmosphere of Bob Dylan's 1966 world tour with the Hawks, this divisive tradition extends to the Style Council's 1989 performance at the Royal Albert Hall, tapes of which capture a palpable divergence between listeners willing and unwilling to be taken on the journey. The tension in the Albert Hall was not entirely incidental. In an interview with Quietus in 2015, Weller speaks of how he played on his capacity to annoy people during the late eighties, when his work was so divisive it was also rejected for release.

Few others in the history of popular music have deliberately challenged their audience in such an overt way. Kate Bush is a critically and commercially successful serial challenger of tastes and expectations, yet that confrontational and exploratory aspect of her work has for a long time been central to the expectations of her audience; it is integral to the art. Self Portrait-era Bob Dylan and Neil Young in eighties label dispute mode have both at times appeared to be intent on producing work contrary to the wishes of their respective corporate and public audiences (Rogan, 2001: 463, 470, 474). In retrospect, it not easy to gauge the degree to which gestures of this kind are, in fact, reflective of the frame of mind of the artist, who can't always be expected to new break ground, or consistently produce work capable of standing up to the rigours of retrospective scrutiny.

Over the years, many aspects of Weller's musical identity have gone against the flow rather than with it; the besuited Jam in the punk era; the European tinged piano pop jazz of early Style Council as The Smiths concurrently led a return to the literate guitar band; the pastoral, acoustic-driven tones of 'Wild Wood' in contrast to the muscular and angular electric pop rock of mid-nineties Oasis and Blur; even in an age flooded with stylistic variation, the Krautrock inspired direction of recordings made since '22 Dreams' appears relatively atypical. This antipathy for convention is ongoing, with Weller inclined to distance himself from others who feature prominently in a postmodern culture he considers lacking in identity. In an interview with GQ magazine, Weller speaks with some bile of the UK celebrity culture in the twenty-first century, claiming to be 'absolutely no part of it whatsoever' (Jones, 2015).

The extent to which Weller's individualism as a musician is knowing or incidental, voluntary or accidental is sometimes easier to gauge than at other times. Invited to join Band Aid to record a charity single in 1985, seemingly unable to conform to pop star tropes, Weller felt entirely out of his comfort zone in the presence of similarly well-known musicians (Sawyer, 2021: 11). When the Style Council were banned for using an image of a black Queen Elizabeth to promote the 1987 album 'The Cost of Loving', Weller will have been aware of the capacity of the image to ruffle conservative feathers in the UK media. A decade earlier, the Sex Pistols single 'God Save the Queen' had been banned, and media and public sensitivities around recontextualised portrayals of the royal matriarch were perennial. The famously camp video for 'Long Hot Summer' is another example of a likely knowing capacity to provoke, in this instance the target being the male, heterosexual Jam listenership. As Weller admits 'Sometimes it's good to have something to kick against' (Du Noyer, 1995: 29).

With reference to his youth as a music consumer, Weller pitches himself as a teenage connoisseur of poetic rock n roll; a fan of the singles of Little Richard, Chuck Berry and The Beatles when most of his contemporaries were into Bowie and Roxy Music (Heatley, 1996: 12). Corroborating this, in the 2015 film 'About the Young Idea', original Jam guitarist and singer Steve Brookes recalls how he and Weller, 'hated' the glam rock scene of the time. Psychological researcher Klandermans (2014) hypothesises that, when pressure is placed upon on those with diverse attitudes to assimilate into normative practices, it is often met with intense resistance. Speaking in 1995, Weller reflected: 'Our family was always tight knit … we were a very insular family. Just us against the world' (Heatley, 1996: 7). Initially an outsider to the music business, Paul's father and manager of The Jam, John Weller, was primarily a psychological manager who developed business acumen in situ. Given his familial dynamic, Weller's appetite for nonconformism may in part be rooted in having been encultured into in the role.

From the outset, The Jam cast themselves, sometimes unwittingly and at others times more knowingly, in nonconformist roles. Towards the end of 1976, ownership of the emerging punk aesthetic was still primarily limited to a relatively small number of individuals moving within London circles. Directing the images of the Sex Pistols and The Clash, Malcolm McLaren and Bernie Rhodes sought to project an unkempt look, replete with spray on graffiti, safety pins and chains. In the Jam documentary 'About the Young Idea' (2015) Weller explains how he sought to differentiate The Jam from the 'left-wing' Clash and the 'Anarchist' Sex Pistols by positioning his band as royalist Tories. Whilst The Sex Pistols were subverting royalism by creating an alternative Jubilee culture, Weller was busy subverting the Pistols (Harris, 2018a: 6–8). A few months earlier, The Jam had quit the Clash's White Riot tour after three dates. According to Harris, The Jam were ostracised by The Sex Pistols and the Clash for four reasons: because they came from Woking; because they were capable musicians; because of Weller's youth and because of their formal attire (ibid.). Rather than adapt, The Jam persisted in wearing suits both on stage and in publicity shots. Unlike their contemporaries,

The Jam busked in central London and played at the renowned jazz club Ronnie Scotts. A paradox, they appeared to be at once acting absolutely in the spirit of individuality whilst simultaneously engaging in activities that were often interpreted in the music media as revivalist.

Weller will have known that London music scenes have long had a reactionary tradition. Writing in 1969, Cohn observed how much of the Mod movement was a reaction against the yobbishness of the Teds in the 50s (1969: 175), and even within the punk movement the scope for solidarity was limited; as Julian Temple (Lydon et al., 1993: 225) recalled, 'If you were to be a punk, then everything that somebody said, you had to do the opposite'. Alternatively, according to Chrissie Hynde, who was present on the London scene at the time and who later went on to form The Pretenders, from January to June 1977, punk was based on a spirit of non-discrimination (ibid: 155). From Weller's perspective, Northern Soul music was more genuinely working class than rock, which in the seventies had acquired a bloated, contented insignificance. A punk scene in which, as Julien Temple (ibid.: 224–225) observed, Shane McGowan would one day wear 'seditionaries' gear, and the next would appear immaculately dressed as Patrick Mc Goohan in The Prisoner, seemed to offer inclusivity for all individuals. Less inclined towards the random, Weller's idea of a kindred subculture was a 'world of skinheads and suedeheads, brogue shoes and loafers, button-down shirts, scooters, soul music and amphetamine induced all-night dancing' (Hewitt, 2007: 48).

Whilst contemporary music criticism can at times be overly deferential, Hewitt (2007) praises the UK music journalism of the late seventies as a golden era. In retrospect, often amateurish in its emotive subjectivity, the culture within music journalism in the United Kingdom was reliably fractious. In any given publication, an artist might be given wild praise by one journalist and be shown contemptuous disregard by another. Scathing in their assessment of The Jam (and in their evaluation of almost everyone else involved in punk) Julie Birchall and Tony Parsons framed them as 'The brainchild of lower-middle-class Tories, abhorred by all self-respecting punks for dissociating themselves from the movement they had no qualms about cashing in on' (1978: 51). Reappraising his mid-seventies peers twenty years later, Weller claims The Jam were never accepted within punk circles, dismissing fellow bands as 'cliquey and art school … mostly middle-class kids with rich parents … (who had) run away to join the circus' (Heatley, 1996: 22). Speaking forty years after the fact, Weller identifies with the energy of punk, but is careful to retain his nonconformist credentials:

> Punk was so much more than just music – it was a cultural revolution…. It was one big explosion and then everyone went off and did their own thing…. For a short space of time punk was very important. If nothing else, it activated people and got them up and out, to strive and attempt to achieve something…. I was a mod anyway.
>
> (Cain, 2016: 432)

By 1978, the sophistication and range of The Jam resonated with new wave acts Elvis Costello and the Attractions, Joe Jackson, Squeeze and Ian Dury and the Blockheads, each of whom combined literate lyricism with a distinctive sound. Stiff Little Fingers from Belfast, Buzzcocks and The Fall from Manchester, The Slits, X-Ray Spex The Pretenders and Siouxsie and the Banshees from London, Swindon's XTC, Gang of Four from Leeds and The Undertones from Derry were equally innovative. Commercially and critically successful, the post-punk movement grew in many inventive directions. In 1979, this explosion of creativity developed a more angular, industrial branch with the emergence of Joy Division as the inheritors to The Sex Pistols in the upper echelons of John Peel's annual Festive 50. Sharing a monochromatic aesthetic, The Specials, The Beat, Selecter and Madness emerged on Coventry's Two-Tone label, marking the commercial re-emergence of Ska. As Weller later reflected, 'Like Madness, maybe the Specials, The Jam were a playground band. That thing of watching it on Top of the Pops on Thursday and talking about it on Friday, that's what it was all about' (Eccleston, 2020: 72). A typical late seventies devotee of The Jam might well own records by Northern Soul singers or singles by Motown artists, but equally likely their record collection might include 'Transmission', 'Anarchy in the UK', 'Complete Control', 'Teenage Kicks', 'Hong Kong Garden', 'Fiery Jack', 'Gangsters' or 'My Girl'.

The late seventies were a time of great eclecticism in UK popular music, and away from new wave the music of The Jam fought for position and public attention with the Bee Gees, Sister Sledge, Earth, Wind and Fire, Kate Bush, Roxy Music, Chic and The Police. Conversely, within this apparently inclusive musical world, the late seventies and early eighties were times of tribalism in UK youth culture, with punks, mods and two tone devotees occupying significant subcultural spaces. Critically subject to endless controversy yet increasingly commercially successful, the music that represented these subcultures was continuously in the throes of reinvention; post-punk emerging from the shadows of the Sex Pistols, bands from the Midlands recontextualising ska, and represented by The Chords and The Merton Parkas, a mod revival. Each movement had its leader and in 1979 Joy Division, The Specials and The Jam emerged from their respective packs.

By 1980 The Jam were by some measures, including an array of music publication reader's polls and the extraordinary chart success of 'Going Underground', the biggest band in the United Kingdom. This stratospheric rise brought with it tensions largely outside of Weller's control. Solt and Egan (1989: 242) cite John Lennon as saying 'My role in society, or any artist or poet's role, is to try and express what we all feel. Not to tell people how to feel. Not as a preacher, not as a leader, but has a reflection of us all'. In a 2018 article by Lois Wilson, Musician Shanne Bradley, journalist Gary Crowley and fanzine editor Phil Jones each recall how, of the bands to emerge from the Punk movement, The Jam were uniquely attuned to their audiences, allowing them access to soundchecks and spending time before and after shows talking to them. Identifying this distinctly nonconformist feature, Lois Wilson discusses how this behaviour was in conflict with major label realities of fame and its implied dimensions of separation; 'a challenge for a group whose emerging principle was that the band and the fans were in it together' (2018: 81).

From 1980 onwards the aesthetic of post punk began to dissipate into electronic areas with the rise to prominence of musicians influenced by punk and new wave including Gary Numan, Heaven 17, Soft Cell, Japan, Human League, Cabaret Voltaire and Ultravox. The guitar driven music of The Jam diverged, with lyric themes and textures often at odds with the new breed. Speaking in retrospect, Weller was disdainful of eighties pop bands, reflecting 'I thought Duran, Spandau Ballet, Depeche Mode and Living in a Box where bunch of wankers.... None of them could sing or play or write a decent fucking tune' (Heatley, 1996: 87). As in 1977 with punk, The Jam found themselves at odds with a concurrent movement. As if to find different ways of confronting the pop fad of the moment, after the vast success of the single 'Going Underground', the sounds used to frame The Jam singles switched haphazardly from the acoustic folk of 'That's Entertainment', to the angular guitar pop of 'Start!', to the hard psychedelia of 'Funeral Pyre', to the consummate soul and funk variations of 'The Bitterest Pill', 'Town Called Malice', 'Precious' and finally 'Beat Surrender'.

A novel sense in which Weller might be considered a nonconformist is within his own band. Writing about The Who, Cohn (1969: 177) characterises Pete Townshend as the one who found Daltrey, Entwhistle and Moon in order to advance his own inherent drive. Cohn perceptively observes that in The Who, like the Beatles, one is cast as an intellectual, one is inarticulate, one is maniacal and one sombre. These caricatures do not translate directly to The Jam, The Style Council or any of Weller's solo bands, where in each case fellow band members subsume their roles to those played out by Weller. As the prominent figure in The Jam, Weller was obliged to fulfil each of Cohn's roles; the avid fan of poetry and intellectual devourer and youthful refractor of Orwell and Sillitoe; the articulate and poised lyricist; the maniacal stage presence; the sombre polemicist. In this light, it seems inevitable that The Jam had a finite shelf-life, that Weller would eventually be unable to withstand the pressure of needing to integrate and absorb so many conflicting collaborative roles into one persona. The Style Council resolved this issue by offering numerous opportunities for Weller to submerge his identity; as a solo artist under increasingly less media pressure, as his solo career has developed in the twenty-first century he finally appears content to conform to the role of bandleader.

In his study of what he calls 'dandyism' Stan Hawkins (2009) cites David Bowie, Morrissey, Adam Ant, David Sylvian, Jarvis Cocker, Bryan Ferry, Pete Doherty and Paul Weller as examples of male artists who portray particular traits of individualism, who in some way stand outside of British popular music culture. Bowie in particular might be considered a kindred outsider spirit. Identifying an arc similar to that experienced by Weller, Perone observes how 'Bowie reached the zenith of his artistic success when he went against the mainstream in the 1970s and the zenith of this commercial success in the early 1980s. In the late 1980s, he went off on one with Tin Machine; and made better records in the twenty-first century' (2007: 145). Whilst arguments can be made for nonconformism in many phases of Weller's career, with regard to Weller's inclusion on his list, perhaps what Hawkins has at the forefront of his mind is the phase that includes The Style Council.

Exemplified by U2, the early eighties saw the rise of stadium bands. Simple Minds offered a similarly limber, anthemic brand of rock, and Echo and the Bunnymen offered a psychedelic and sardonic northern alternative. Within this bombastic environment, The Style Council responded with an eclectic album of instrumentals and vignettes that evoked a café more than an arena. Recalling Weller's insistence that he no longer considered himself British but European, Ian Munn writes: 'The European obsession was stretched to the limit, the 'Long Hot Summer' video mimicking watercraft in Venice, 'The Paris Match' and 'Le Depart' song titles, the European photo shoots, the 7" UK sleeve notes and newspaper adverts written entirely in French' (Munn, 2016: 53). Culture Club, Kid Creole and the Coconuts and Wham! were among contemporary acts offering a colourful, hook laden style of pop with no axe to grind that reflected the mood of The Style Council's languid 'Long Hot Summer' and 'You're the Best Thing'.

Reflecting on the Post Punk era Weller recalled: 'If you wore a certain uniform everyone recognised what you were about.... It's not as tribal as it was ... everything went up to the mid 80s and then faded away' (Cain, 2016: 431). In the mid-eighties there was much cross fertilisation between styles and genres (Winterson, 2003: 75), and pop continued to develop postmodern branches, with Orange Juice, Scritti Politti and Prefab Sprout at the forefront of intellectual guitar pop scene that co-existed with a short lived but influential US-led guitar band revival led by Green on Red, The Rain Parade and the Dream Syndicate. Tom Waits' 'Swordfishtrombones' melded Indonesian and Eastern European tones with an observational poetry style in the tradition of Charles Bukowski and Raymond Carver, while Nick Cave's raucous update of post-punk with The Birthday Party and New Order's epochal 'Blue Monday' offered further stylistic variations. As singer Alf Moyet observed 'Nothing was very concrete in 1983' (New Musical Express, 1983: 24). Within this popular music culture of extreme diversity, by simultaneously writing and recording hits and making albums that defied prediction or categorisation, the Style Council were able to remain both popular and resoundingly remote. Unlike The Jam, who emerged and developed during eras dominated by punk, new wave, post punk and mod revivalist scenes, The Style Council existed during a period of popular music characterised by individual artistic styles largely untethered to movements. In the Style Council, Weller was able to subsume himself into a crowd of eclectics and eccentrics, a nonconformist surrounded by nonconformists.

In the eighties, the once prohibitively expensive technology available to musicians became more accessible, and producers developed textures that enabled bands and artists to add greater individuality to their sound. Later in the decade, these technological advances enabled the Chicago house and Detroit techno scenes in the United States to flourish, and Giorgio Moroder and others led cutting edge popular music away from form to feel; away from the radio to the dancefloor. In the United Kingdom, Acid House and the Ecstasy-infused guitar dance pop of Manchester's Happy Mondays acquired critical and commercial prominence. As always in the United Kingdom, division was near to the surface and when the link between dance music and drugs became apparent, media attitudes became antagonistic (Bricheno, 2003: 101). The nineties saw dance filter into myriad innovative subgenres. Ambient chillout made by LFO, Orbital, Leftfield and Aphex Twin gained substantial audiences, and from Bristol, Portishead, Massive Attack, Tricky and Roni Size innovated with trip hop and drum and bass.

By then the eclectic adventure of The Style Council had run its course. As a solo artist, Weller gradually re-emerged, reinvented, still in thrall to numerous influences, still capable of creative heights and prone to the occasional lapse in artistic quality, still unflinchingly committed to self-expression and to the authentic and unsparing chronicling of his condition. Concurrently, in the slipstream of REM, bands including Mudhoney, Nirvana, Korn and Slipknot provided a flourish of noisy, brash American guitar rock, and in the UK Radiohead and Manic Street Preachers began to emerge as counterparts. Within this context, the Britpop explosion of the mid-nineties was significant in that it marked a brief return to UK youth music tribalism. Unlike the majority of music recorded by The Style Council, Weller's first three solo albums 'Paul Weller', 'Wild Wood' and 'Stanley Road' are in synch with much of the successful music made in the United Kingdom at the time. Like the solo Paul Weller, many of Britpop's best bands were reliant upon imaginative guitarists capable of establishing a dominant tone, and who could write and play harmonic rhythm and lead lines as immediate and memorable as the accompanying vocals, words and melodies. Combining and balancing virtuosic and understated playing with relentless pulse, Noel Gallagher, Graham Coxon and Bernard Butler emerged at the forefront of a rejuvenated guitar-based scene.

With the rise of MP3 culture, the 2000s saw further evolutions in production, reception and consumption. Subsequently, in the twenty-first century the cultural influence of music, and consequently the critical pressure placed on leading pop musicians has steadily diminished. Speaking to Barry Cain, Weller explains:

> There are some artists that change the landscape and the time – The Beatles, Bowie. We may never see the likes of them again. They were

> pioneers, but it was probably easier to be a pioneer then, because there wasn't any rule book.... Music definitely hasn't got the same cultural influence and power it once had. There are other things that have taken its place with young people, like social media, like football.... They never sit down and focus or concentrate on a song like we used to ... you were completely immersed in the experience.... It doesn't define people like it used to.
>
> (2016: 423–425)

An underground capital centric scene with a do-it-yourself punk ethos, in the early twenty-first century Grime provided a way for London's young black and ethnic minorities to find a voice and define their own high tempo culture. Dubstep developed, drawing its character from a much wider spectrum of music, taking influences from genres as diverse as new metal and bhangra and spawning its own subgenres (Bricheno, Kaye, Winterson 2003: 132). Adapting his mod credentials to incorporate disparate influences, in 2008 Weller began to develop his own new hybrid form of music with '22 Dreams'. With its emphasis on stylistic fluidity, this creative direction unwittingly met well with the Spotify era. Generating an ever-increasing number of options that erode the capacity of pop musicians to conform or not conform, the culture of instant access to all music past and present has underpinned recent developments in consumer culture.

Whilst this sub-chapter primarily focusses on non-conformist traits, in some ways, Weller can be argued to be relatively conformist. Like Bowie, he has always tended to follow major label protocols in releasing and promoting music; from the singles, albums and cassettes of The Jam, through the CDs of The Style Council and the MP3s and streams of the Paul Weller solo era. As the twenty-first century continues to dissolve into myriad genre types and niche platforms, Weller's incursions into the avant-garde are less critically divisive than his decision to embrace classical music in the later phases of Style Council. Having assimilated and absorbed many aesthetic impressions, it is evident that Weller can easily move inside or outside of genre or field of expression without compromise. Indeed, the ease with which his post 2008 work has crossed boundaries has led observers to consider him an outsider in the current milieu; no other popular music artist has shifted musical shape with comparable levels of critical success. Little of this activity seems to have to do with a wish to be seen as a nonconformist, rather it relates to a need to follow instinct.

Weller's inclination to defy expectation mirrors that of Pete Townshend who writes of his experience at Woodstock:

> Before I knew it, Roger was singing 'See me, touch me, feel me, heal me' to waves of young people who suddenly realised that Tommy was music unwittingly designed from precisely this kind of festival, for

this particular moment, for them. At one point Keith shouted, 'For Christ's sake Pete, no more!'. I went into this long feedback rich guitar solo as the sky behind the hillside began to pale with the first signs of dawn. Ebullient but weary, I struck my guitar on the floor a few times, tossed it into the audience and The Who went back home to London.

(2012: 181)

2 Idiolect

2.1 Curation

From the perspective of both the artist and the analyst, understanding how influence is brought to bear in the making of original works can be a complex task. Weller's 'Start!' was certainly initiated with reference to The Beatles 'Taxman', but whether 'Sunflower' arrived as a consequence of Weller having previously embodied Eddie Floyd's rhythmically similar 'Big Bird' as a performer in The Jam is less clear. As Frith observes 'Pop music may come from no particular place, but it absorbs musical sounds from everywhere … the history of pop is marked by the traces of all sorts of musical form … (it is) a social storehouse from which musicians of all sorts, draw and quote and sample' (Frith, Street and Straw, 2001: 97, 106). Away from the world of music, a number of fiction writers and poets are acknowledged by Weller to have helped shape his outlook as a songwriter; these figures, including the authors Colin McInnes and George Orwell and the poets Adrien Henri, Brian Patten and Roger McGough often leave aesthetic imprints that can be sensed more than traced in Weller's music. Consequently, the influences on Weller's songs tend to be fragments, impulses and resonances sifted and integrated with a modernist eye from an array of resources. While Weller's mod sensibility references Ray Davies, Steve Marriot, Pete Townshend, Curtis Mayfield, and Marvin Gaye (Hawkins, 2009: 187), in the latter phases of his solo career, much of Weller's listening focuses on current releases. Weller's tastes as a music consumer are broad, and the scope for threads of his listening to be integrated into his music vast.

From a young age, Weller recalls how he was very impressionable, and would immerse himself in the music of his favourite artists one by one, settling on a new favourite and listening to their music continuously. Weller reflects: 'I guess the first things you hear are always the most influential' (Du Noyer, 1995: 29). Speaking to Records in my Life in 2017, Weller recalls how, after watching The Beatles in the 1963 Royal Command Performance on TV 'my life was irrevocably changed', and many of the artists whose records Weller bought as a youth have remained indelible. As he revealed to a journalist in 1996, 'I like all the soul of Motown and Stax and the English

DOI: 10.4324/9780429281730-3

stuff like The Kinks, The Who, Small Faces' (Heatley, 1996: 11). Away from singles and LPs, being present at a musical event brought a different level of influence; Weller describes seeing the Sex Pistols as 'an epiphany.... They were of my generation, speaking to me' (Wilson, 2018: 79).

By 1981, having weathered the intense focus of the credibility obsessed UK music press, Weller was secure enough in his own artistry to acknowledge The Who's first album 'My Generation' as a direct influence on The Jam. As heard on the 'In the City' LP in particular, this influence can be heard in the song 'In the City', whose title was borrowed from a Who track; in the instrumental cover of Neil Hefti's 'Batman Theme' (a copy of a Who cover), and in Weller's overt homage to Pete Townshend in the epic coda of 'Away from the Numbers'. The modernist outlook of The Who may have been as influential as the music itself. As Nik Cohn writes on the ethos of The Who: 'intelligent, musical they do keep moving forward.... They make good music that somehow is still pop. That's almost a contradiction in terms, but somehow they make it' (1969: 175). Similarly, 'All Mod Cons', written as Weller reviewed The Kinks back catalogue, included a cover of The Kinks 'David Watts'. Uniquely within the landscape inhabited by his contemporaries, Weller's influences, particularly the Kinks, were hidden in plain sight. Illuminating the most pervasive influence of all, asked in 1996 if he had a favourite teacher, he replied 'Yeah, there were four of them – the Beatles' (Heatley, 1996: 11–13).

In a 2005 playlist of 'songs that shaped his world' published by Q magazine, Weller lists Emmitt Long, Lee Moses, The Gaturs, John Coltrane, Lee Morgan, Charles Mingus, John Holt, U-Roy, The Wailers, Muddy Waters, Howlin' Wolf, Sonny Boy Williamson, D'Angelo, Mary J Blige, Chic and Kelis. Interviewed for the self-explanatory online series 'Records in my Life' in 2017, Weller cites 'Something's Changing' by folk singer songwriter Lucy Rose, 'Modern Kosmology' by the experimental musician Jane Weaver, the debut album by Nashville based garage-rock band Savoy Motel and 'Wildflower' by the Melbourne based electronic music group Avalanches. Interviewed in 2013 for the online Amoeba Music 'What's in my Bag'? series, Weller highlights 'Tropicalia - A Brazilian Revolution in Sound'; John Coltrane's 'A Love Supreme'; 'The Slider' by T Rex; Tame Impala's 'Lonerism'; Traffic's 'Heaven is in Your Mind', 'Sugar Man' by Rodriguez and a compilation by Dinah Washington. Elsewhere, Little Richard's 'Here's Little Richard', The Libertines 'Up the Bracket' and Buju Banton's 'Til Shiloh' are cited as favourites in a 2018 article in Mojo authored by David Cavanagh.

Unlike many popular musicians who remain diplomatically neutral or decline the opportunity to profess any peer favouritism one way or the other, Weller's critical judgements of his musical contemporaries tend to be decisive. Invited to be a guest singles reviewer for the UK music weekly Melody Maker in their November 4, 1978 edition, Weller dismisses Adam and the Ants 'Young Parisians', with a curt 'maybe the French will like this one', and describes 'Germ Free Adolescents' by new wave contemporaries X-Ray Spex as a 'basic song about deodorants, mouthwash, antiseptics, etc, etc' (1978: 18). Offering more forensic opinions in the eighties or nineties, Weller dismisses REM as musicians but says he likes them as people; praises Sheryl Crow's voice but not her songs, and is a fan of The Smiths live but not on record. Similarly, as a critic of his own work, Weller enjoys selected aspects; his voice on 'Town Called Malice', the lyric of 'Porcelain Gods'; the feel of 'Tales of the Riverbank' (Heatley, 1996: 80–82).

Weller's critical perspectives are temporal and subject to re-evaluation over time. Within Heatley's (1996) collection of quotes, on two separate occasions in 1979 and 1981, Weller claims to have loved the Sex Pistols, yet by 1985 he concludes 'they turned out to be real wankers in the end' (ibid.: 12, 15, 18). Returning to the subject again in 2017 for the online series 'Records in my Life', the initial positive perspective is reinstated. Retrospectively reviewing formative releases by The Sex Pistols, the Damned, the Stranglers and the Clash in Barry Cain's book, Weller is either enthusiastically supportive or conclusively dismissive, there is no room for ambivalence or ambiguity (Cain, 2016: 442). Speaking to Du Noyer, Weller expresses his dislike of Pink Floyd's 'Dark Side of the Moon' or anything by Led Zeppelin, claims to have 'hated' Electro-pop in the mid 1980's (1995: 29, 30, 34) and later appraises Marilyn Manson as 'fucking appalling' (Kessler, 2006: 60). In each instance, the modernist instinct is at play; the free reign to pick and choose, to embrace or discard.

At an analytical level, resonances can frequently be found in Weller's music. Several lines from Adrian Henri's poem 'Tonight at Noon' (the title of which was initially borrowed by Henri from a Charles Mingus record) appear in the lyric text of the song of the same name. Elsewhere, Weller acknowledges the influence of Jack London and Jeffrey Archer on 'Life at a Top People's Health Farm', William Blake on 'Set the House Ablaze', Herman Hesse's 'Siddhartha' on 'Black River' and even figures from classical Greek literature on 'Peacock Suit'. The scope of influences imbibed through reading is eclectic, and since in each instance the flavour of the written word undergoes prismatic change through interaction with melody, phrasing and textural context, such 'borrows' never invite accusations of plagiarism. All musicians borrow from other musicians, sometimes perceptibly and sometimes imperceptibly. Particularly in The Jam, where the limited instrumental scope left less room for ambiguity, critics have pointed out how 'Standards' borrows from 'I Can't Explain' and how 'This is the Modern World' borrows from 'Pictures of Lily' and in the Style Council era comparisons were drawn between 'The Lodgers' and Marvin Gaye and Tammi Terrell's 'Aint No Mountain High Enough'. In the solo era, Snowball identifies the textural presence of Krautrock, Neu!, Kraftwerk and Can in 'Wake Up the Nation' and 'Sonik Kicks' (2017: 39), while Du Noyer hears stylistic traces of Neil Young's 'Harvest Moon' and Free's 'Fire and Water' in Weller's early solo recordings (Du Noyer, 1995: 34).

Embodiment plays a key role in curation. As a singer, guitarist and avid listener, Weller has formally and informally played many songs by others. In doing so, the part of the music relating to the voice and guitar is embodied, and to a greater or lesser extent a similar phenomenon applies to all the musicians who work with Weller, whose learning trajectories are invariably signposted by learning and mastering other's basslines, drum patterns and so on. Green (2002) proposes that music identities are forged from a combination of musical tastes, values, skills and knowledge, and from the musical practices in which an individual or group engages. In their pre-Polydor years, The Jam played songs originally recorded by Chuck Berry, Motown and The Beatles, while Weller also absorbed Dr. Feelgood's 'Down by the Jetty', which he considered 'a great English RnB record' (Du Noyer, 1995: 29). Consequently, Weller's guitar style borrowed directly from Wilko Johnson of Dr Feelgood (Hawkins, 2009: 187) and the chord sequences, rhythms and arrangements initiated by Johnson formed part of a wider 'muscle memory' that comes into play in the creation of new ideas.

By learning the songs of others, Weller was able to develop the guitar rhythm of The Beatles 'Fool on the Hill' into 'Wild Wood' and the chordal pattern of The Rolling Stones' 'You Can't Always Get What You Want' into 'Time Passes'. Here, the feel of the rhythms and chord sequences on the guitar or piano become transposed by the energy of the revisitation. Similarly, 'Ghosts' follows the descending line of 'Sweet Soul Music', initially recorded by Arthur Conley in 1967 and subsequently covered by Weller's first band, The Jam in 1977. Whilst the two songs are very different in terms of energy, with Conley's frenetic pulse replaced by Weller's solemn march, given the motific likeness it seems impossible that Weller's embodiment of the earlier performance was not influential. Other resonances originate from music written and recorded earlier by Weller himself. The melodic refrain of 'Long Hot Summer' is heard again on 'With Everything to Lose' and again on 'Have You Ever Had It Blue'. Elsewhere, the brass line on 'Just Who is the 5 O' Clock Hero' is almost identical to the melody of 'That's Entertainment', which in turn is almost identical to the refrain of 'Speak Like a Child'. That each song has a very different lyric theme illustrates the capacity of melody to support verbal meaning with metaphorical ambiguity.

To analyse a popular song is, by its very nature, to offer an interpretation of it, to determine what range of meaning it has, to make sense of it (Moore, 2012: 5). In some instances, the range of meaning can be quite broad; the popular music songwriter is negotiating impulses and sources from across the spectrum of song text, instrumental texture, arrangement and feel. Some influences that make their way into new works are likely to be conscious and others more subliminal. Sometimes a number of influences can combine to create a novel aesthetic tinged with familiarity. This is true of 'Speak Like a Child', written in the immediate aftermath of The Jam split in December 1982 and released as the debut single by the Style Council in March 1983. Built upon a descending two bar major to minor chord sequence, 'Speak Like a Child' has a number of musical and experiential resonances with John Lennon's 'Instant Karma!', recorded in the aftermath of the Beatles split in late summer 1970. The two songs are not alone in their use of the chord sequence; different sources have attributed the chordal genesis of 'Instant Karma!' to 'All You Need is Love' (Edmondson, 2010: 133) and perhaps less flatteringly 'Three Blind Mice' (Blaney, 2007: 28). In the early seventies, after the release of 'Instant Karma!' and long before 'Speak Like a Child' took shape, T Rex had used an identical major to relative minor chord sequence on 'Metal Guru' and later, in 1986, The Smiths used the same chord sequence for 'Panic'. Unlike Bolan, Morrissey or Marr, on 'Speak Like a Child' and 'Instant Karma!', both Weller and Lennon were in the process of re-establishing their respective creative identities.

Whether Weller has ever made any connection between the two songs is unknown. Analysis, however, reveals that the descending major to minor sequence opens both verses, and that both songs then follow identical structures. Both vocals enter at the same interval after the beat, and both play out with codas that emphasise refrains. In both instances, the inference of the structure and vocal phrasing may be key, since they convey unhurriedness. Emphasising a sense of joyous contentment, both recordings have sustained arrangements that remain at their respective expressive altitudes; they are happy to be where they are. Given his imminent move towards a jazzier aesthetic, it is more than likely that Weller had been aware of Herbie Hancock's (1968) Blue Note album 'Speak Like a Child', whose liner notes indicate a further significant link, with Nat Hentoff citing Herbie's intention for the music to represent 'a forward look to a bright future', a rediscovery of childhood qualities, to 'purity, spontaneity'.

As a songwriter and avid listener, Weller will have had an early awareness of the significance of structure in shaping songs. Conforming to Sondheim's edict that 'content dictates form' (2010), songs such as Holland, Dozier and Holland's 'You Can't Hurry Love' have extraordinarily complex structures that are shaped and edited to make the song flow naturally. What is complex from the perspective of the songwriter is often simple from the perspective of the listener. At other times, song structures conform to more traditional structures. In each individual instance, every sonic element that exists around within and around the text of the song has an influence on its most effective structure. Winterson, Bricheno and Nickol (2003: 182) note how Radiohead's 'Paranoid Android' is a complex song which changes tempo and modulates several times, shifting between two-time signatures, 4/4 and 7/8. Avoiding sectional repetition, it is highly untypical. 'Paranoid Android' and Weller's 'Trees' appear to have been influenced by two earlier Beatles recordings, 'Happiness is a Warm Gun' and 'You Never Give Me Your Money'. In 'Revolution in the Head', Ian MacDonald (1994: 254, 281, 282) calls 'Happiness is a Warm Gun' 'the darkest song on The Beatles (White Album), strung together from random associated phrases, real characters and incidental slogans. Conversely, in 'You Never Give Me Your Money',

MacDonald writes of how 'an entire era – the idealistic, innocent sixties – is bravely bidden farewell'. In this latter song, MacDonald perceives a salvaging of spirit for the future, a psychological opening that chooses celebration over recrimination. Whether consciously or subconsciously, on 'Trees', which shares a non-repetitive structure, Weller integrates the darkness of old age as experienced and conveyed by real characters, and celebrating the magic of their time together, bids farewell to his father. Structurally related as compositions, each song uses form to project bleakness and euphoria, extremes of the human condition.

As previously mentioned, in a curatorial sense, influences tend to be fragmented. Discussing his approximation of The Zombies 'Odyssey and Oracle' Weller recalls how, by figuring out how to play songs from that record, he and Steve Brookes discovered major 7th chords: 'That was like finding a whole new universe to us, and we discovered minor ninths and lots of other jazz chords through them' (Wilson, 2018: 93). While many technical and stylistic threads within his music are imperceptible, particularly in the solo era Weller is typically unconcerned with hiding or denying his influences. Discussing 'Equanimity', a track from the LP 'On Sunset', Weller describes it as 'A bit of Pepper, a bit of 30's Berlin, a bit of Mills Brothers harmonies' (Eccleston, 2020: 76). Some influences underpin entire tracks while others are temporal. In Weller's 'Fast Car, Slow Traffic' the pulse of 'Hallogallo' by the German band Neu! is insistent, while an approximation of the piano of Stockhausen's 'Klavierstuck V. Work no. 4' is temporal. Similarly, on later solo recordings, the distinctive cut up techniques favoured by The Focus Group occasionally add a disembodied aspect to more conventionally assembled pieces.

Explaining how influences make their way into Weller's songs, drummer Steve White says:

> I remember being at the soon-to-be-renamed gig in Bristol that was once known as the Colston Hall. Paul was on stage playing a song and he asked Yolanda Charles and I, the bass player, to join in. We joined in and he made a couple of minor adjustments and he said, 'We're going to play that tonight'. We played it, and it was a song called 'Time Passes', which is one of his favourite ballads. Now, the thing that Paul came up with was that descending riff. I used to sit and look at him and just tap away at rhythms. He said, 'I don't want anything straight on this. I don't want anything standard'. The whole idea of playing a conventional grove, which would have worked perfectly well, he didn't want that.
>
> I actually took the influence of one of my all-time favourite drummers and slightly lifted something that's called the 'King Kong Beat'. Now, the 'King Kong Beat' was brought to prominence by the great David Garibaldi. It's a paradiddle sticking, and the first half of the paradiddle

is right-left, right-right but the second half of the paradiddle is left-right, right-left. Now, that particular rhythm fits absolutely brilliantly with pretty much any combination of bass drum, idea or pattern you can come up with, a four on the floor, a rock feel. You can play it with unison with the bass drum and the hands in a New Orleans sort of feel. Or a samba, even. It's incredibly versatile and fits so perfectly in so many situations.

I was listening to Paul play and I was just playing the beat of the hi-hat and he said, 'Yes, that's works, but it's not really feeling as powerful as it should be'. I said, 'Right, okay, I'll come up with a few ideas'. I just literally lifted my right hand over and played the beat on the floor tom. 'That was it', he said, 'That is the groove for the riff. I want you to play that pattern'. The bass drum was fairly simple, a little syncopated skip thing, and the hi-hat was playing straight eights all the way through, which is something I do a lot on records because it gives you a shaker type feel, which I think just gives you that sonic relevance at the higher frequencies.

The whole thing came together, and I played this as the verse and chorus groove. That became the verse and chorus pattern. We had a bridge, a middle eight section that I had to come up with. Again, when it got to that particular section, I came off of the floor tom and I played a conventional two and four-beat. Paul just went, 'No, I don't want that. Do something different'. Again, I am not frightened to wear my influences very, very much on my sleeve and I drew on my love of the great Ginger Baker, who I adore as a drummer and as a friend, now passed. I stole a little bit of one of his most famous drum licks, which is to a song called 'Sunshine of Your Love', where he reverses the bass drum and snare drum … and just goes completely against the grain of what you're supposed to do with drumming and just reverses the back beat onto one and three. I just lifted that really. I just thought, 'I'm going to do a little bit of Ginger in there'.

When I got to the middle eight- … and then back in for the choruses, the little refrain that we did on the end of the middle eight, the slight accent, was a nod to 'The Wind Cries Mary' by Jimi Hendrix. We wore our influences fairly high on our sleeves for that particular song. Paul used to have a phrase, a very, very intellectual musical phrase, and he called it 'Just do the big F off fill'. That was his musical terminology, if you get my meaning. There's a song called '5th Season' that was on the same record. At a certain point in the song, he said to me, 'Just do one of those big F off fills', so I got to do it in that particular song.… I was quite grateful to that, to get my little Billy Cobham type influence.… There's a song called 'All the Pictures on My Wall' where I'd play a

> New Orleans kind of beat. Then I'd go into a half-time thing, which I completely lifted off of Steve Gadd on an album by Chick Corea called 'The Leprechaun.

Another more easily identifiable form of influence is covers, or songs Weller has admired enough to reinterpret. Shuker (2008: 129–131) discusses how covers were originally used by record companies to capitalise on the ethnic divides in American radio; this, he explains, ultimately contributed to the perception of covers as being unoriginal and lacking creativity. Covers, however, have always been used to introduce new generations of listeners to old songs. The reinterpretation process allows for the artist to convey material in a new way, to model the text in a fashion that makes it congruent with the times. As Herman observes 'When the Who play 'Young Man Blues' it becomes the anthem of outraged young men, lost and defeated, trodden upon. (Mose) Allison throws the line away, but The Who shout it' (1971: 60).

Dai Griffiths (2002: 51) writes how:

> Cover versions emerge in industrial conditions, but nevertheless mount dialogues and debates between texts and performers. They help to raise retrospectively for the textual study of popular music useful points of comparison around questions of identity and political power.... The musicologist's specific task in this complex framework is, it seems to me, to suggest how texts, in this case often consisting of the pair, original and cover, in some way describe or 'call into being' the social within given industrial conditions.

Griffiths (ibid.) notes how covers illustrate identity in motion. From a curatorial perspective, some of Weller's covers appear to have been chosen to augment original material. Early soul covers like 'Sweet Soul Music', 'Slow Down' and 'Back in My Arms Again' have a directness of expression that leavens some of the lyric and compositional density of songs in Weller's mid-seventies catalogue, for instance 'I Got by Time' and 'I've Changed my Address'. Where the immersive Weller original 'Away from the Numbers' provokes thought, Arthur Conley's 'Sweet Soul Music' appeals to the feet. Similarly, while 'I Got by In Time' requires repeated listening to access the full dimension of the expression, 'Back in My Arms Again' needs one listen to be absorbed. The original Weller songs recorded in 1977 are not necessarily flawed, but the covers offer an immediacy Weller's writing has yet to acquire. Embodiment may also play a role; from Weller's perspective as a singer and guitarist, on covers like Larry William's 'Slow Down' and Wilson Pickett's 'In the Midnight Hour', it is not necessary to look at the fretboard or think about dynamic cues; they feel good to play, they are easy to play and this allows the performer to become more immersed in the communal live experience.

Alternatively, covers chosen in the latter phase of The Jam seem to involve the selection of existing expressions that convey a perspective on the social conditions of the time. Edwin Starr's 'War' reflects the prevalent cold war rhetoric, while the Small Faces 'Get Yourself Together' and Curtis Mayfield's 'Move on Up' seem to have been chosen as part of Weller's appeal to his live audience to look inwards to find a way to ascend above their condition, a theme explored in his notes for the 1982 tour programme. Aside from a narrow coterie of well-known English bands, Weller's covers during The Jam are curated from the catalogues of Black American artists. In addition to covers already mentioned, by 1982, Eddie Cooley's 'Fever', James Brown's 'I Feel Good', Percy Mayfield's 'Hit the Road Jack' (made famous by Ray Charles), Brenda Holloway's 'Every Little Bit Hurts' and The Chi-lites 'Stoned Out of My Mind' had been either recorded or played live by The Jam. It is likely that these covers are recordings with atmospherics Weller will have aspired to, but that perhaps felt out of his reach. As a songwriter and record maker, unable to draft originals to authentically replicate the feel of the cultural contexts in which their records were made, Weller effectively transports Black America to White London, from a variety of known and obscure black American soul artists to an English three-piece band of white popular musicians.

According to Billboard, Soul music was at its peak from 1965 to 1967 with the advent of Stax and Motown, Muscle Shoals, James Brown and Aretha Franklin. From October of 1965 a sudden influx of R&B tunes by the Temptations, Joe Tex, Supremes, Marvin Gaye, Sam Cooke, Mary Wells, Ray Charles, Marvelettes, Impressions and Contours necessitated that soul music should have its own chart (Brackett, 2016: 235–237) and the influence of these and many other black musicians on Weller's music is of lasting significance. A link between the punk movement adjacent to The Jam and black culture was visible from the outset; the Clash were heavily influenced by reggae, recording Junior Murvin's 'Police and Thieves' on their first album, while John Lydon's love for dub reggae is imprinted on 'Metal Box' by Public Image Limited, not least in the form of Jah Wobble's hypnotic bass lines. As Negus writes (1996: 108) 'around the time of the Clash, a number of white musicians were using reggae to construct a sense of their own 'ethnicity' and their relationship to blackness'.

Dyer (1988) observes that there are far more definitions of what is black than what is white. Drawing the scope of definition towards Weller's practice, Negus (1996: 107) writes: 'Like white music, black music should be approached as part of a more discontinuous process in which cultural traditions are continually remade and new 'hybrid' identities are created'. In his analysis of The Jam, Hawkins (2009: 186) discusses how they drew upon distinct African-American influences whilst upholding a sense of Britishness. Emphasising a commercial imperative, Frith (1983: 16) notes how white popular musicians have drawn from historical styles and values drawn from black culture to enable them to be discovered by new audiences. Observing how the reverse dynamic can also be significant, Griffiths (2002: 57) discusses how Ray Charles's 'Modern Sounds in Country and Western

Music' updated many of the sparse arrangements of originals made by white musicians.

In the United States, black musicians served and continue to serve as counsellors, politicians, historians, entertainers, and role models for the black community and through song, black musicians address concerns, problems and social issues that pervade the black community (Maultsby, 1985: 46). Griffiths (2002: 55) discusses how racially based covers raise a series of comparisons which ask us to consider carefully questions of power and exploitation, and Negus (1996: 112) offers a reminder that it is out of struggles arising from unequal relations of economic and cultural power that black music has been made.

The discussion is broad, as Shank writes:

> In all forms of popular music racial identity has been asserted, defended, negotiated and denied.... In every case, within every popular musical genre, crossover exceptions to the typical racial identification exist; for in the very vibrations of its being, music doesn't know race.
>
> (Frith, Straw and Street, 2001: 263)

After having a batch of new songs dismissed by Chris Parry at Polydor in early 1978, Weller retreated with his girlfriend Gill to his parent's house in Woking and sought inspiration in the music of his youth. Originally recorded by The Kinks, 'David Watts' was one of the songs Weller reviewed. It seems likely that, by embodying the song, by figuring out the chord sequences and singing and playing it on his guitar, that Weller will have discovered a sound, and with it, possibilities for further adaptation. Voiced from the perspective of an envious and ambitious young man, 'David Watts' is likely to have inspired Weller to sketch the similarly aspirational 'Billy Hunt', recorded around the same time. As a cover, 'David Watts' was a knowing choice; unlike many other songs in the Ray Davies catalogue, it was not widely known by UK audiences. Many fans of The Jam will have heard it as an original Jam song before discovering its origin, and those who became aware of its origin as a cover after the fact will likely have considered it a deft example of curation on Weller's behalf; the tasteful unearthing and reimagining of a great song. A similar curatorial dynamic applies to the selection of 'So Sad About Us', a fine Who album track featured on 'A Quick One'.

Style Council covers were primarily integrated into live shows rather than recorded for release. Global in outlook, they predominantly focus on inclusive themes, with The Isley Brothers' 'Harvest for the World'; 'Promised Land' by Joe Smooth; Funkadelic's 'One Nation Under a Groove' and 'Meeting Over Yonder' by The Impressions all appearing to have been selected to convey themes in which the singer, band and listenership are cast as a collective, with a handful of contemporary originals including 'Internationalists' and 'Walls Come Tumbling Down' aspiring to convey similar themes in Weller's own compositional voice. Unusually for Weller, a number of covers from the Style Council era are contemporary, with Anita Baker's 'Angel' and Willie Clayton's 'Love Pain', both originally recorded in the mid-eighties. Elsewhere, David Sea's 'Night after Night' and 'Hanging on to a Memory' by Chairman of the Board are, like many of the covers selected for The Jam, gestures of taste drawn from American artists for reinvention and consumption by a predominantly British popular music audience. Citing Elvis Presley's Sun-era performances of regional RnB and bluegrass tunes, Shuker (2008: 130–131) notes how playing and recording covers enables artists to appear authentic to the aficionado element of their audiences by displaying a virtuous ability to skilfully mine the past. Chrissie Hynde's version of The Persuaders 'Thin Line Between Love and Hate', and Elvis Costello's earlier reading of 'I Can't Stand Up for Falling Down' helped to project both artists to devotees as curators, capable of finding rare gems beyond the reach of other, seemingly less authentically immersed contemporaries.

Covers in the Paul Weller solo era are more wide ranging in terms of stylistic reference and genre. Like 'David Watts' and 'So Sad About Us' from the Jam era, Nick Drake's 'The Riverman', 'Pearly Queen' and 'Paper Sun' by Traffic, 'Black Sheep Boy' by Tim Hardin and the traditional tune 'Black is the Color' as interpreted by John Jacob Niles are all covers that reflect contemporary directions Weller is moving in; embodiments integrated into collections of original work. Most notably, Dr. John's 'I Walk on Gilded Splinters' is threaded seamlessly into side one of Stanley Road. As Weller turned to covers to disguise a lack of creativity in 1981, he did so again in 2004, recording multiple covers for 'Studio 150'. Here, as with many other covers recorded during the solo era, Weller seems less concerned with the artistic statement, and more with embodiment and enjoyment. In that sense, the role of the cover turns full circle to that played by 'Sweet Soul Music' in 1977.

2.2 Impetus

As collaborators, other musicians bring varying degrees of influence to Weller's recordings. Excepting a brief period in which Simon Dine originated song ideas with textural prompts for Weller to build upon, Weller's role in each iteration of his career has been to be the initiator of song ideas. Collaborators typically build upon those ideas and add their own tastes, with Weller as the final arbiter in terms of how the songs are developed. He begins and ends the process, but collaborators are usually heavily involved in the phases in-between. On his songwriting role in The Jam, speaking in 1992 Weller explained: 'Eton Rifles I wrote in its entirety, but it was an exception. Most of the time all I had were rough ideas and fragments, and we'd hammer them out together, with everybody contributing ideas' (Heatley, 1996: 21).

Psychologically, Weller's approach to collaboration is to encourage, as Mick Talbot testifies: 'he has a very nurturing way with musicians, where it's like he has more belief in you than you have in yourself. I've seen it work on other people and I know it's worked on me' (Cavanagh, 2018: 79). Steve White adds: 'Paul wants everyone to be in the same space to make the music' (West, 2007: 48). From a listener's perspective, it is tempting to assume that works of great musical harmony are made by musicians in great personal harmony. However, numerous interviews with members of Crosby, Stills, Nash and Young testify to the co-existence of animosity and alignment in the making of lasting works of art. Similarly, in The Jam as Weller explains:

> It's hard to find all members of a band that think the same way.... The Who were four of the most disparate people you could ever get.... In the final six years The Jam were working and recording, Rick and I probably only exchanged about three conversations and they wouldn't have lasted much longer than a sentence each... the only bond between the three of us was a love of playing music.
>
> (Cain, 2016: 420)

Extraneous to personnel, the creative processes of a successful popular musician are always subject to external conditions that can move the parameters of the process away from the artists' control. During the recording of 'This is the Modern World', Polydor boss and producer Chris Parry recalls how 'Paul was looking to The Beatles for inspiration musically, but there was not time to give it the attention it needed due to the schedule' (Wilson, 2019b: 21). Conveying his perception of early Jam recording sessions, bassist Bruce Foxton recalls time constraints on both 'In the City' and 'This is the Modern World', but with the debut recording being 'intense' and the sophomore release 'rushed' (Wilson, 2018: 81, 84). According to producer Peter Wilson, 'The Gift' was subject to the constraints imposed by fame and constant touring (Hoffman, 2012). In an unscheduled return to restrictive practice, during the worldwide covid pandemic of 2020, Weller was obliged to record his guitar and vocal parts for 'Fat Pop (Volume One)' at Black Barn and send them to Steve Cradock, Andy Crofts and Ben Gordelier to overdub (Sawyer, 2021: 8).

Location is widely considered integral to creative process. RAK and Townhouse studios in London where The Jam recorded 'All Mod Cons' and 'Setting Sons' were said by Foxton to have a good vibe that promoted creativity (Peart, 2019: 45). Having his own studio Black Barn at his disposal has enabled Weller's creative processes to be more freely collaborative and lateral. As he explains to Ted Kessler: 'There's no time limit. It's peaceful. Space to think' (Kessler, 2021: 70). An obvious role model for choosing to record on one's own clock is The Beatles. Wilco, who own their own studio The Loft in Chicago, enjoy the idea that extraneous performances can be captured; that the option to capture and integrate the accidental with the intended is always open (Verlinde, 2011). With a similar latitude in mind, Shangri-la in Malibu, California was designed and built to the specifications of Bob Dylan and the Band. In Stephen Davis' book on The Band, drummer Levon Helm describes it as 'a clubhouse and studio where we and our friends could record albums and cross-pollinate one another's music' (Davis, 2013: 245). To illustrate a similarly porous culture within the context of Weller's practice, drummer Ben Gordelier was recording at Black Barn with his band The Moons when he was asked by Weller to contribute percussion to some new demos. Following the session, he was invited to join Weller's band (Snowball, 2017: 24). Guests featured on the solo album 'On Sunset' include Col3trane, who Weller recalls having stopped by one day and who 'did a really nice little part for it. It's the spirit of the record. The sun was coming down, so we just tried it out. And it worked' (Mills, 2020: 13). Such an informal collaborative process in not without risk, as Moorefield writes: 'On 'Music for Films' Brian Eno would ask people to come at different times to record on a couple of cuts. As such, the spontaneity of group performance can be lost, and the producer needs to be careful not to make the resulting music sound artificial or cold (2010: 55). The atmospheric of a concert hall can also provide impetus, and as discussed by Steve White in the previous sub-chapter, on tour he, Weller and Yolanda Charles would work together to develop song ideas on stage. Writing on stage, surrounded by seating, lights, floorboards and the storied history of many venues, it is tempting to imagine enhanced access to the creative impulse.

Momentum, and a focussed work ethic are integral to the creative process. As Steve White (2020) recalls:

> There was a lot about the Paul Weller band that I think was comparable to people like James Brown, that we were very, very hard working, lots was expected from us. As wonderful as Paul was, he would record shows. We would get on the bus and he would listen to the show, tweak a BV, watch the tempo, check the tuning, 'What snare drum are you using'? Lots of that kind of stuff, which essentially added up to the fact that when we first started playing in Newport to 240 people, over 7 years, 3 studio albums and 1 live album, we went from 240 to playing to 38,000 for 2 nights at Finsbury Park or Crystal Palace. That was that old-school style of working, which there is no substitute for.

On the autodidactic nature of his creative process, Weller says: 'Some people may learn music by reading and writing it, I think that approach is a bit clinical, a bit soulless, and The Jam, along with a lot of other bands just seemed to develop' (Heatley, 1996: 20).

Enculturation into music enables almost everyone, musician and non-musician, to become a music expert (Sloboda, 1985: 248) and as Hoskyns concurs, an education in music might involve a series of formal processes or be more to do with informal development in understanding the nature and mechanisms of music (1992: 144). Within this spectrum, songwriters such as Paul Weller don't create scores; rather they work directly with sound and music (Moore, 2012: 14). One consequence of autodidactic creativity is that Weller has his own idea of how his songs are structured, and this idea may or may not correspond with others involved. Discussing the structure of 'That Dangerous Age' producer Jan Kybert reveals how 'Paul says that the song doesn't have a chorus, just a verse and a bridge, but in my mind, the verse is the chorus' (Tingen, 2012). Speaking to Mojo magazine, arranger Hannah Peel notes how Weller 'describes things metaphorically' (Cavanagh, 2018: 79).

When approaching Paul Weller's music, it is important to bear in mind that not all of his work is written consciously to communicate meaning; to a greater or lesser extent much of it is the sound of an energy being captured. At these times it is not meaningless to describe the music, but it is good to be cognizant that it exists to be heard and felt, rather than classified. On the subject of lateral thinking, the Maltese philosopher Edward De Bono writes:

> Rightness is what matters in vertical thinking. Richness is what matters in lateral thinking.... One does not have to be moving towards something, one may be moving away from something ...... the vertical thinker says 'I know what I am looking for'. The lateral thinker says 'I am looking but I won't know what I'm looking for until I have found it.
>
> (1970: 37–39)

Writing in 'Suburban 100' (2010: 25), Weller reflects that he doesn't always know what he is going to write at the point of inception. There are often no ideas to begin with, no need to express or convey an impetus or meaning. In those instances, the words and music flow and meaning, if there is meaning, follows afterwards.

Where there are starting points, the stimuli for Weller's songs are extensively varied. After a few hours of listening to Krautrock pioneers Neu! and Cluster, Weller flew to Berlin's Hansa Studios with collaborators Simon Dine and Graham Coxon to lay down some ambient landscapes for use in the preparation of 'Sonik Kicks' (Quantick, 2020: 122). In preparing to make 'Wake Up the Nation', collaborator Simon Dine recalls that Weller sought to evoke the aesthetic of 'Sound Affects', the initial writing of which was prompted by a number of disparate sources, including 'the jagged and minimalist paired down pop of Gang of Four and Wire, The Beatles 'Revolver', Michael Jackson's 'Off the Wall', a book by Geoffrey Ashe titled 'Camelot and the Vision of Albion' and the English landscape, particularly pylons' (Harris, 2018b: 16). The song 'The Butterfly Collector' is based on John Fowles (1963) novel 'The Collector' and, as previously mentioned, 'Tonight at Noon' is based on Adrien Henri's book of poems.

Weller has never used a singular creative process. Songs are sometimes written words first; sometimes using piano first; sometimes using guitar first; and sometimes vocal melody without words first. Speaking in 1984, Weller claimed that his songs usually start with a title (Heatley, 1996: 79). 'Down in the Tube Station at Midnight' started as a long prose poem, a story without music. Alternatively, 'You Do Something to Me' was written by appropriating some chord symbols from a piece of sheet music lying around in a recording studio. Weller says a song like 'Wild Wood' is likely to have come more from the voice than from the chords, and speaking in 1995, Brendan Lynch recalled how Weller wrote most of his first solo album on piano. At other times, for instance with 'Headstart to Happiness', the process began with a guitar. 'From the Floorboards Up' was initiated by a discussion Weller had backstage with Steve White, and 'Broken Stones' originated from a conversation on a beach with his son Nate (Rachel, 2013: 192, 198–199).

It is frequently possible to link Weller's creative processes to outcomes. In 1992, Weller reflects that he wrote differently at different times during The Jam, and that after 'Setting Sons', which he predominantly wrote as a series of completed, self-contained songs, the songs were scraps of ideas and images (Heatley, 1996: 82). As a consequence of this change of creative process, 'Sound Affects' took longer to make. Mostly written alone on guitar, 'Setting Sons' is compositionally condensed, reflecting an impetus to forefront the voice in the absence of the immediate presence of other instrumentation. A year earlier, disturbed by the sudden limelight, Weller had suddenly stopped writing for the third Jam album. Spooked into hibernation, many of the songs for 'All Mod Cons' were written while holed up in his parent's house hiding from a stalker with his girlfriend Gill (Gilbert, 2018a: 11). Prompted by this return to his childhood home, Weller's songs began to coalesce around oppositional themes of dreams and reality, of imprisonment and escape. Discussing the mood of True Meanings, Weller links the fact that, as a busy husband and father, he only has time to write late at night, hence the recurring lyric references to solitude and lateness of the hour. 'Once you put an acoustic guitar in someone's hands it always goes that way', he says, 'An introspective time. The witching hour' (2018: 76).

In a wide-ranging interview with Daniel Rachel in 2013, Weller sought to expand upon his own creative process. From the transcript, it is clear that the process is elusive by nature:

> A lot of the time that's what writing is: picking up what's floating in the air. Generally speaking, it's more luck than judgement, I think. You seize on something and just capture it or it comes to you: some words, a couplet, a title, a theme and then a melody. People always ask me how I write: no idea, it's just something that's in me. It seems the most difficult insurmountable thing to do until you're doing it and then it just seems so natural, just like walking or breathing.... Fragments come to me and then after, once I've got the idea, I will run with it

> and work it and possibly see where the melody should go to.... I think writing is a bit of a waiting game: you have to wait for the inspiration.... Sometimes I get a feeling, an inkling of some kind, a physical sensation where you think 'I'm going to write' but I can't say it happens every day of every week. I couldn't say why that should be or what causes it.... I write some songs by just making stupid sounds playing along to some chords and waiting for words to form ... sometimes you might have to go back and edit those words to make them fit rhythmically into a musical piece.

John Lennon spoke of a cathartic relationship with songwriting, claiming it 'is about getting the demon out of me. It's like being possessed. You try to go to sleep, but the song won't let you. So, you have to get up and make it into something, and then you can sleep' (Solt, 1989: 169). Weller speaks of how he might have a fragment of a song in his head for weeks before he starts writing or working on it. He says it's hard to describe the process because it's always the same, but always different. He writes down bits and pieces of lyrics on scraps of paper and tends to write songs over varied lengths of time. He doesn't use a tape recorder, saying if it's good enough, it always comes back to him. He is not worried about going for periods of time without writing, rather he waits for the impulse to return. He summarises: 'I just follow my nose and take it where the music takes it. The only limitation is what you put on yourself. If you keep an open mind, you can go anywhere with it' (Rachel, 2013: 189–194).

During some phases of his career, Weller has written or played songs as 'dry runs' to acquire focus, a process known to songwriters as 'woodshedding'. As De Bono writes: 'In lateral thinking one does not mind being wrong on the way to a solution, because it may be necessary to go through a wrong area in order to get to a position from which the correct path is visible' (1970: 203). On a series of unpublished, later unearthed studio recordings from Woodstock in Spring 1967, Bob Dylan can be heard easing himself back into songwriting by 'writing in a panoply of styles that directly influenced him, all the while showing The Band how they might integrate such influences themselves' (Heylin, 2010: 395–396). Prior to some recordings, Weller has been known to 'woodshed' ideas; to write without critical focus as a means of attaining creative focus. Speaking in 1979, he recalled a period in early 1978 when his songwriting refracted into a range of unlikely stylistic areas before coalescing into the shape of 'All Mod Cons' (Heatley, 1996: 18). In an NME interview with John Hamblett in November 1978, Weller explains: 'I wrote a lot of songs in America but they were all crap.... We went through Harlem and that was really inspiring, but that has nothing to do with me.... We've got Harlems of our own' (Hamblett, 1978: 31). Significantly, Weller considers this unreleased material to be integral to the quality of 'All Mod Cons', a necessary phase of development leading to a focussed creative realisation.

Perhaps having been seeded the idea by Pete Townshend, whose 'The Who Sell Out' and 'Tommy' coalesce around a series of themes, occasionally, Weller seeks to write to concept. In a retrospective review, Pat Gilbert (2018b: 13) refers to 'Setting Sons' as:

> The new wave's reply to The Who's 'Tommy' or The Kinks' 'Arthur'…. An ambitious concept album that would explore the idea of English class identity and the twentieth century social and political experience, or in Weller's words 'about three close mates who get split up when the Civil War occurs: one joins the left, one veers off to the right, while the third one doesn't feel any particular affiliation. After the war's conclusion the splintered comrades plan to meet up again.

The subject echoed an earlier one; Ray Davies describes The Kinks 'Do you Remember Walter' as about the process of growing up, and what happens when people drift apart and then meet up again years later to find they have nothing in common (Jovanovic, 2013: 149).

In 1967, The Beatles attempted to write a concept album on the theme of Liverpool, an idea that yielded 'Penny Lane' and 'Strawberry Fields Forever' but was unsustainable. Similarly, the concept for 'Setting Sons' was ultimately over-ambitious. After completing work on four songs, Weller began to write about other themes, the recording budget almost doubled and the partial completion of a surfeit of unfinished ideas led to the late inclusion of a cover of 'Heatwave' (Gilbert, 2018b: 12). During the DVD on the making of 'As Is Now', Steve White recalls how: 'Paul said to me, I want to make a record that sounds like a piece, like one continuous piece'. '22 Dreams' was initially planned to be a duets album with singers including Dot Allison but eventually became a concept around the idea of capturing a year in someone's life. Under less time pressure, this concept was more fully realised. Occasionally, songs, or parts of songs that don't fit initial concepts are kept for later use. Written as a demo in 1977, 'Worlds Apart' was never released in its original form yet the melody of the middle eight resurfaced the following year in 'Strange Town'. 'Mirrorball' was originally written as a bonus track for 'True Meanings' and eventually released two years later (Mills, 2020: 13) and prior to its recording, 'Gravity' had existed for five or six years, with Weller telling Mojo magazine 'I didn't feel I had the right album to put it on' (Cavanagh, 2018: 76).

Weller is averse to what Amabile (1996) calls 'surveillance' when writing songs; he does not think of the audience reaction in the initial phase of the process, leaving any consideration of reception until the editorial phase. His solo career has generally been less shackled by audience considerations. As Weller reflects: 'I felt that with The Jam and The Style Council I'd boxed myself into a corner lyrically with what people think you are about and what they expect, or what you think they expect from you, and I was just 'Fuck this, I'll sing and play how I feel' (ibid.). Of the difference between the creative processes in The Style Council and during the solo era, Steve White explains:

> I think the difference is that in The Style Council there was probably more of a democracy in terms of the fact that we were musically more equal partners. Obviously, Mick Talbot was much more integral to the songwriting, but when Paul went solo, I think with the first solo album the way that he explained it to me was, 'This is my show, Whitey. It might not be for you, but this is how it's going to be'. He was always completely honest about it. When he went solo, I knew who the boss was, and it was my job to keep the boss happy and I was completely fine about that.

Ray Davies (2013: 148) admits that when he has 'writers block' he will 'take anything I get' and Weller makes a similar admission to Barry Cain (2016: 437). When songs do arrive, the notion of developing a raw composition to meet the unforeseeable elements of the building process that will follow is daunting: 'Whenever I'm starting a record, it's always feels insurmountable.... Then all of a sudden, before you know it, you've got six songs on the go' (Doyle, 2015: 110). At times, songs originate by unlikely circumstance. Following a 2-year hiatus, 'As Is Now' was written in October 2004 while Weller was diagnosed with Quinsy and Chronic tonsilitis. He later reflected:

> My neck and face swelled up and I looked like a fucking zombie. I got out of hospital and was told to take extended rest, leaving me three or four weeks with nothing to do. I started bashing around on the piano and guitar and suddenly, miraculously, I had six or seven songs.
>
> (Lewis, 2020: 112)

Once writing, Weller says he is immersed in the activity, that his frame of mind is focussed on honing in on the problem-solving task of completing the song. This can result in recordings being made very quickly; Rick Buckler remembers that 'Setting Sons' was all recorded in one or two takes (Peart, 2019: 48). Recalling his induction into The Style Council, Steve White remembers: 'When we got to Radio One, he (Paul) was still writing the song. It was 'The Paris Match', and I played it after knowing these guys (Paul and Mick) for 30 minutes' (West, 2007: 47). On a related note, collaborator Erland Cooper told Mojo magazine 'he doesn't sit down for very long when he works. 'Right, straight in, let's go'. And then he moves on to the next one. It's a great pace, a great energy' (Cavanagh, 2018: 79). In the same article (ibid.: 78) fellow founder member of The Jam, Steve Brookes comments on what he calls Weller's amazing level of concentration, saying 'it's always completely what he intended. There'll never be a situation where a producer got the better of him'.

Because of Weller's aversion to click tracks, many of his studio recordings are live performances with overdubs added later. Weller's creative process is argued by Steve White (ibid.) to be at its most fluent when songs have been road tested first, since it allows for the experience of having embodied the music and evaluated a response to it. This method stretches back to an earlier point in Weller's career; Bruce Foxton recalls how the preferred recording method for The Jam was to road test material first and then record live guitar, bass and drums, preferably in one take (Ogg, 1993: 110). On some recordings, the absence of road testing is detrimental. Of 'Hung Up' producer Brendan Lynch says 'If we had left it for a couple of months and let them play it in, it could've been better' (Hewitt and Watson, 1995: 81). Road tested extensively, the backing tracks for 'Wild Wood' were recorded in a week. Steve White explains:

> The album has a very muscular feel about it because it really, truly benefited from the amount of touring that we did. At a certain point we were doing pretty much 200 shows a year and they were very high-energy shows, two and half hours, sometimes longer if Paul got into some hefty guitar soloing. I'm not talking about a macho muscularity because half the band were women. At a certain point we were a four-piece and at a certain point were a five-piece, Helen Turner, Yolanda Charles. It was a very, very hard sounding band, in a good way, a soulful band.

At one end of the production spectrum, the producer of 'In the City', Chris Parry, might be considered the conduit, or vessel through which the expression is delivered, more or less in-tact. More involved in the shaping of the sound, on mid-era Jam recordings Vic Smith and Peter Wilson bring touches of arrangement that transform, and add dimension to the song text. Psychological input can be key, and sometimes the main role of a producer is to create the right environment for music to be made. Technological insight can also be influential; with reference to the formative phase of Weller's solo career, producer Brendan Lynch credits engineer Juan Atkins with turning off all the expensive computer gear and the SSL console at Solid Bond, in order to 'break all the rules of conventional studio practice … working fast and getting a vibe going, not worrying about the overall levels, not being a slave to the equipment – just going for it and forgetting about all the bullshit' (Munn, 2014: 17).

On the evolution of recording, Moorefield (2010: 54, 55) writes:

> Since Sgt Pepper it has become quite clear that performances and records are not necessarily linked. For Eno, the studio is where composition takes place, and what is being made is not a replication or extension of the concert experience, but something altogether different … beginning with albums such as Discreet Music (1975) and Music for Films (1978) Eno effectively removed stage performance as a metaphor,

> taking the listener instead on imaginative sonic journeys unbounded by physical limits.... Realism, or the model of replicating a concert experience, isn't the point any more. What matters is the sonic experience the record offers, on its own terms, as sound. The producer is the director of the aural movie ... he is himself the artist.

Moorefield (ibid.: 62) observes the increasingly common role of the pop producer as someone who does not merely oversee the recordings of others, but is also a recording artist on the project. In the post '22 Dreams' era, producer Jan Stan Kybert and recording engineer Charles Rees are given latitude to make and alter textures and structures; to affect a metamorphosis of sound. Although Weller is a seasoned and skilled multi-instrumentalist, synthesised textures are integral to the sonic depth of many of his later recordings. While reviewers of Weller's music since 2008 often focus on the apparently extensive use of electronics, Kybert (Tingen, 2012) explains that Weller goes through several guitar pedals, using his Danelectric guitar to create synth sounds. Occasionally, as on 'Sonik Kicks', Weller has been known to add multiple layers of instrumentation, entrusting producer Jan Stan Kybert with the process of sifting and selecting sounds (Quantick, 2020: 122), and writing in Mojo, Paphides describes Kybert as a 'de-clutterer' of Weller's ideas (2021: 18).

For some of his album projects, Weller has recorded demos of songs that were eventually re-recorded as masters. Here, the demo is an early iteration of the master, but it may or may not be the *earliest* iteration, which is likely to have been constructed with voice and instrument. Some masters, most audibly the raw live takes on the album 'In the City', have no overdubs, in which case the recording is a reflection of a live performance. More commonly, the original iteration of the song is conveyed as a live performance and extensively overdubbed, gradually evolving into a master recording that constitutes elements of performance interwoven over time. Iteratively, some overdubs lead to elements of the original live performance being replaced, or withdrawn. As Schechner (1998: 28) proposes, the intention is to explore relationships among related forms. For listeners who have never made sounds, or explored the genesis and development of master song recordings, an understanding of how the recording was made can lead to profound changes in their listening (Kassabian, 2016: 198). Providing potential insight into the thought processes of artists and producers, comparative analyses of demo and master recordings can enable inferences to be made on creative trajectories.

How much of Weller's songbook was re-recorded on its way to public release is difficult to quantify. The Style Council recorded some demos for 'Our Favourite Shop' but for the most part seem to have preferred to record straight from sketch to master. Perhaps reflecting Weller's level of trust in the capabilities of those around him, his post '22 Dreams' material is often constructed and deconstructed 'on the spot' without recourse to demos. Confidence is integral to the approach; in 1995, having recently emerged from a fallow creative period, Weller was less inclined to leave the process to chance. Recorded live and limited to drums, bass, guitar and vocal, the demo of 'Porcelain Gods', establishes the feel, tempo and basic structure as eventually captured on 'Stanley Road'. Between the demo and the master recordings of 'Porcelain Gods', a number of creative decisions are audible:

- To increase the guitar motif introduction from two bars to four. Demo versions are often used to create album playlist templates that enable artists and producers to listen back to songs in sequence, to hear the tracks as a continuous set. It may have been decided to double the intro to create compositional space between the eventual arrival of the vocal of 'Porcelain Gods' and the coda of the previous track 'The Changingman';
- To add a near-identical double tracked lead vocal. Not viable on the live demo, this recording method, extensively used by The Beatles, enables the vocal to sit more easily within the instrumentation. Its effect is to allow the sound of the track to project as a singular force;
- To introduce a second, interwoven lead guitar. This intricate and often exacting task thickens the sound, creating another channel for the listener to follow upon repeated listens;
- To add gospel backing vocals in the refrain. This makes Weller's singular voice project as less introspective;
- To introduce a piano in verse two. A long-standing arrangement method in popular music, this is to sonically differentiate verse two from verse one. Creating compositional momentum, a new sound is added and mixed with subtlety, so as not to distract from the vocal;
- To increase the number of bars in the instrumental section from 6 to 8, and to add a 2-bar descending vocal section to bridge the instrumental section and the guitar motif. This subtle structural amendment extends the heightened energy and spirit of the instrumental section, and creates a more convincing and dynamic conduit for the switching of moods;
- The addition of overdubbed guitars, effects and harp on the final verse and coda. Significantly, these ornamentations ensure that, unlike the demo, the palette of sounds remains in motion, that the sound of the song is ever evolving.

The demo structure of 'Broken Stones' is retained in the master version, but the feel and instrumentation are both entirely different. A new drum rhythm precipitates a decision to switch the guitar used on the demo for a more simpatico electric piano. This new arrangement in turn invites the introduction of a Hammond organ at the bridge and a tambourine from verse 3. Ultimately, the new rhythm leads to a complete re-evaluation of the arrangement.

The demo and master of 'You Do Something to Me' have a very similar feel and tempo, and an identical structure. On the demo, the acoustic guitar is featured high in the mix, but on the final version it is mixed lower and is more strummed than picked. This change is made to accommodate the introduction of Hammond organ from the start of the song rather than from verse 2 as on the demo, bringing an immediate, rather than an eventual warmth. At the start of verse 2, replacing the new texture provided by the Hammond on the demo, an electric guitar is woven around the vocal. As on 'Porcelain Gods', momentum is created by differentiating the sounds of verses 1 and 2. Later, the newly introduced electric guitar, reminiscent in tone and style to that of Fleetwood Mac's Peter Green, is seamlessly extended to play an evocative solo that replaces the slower moving and now aesthetically redundant string synth used on the demo.

Where the demos of 'Porcelain Gods' and 'Broken Stones' were clearly intended as initial sketches, the demo of 'The Changingman' is a more overt, multi-tracked attempt to make a demo that sounds close to a master. Here, the textures of the demo are retained for the master version and essentially only the compositional furniture of the song is rearranged. Similarly, the demo of 'Start!', recorded with The Jam fifteen years earlier, is an audible attempt to create a blueprint for the eventual single. Close to identical in tempo, structure and instrumentation to the demo, the single has a thicker bass sound, a more subtle and less intrusive use of shaker and a triangle strategically placed to provide top end in the middle sections. For both 'The Changingman' and 'Start!', only cosmetic changes were required.

Listening back to the demo of 'Pretty Green', Weller appears to have been moved to change the melody of the refrain; the version on the album is notably less angular and more melodic. Other significant changes to 'Pretty Green' include; the removal of overbearing hand claps intended to provide percussive dimension; the absence of the revolver-flavoured sitar used on the demo, and the addition of the signature detuned guitar string used on the coda. As would be hoped, are all improvements, presumably as a consequence of Weller's dissatisfaction with their content and/or capacity to scan, on 'Boy About Town' the original demo lyrics were updated for the master recording. Evidencing the intense work ethic attributed to Weller by Steve Brooks, 'Boy About Town' was recorded at least three times with a full band. Version one, featuring only the trio, has a lengthy introduction, while version two features the introduction augmented by a brass section. Ultimately, the introduction was considered surplus to requirements and a decision was made to bring Weller's vocal straight in.

Performed with kinetic enthusiasm, the demo of 'That's Entertainment' has a joyous lustre that conveys the excitement of discovery. Live to tape, its arrangement is basic, and once the chord sequence and beat have been established and the vocal begins, there is nowhere new for the ear to go. Conversely, on the master recording, each verse is arranged to give it a bespoke identity, to create unobtrusive new chapters of sound. What we hear as listeners sounds very simple, yet from the perspective of those making the record the process is complex and exacting. To illustrate, in developing the song from demo to master, the following are decisions made by the band and producer to vary the soundscape:

0.00 Soundscape 1: Intro: 1 × acoustic guitar.
0.05 Soundscape 2: Intro: bass, 2 × acoustic guitars, shaker.
0.14 Soundscape 3: Verse 1 and refrain - addition of single lead voice.
0.35 Soundscape 4: Verse 2 and refrain - addition of vocal harmonies on lines 2 and 4.
0.58 Soundscape 5: 'la la la' backing vocal, temporal addition of snare drum.
1.03 Soundscape 6: Verse 3 and refrain - lead voice with backing vocal; added unison vocal on line 4.
1.26 Soundscape 7: Verse 4 and refrain - with vocal harmonies on lines 2 and 4, temporal reintroduction of snare drum.
1.56 Soundscape 8: temporary introduction of wood block.
2.04 Soundscape 9: Verse 5 and refrain with introduction of backwards guitar.
2.25 Soundscape 10: Verse 6 and refrain with single e-bow guitar line, reintroduction of snare drum.
2.46 Soundscape 11: Coda with occasional snare drum.

To emphasise the intricacy of the attention to arrangement detail, note the single tambourine rattle at 0.01, 1.22, 1.48, 2.25 and 3.15.

Writing on Cage's chance music, Wolff (Duckworth, 1999: 97) refers to the intellectual shock of the notion of composers operating randomly, or giving up control. David Bowie, whose cut-up lyric technique was viewed as part of a random 'chance' approach, was lauded by critics and fans alike for the quality of the finished work, over which he ultimately had *editorial* control. Similarly, the musicians, producers and engineers who work alongside Weller are subject to the final say of the artist, whose name will be attached to the finished work. Adelt notes how in the German band Can, Holger Czukay, who studied with Stockhausen, added sounds from radios and tapes to the mix, Michael Kerny made his Stratocaster sound like a violin and Jaki Liebeziet was a free-form jazz drummer playing straight (Adelt, 2016: 18). On his later solo recordings in particular, the musicians Weller works with often take on multiple roles. Initially a keyboardist on stage with Weller and then a bassist, on Sonik Kicks Andy Crofts sings on 'Green', arranges strings on 'Drifters' and plays guitar elsewhere. On 'Up the Dosage' on 'Wake Up the Nation' the guitarist Steve Cradock plays drums and bass (Snowball, 2017: 39, 51). This predilection for musicians to switch instruments also helps to keep the sound and feel of the recordings moving, to avoid the type of stasis created during the latter phases of The Jam and revisited in the more formal solo recording phase from 'Heavy Soul' to 'Illumination'.

In a text on experimental and electronic music, Holmes (2002: 237) reflects upon how the renowned composer Wendy Carlos invariably arrives at a point in the creation of her work when the physics of the sound become as important as the text; the construction and refinement of the timbre becomes of equal significance to the composition of the pitches. As a consequence of their extensive use of exploratory sound, there is a sense that Weller's post '22 Dreams' material could belong anywhere and to any time; its textural source is consistently elusive and this in itself creates a sense that the artist is *moving*. Working in his own studio environments in his own time, the economies of scale found in Weller's earlier work fade as time stretches out; the music becomes less predictable as the sound palette broadens. As producer and artist Brian Eno explains:

> Once you become familiar with studio facilities or even if you're not, actually, you can begin to compose in relation to those facilities. You can begin to think in terms of putting something on, putting something else on, try this on top of it, and so on, then taking some of the original things off, or taking a mixture of things off, and seeing what you're left with – actually constructing a piece in the studio.... You're working directly with sound, and there's no transmission loss between you and the sound – you handle it. It puts the composer in the identical position of the painter – he is working directly with the material, working directly onto the substance, and he always retains the option to chop and change, to paint a bit out, add a piece, et cetera.
>
> (2005: 127–129)

Reynolds advises that listeners who immerse themselves in Krautrock will find a paradoxical combination of discipline and freedom (2000: 27). This is the essence Weller seems to be aiming at, and regularly achieving in his later works. Seeking to move from the reflected glory of Brit-pop out into an as yet unchartered sonic landscape, the Paul Weller band post 2008, with its vast, psychedelic use of electronics avoids the kind of exclusive instrumental virtuosity Reynolds attaches to fusion acts, instead creating a clean, hard and immersive *soul* music. As Reynolds infers (ibid.), there is a spirituality at the heart of Krautrock, and this resonates with the older, more mature Weller, less personally concerned with setting things straight, and more immersed in the equally elusive, but progressively more pressing matters of the spirit. Importantly, as Reynolds acknowledges, guitars were used to provide instantly memorable texture on the seminal Krautrock recordings, and as an electric guitarist working within the sonic confines of synthesisers, this combination enables Weller, a consummate electric guitarist, to place himself at the centre of the sonic picture. Rooted in exploration and entrusted to kindred spirits, each reinvention is calibrated to suit his evolving frame of mind. Each direction works well because, to Weller's instinctive ear, it belongs in the here and now.

3 Image

3.1 Evolution

In the late 20th century, Sounds, NME and Melody Maker dominated the UK popular music critical landscape. Positive reviews were not guaranteed. Less closely bound to the more promotionally oriented ecology that has developed in the 21st century, journalists were opinionated and unafraid to be polemic in their summative judgments of bands and artists. Weekly music magazines were central to the discourse around popular music, critical responses to new works were awaited with trepidation, and fans and musicians, including Weller, paid close attention to reviews. On preparing to premiere 'Tommy' to an audience of journalists at Ronnie Scott's in London, Pete Townshend writes: 'As critics gathered like a pack of baying, snarling dogs we prepared to face them' (2012: 55). The Who's ultimate success on that occasion owed much to the undeniable quality of the material, yet it is clear that unanimous praise was never a foregone conclusion within UK music critical circles, that no matter the reputation of the artist, new works could equally be praised or dismissed. As an interviewee, Weller's reputation with the music press was for a long time frosty, and antagonism regularly comes into play throughout The Jam, The Style Council and Paul Weller reviews. This confrontational dynamic was initially established in 1977, when Weller burned a copy of Sniffin' Glue on stage because the fanzine editors failed to print an interview with him. Years later, upon his arrival after a long journey to cover Weller's tour of Japan for Q magazine, Cavanagh reports that Weller greeted him with the line: 'I can't stand Q, it's a load of intellectual bollocks' (1994: 26). The following year, Weller explained: 'I get the impression that most people dislike me anyway, so I will start the conversation from that point. It can only get better' (Watson and Hewitt, 1995: 44).

Despite this rancour, Weller was an avid reader of music journalism to the extent that he arranged for his record label to save copies of the NME for him when he was touring overseas (Hewitt, 2007: 62). Research by Wilderom and Van Venrooij (2019) shows how, in the late seventies, along with Sounds and Melody Maker, the New Musical Express, or NME was a key source of

DOI: 10.4324/9780429281730-4

music news in the United Kingdom. In 1980, its circulation was over 200,000 per week, while Melody Maker circulation figures were around half that number. By 2000, the circulation of NME had fallen to 80,000 and by 2014 to 15,000. Finally, in September 2015 by which time its rival publications Melody Maker and Sounds no longer existed, the NME was relaunched as a free publication. During the heyday of UK music journalism, readers' polls were an annual opportunity for music fans to voice their opinion. The cover of the NME on January 19, 1980 featured the title 'The Jam: Number One in Your Hearts; Paul, Bruce and Rick clean up NME readers' poll'. That year, following the release of 'Setting Sons' and three Top 20 hit singles, The Jam were voted best group, best album, best writer, best drummer, best bassist and best guitarist. In 1981, following the release of 'Sound Affects' and a further three highly successful singles including 'Going Underground', The Jam were voted best band, best male singer, best guitarist, best songwriter, best single and best album, above both Joy Division and David Bowie. In 1982, The Jam were voted best group, best songwriter, best guitarist, and Weller was voted most wonderful human being, beating John Peel, Tony Benn, Ken Livingstone, Clare Grogan and Lech Walesa.

Joe Boyd (2005: 35) writes of how Dylan transformed folk music in the United States of the 1960's: 'It was far more now than just a soundtrack for students and liberals, it was affecting national politics and creating huge cultural waves'. On a domestic scale, the potential for The Jam to effect social change was palpable; prior to its release the single 'Going Underground' had pre sales figures of over 200,000, numbers that more than doubled post release. Radio has always been, and continues to be influential in the reception of singles. Writing an article on John Peel (1979: 26–27, 53), NME journalist Paul Morley describes Radio One's daytime musical focus as centred on 'nostalgia and imbecility', while its evening programming offered 'a systematic, perceptive and constantly changing survey of the current massive excitement'. Morley reports that Peel, who broadcast on Radio One from 10.00pm each weekday, had listened to 135 demos that week, and had offered his favourite bands and artists, including The Jam, to record forthcoming sessions for the show. Effusive in its praise for Peel, Morley's article illustrates the chasm between commercial and alternative forms of music in the late seventies. Atypically, The Jam were soon to acquire vast followings among both audiences.

As a mass-market music, pop reflects the changing nature of its audience (Frith, 2001: 97). Between 1977 and the present day, the impact of recording technology on listening practices has been profound. Music has gradually been removed from its original contexts; in 1977 a fan of The Jam would typically buy a single (on vinyl), buy an album (on vinyl or cassette) and attend a concert. Whilst in the charts, the single would likely be played on national radio, promotional television appearances on shows including 'Top of the Pops' and 'The Old Grey Whistle Test' would often be announced in newspapers on the day of broadcast, the album and single would be listened to at home, and the concert would happen in a concert hall. Taking a share of ticket and record sales and entitled to performance royalties, the artist would expect to profit from each of these transactions. Some income streams have always been diverted away from musicians, however, as Laing (2003: 310) observes, dedicated fans of The Jam also had access to bootleg releases and unofficial live recordings at places such as Camden market.

Elborough (2008: 6–14) discusses how the LP revolutionised the way music was produced, packaged marketed, sold, purchased, listened to, and performed. As Elborough notes, it offered consumers more value for money, placed complete collections of songs within easy reach of millions, spawned the seven-inch single, encouraged many enthusiastic amateurs to make records, forced us to buy tracks we didn't really want, persuaded musicians to make sustained artistic statements, encouraged levels of indulgence unequalled in other arts and gave obsessives something to be obsessive about. Over time, the commercial value of the long player has eroded; a vinyl edition of The Jam album 'In the City' initially retailed at £4 in 1977, whilst 'Fat Pop Volume One', released in 2021, retails for £10. In keeping with inflation rates, to meet the retail valuation of 'In the City', 'Fat Pop' would need to retail at £17.50. Conversely, while a ticket to see The Jam at the Music Machine in Camden on December 12, 1980 would have cost £3.75, a ticket to see Weller live in 2021 retails at £45; in keeping with inflation, the 2021 ticket would cost just £9.50. Relatively transient and intrinsically linked to the rise of the experience economy, live music has become increasingly central to the incomes of many popular music artists.

In 1982, the Compact Disc was introduced alongside vinyl and cassette formats, eventually overtaking vinyl sales in 1988. Consequently, while Jam recordings were produced for vinyl and cassette, Style Council recordings were produced to be heard in digital formats. CDs reached their commercial peak in 2000 and became the dominant album format until 2014, when CD sales were superseded by digital music revenue. Untethering the listener from the physical constraints of music ownership, in the early 2000s, MP3 downloads and streams diffused the established notion of the album as a linear, unalterable whole. Writing in 2008, Elborough predicted that this dynamic would continue to change how music was composed and consumed and in the intervening years, it has. On streaming platforms, albums are systematically cannibalised, and one effect of this is that songs once considered to be 'growers' are subsumed by skip rates that relegate material down playlists. As a consequence, songs that are not immediately popular among digital audiences tend to be lost. The ubiquity of material available through streaming has both released artists from the tyrannical control of critics and also led to the devaluation of recorded music. Writing at the end of the 20th century, the Australian academic Peter Conrad (1998: 713–714) reflects:

> We are surrounded by new Romes, squeaky clean facsimiles of the antique original. Architects, experts at abolishing both time and space,

> can rebuild this or any other mouldered city in not much more than a day.... Time, rather than compliantly expiring, lives on in space, while space, no longer tethered to the inflexible coordinates of geography, has become as mobile and footloose as time.... We have learned how to rewind time, and how to dislocate space.

This existential change, involving the flooding into consumer life of previously inaccessible or overlooked historical, cultural and social perspectives along with an increasing breadth of qualified and unqualified opinion has coincided with the dilution of the significance of the LP. Practices and technologies are inseparably intertwined and downloaded MP3s, with what Kassabian (2016: 197) calls their 'lossy compression' were considered by many consumers to be inferior to the 'correct origin' of live performance.

As music business expert Steffan Geldner (2017) notes, musicians are increasingly inclined to distribute music across numerous platforms. Using a singular means of distribution to an audience, for instance *only* Google or *only* YouTube, is increasingly rare. Examining the dynamic from an audience perspective, Scott Cohen, co-founder of the Orchard, observes that individual listeners do not typically surf across platforms in search of music, but rather use their preferred platforms before interacting to discuss content. In terms of consumer behaviour patterns, audience demographics are unstable; Cohen (2019) argues there is a dis-connect between older fans who are encultured into standing in halls with sticky floors holding a beer, and younger audiences who prefer to be a part of digital communities that share insight into artist development.

Modern consumers live in what Simon predicted in 1971 would become 'The Attention Economy', characterised by a move from the world of product base systems to a world of access. Consequently, successful artists need to provide consumer access by delivering bespoke materials native to the platform; from the perspective of the artist there is an increased incentive to generate multiple versions of, and variations on releases. To engage existing audiences *and* draw new listeners in, popular music is obliged to thrive in an ever-increasing number of listening situations, leading to greater competition for consumers' time. Particularly since the outbreak of covid, more musicians are making and releasing music and to attract the attention of the audience, artists are obliged to make a plethora of listening and viewing experiences for free. In turn, it is hoped these loss-leading tasters will lead to sales of other more tangible items of music and merchandise.

In 2021, a typical Paul Weller fan might see a short, impactful bright video clip of a song excerpt on Instagram; this would seek to draw the viewer to the full video on YouTube, where the fan community will be encouraged to post and share reviews. An adjacent platform might host a lyric video. The official website may offer exclusive access to a pre-release stream of a single to promote the forthcoming album, which once released will be available on vinyl, CD, cassette, download or subscription. The website will likely direct fans towards promotional media appearances on radio and TV and to exclusive subscription only live performances. A behind the scenes video will be posted online to cater for fans who enjoy the metanarrative, or story around the album. The single will be played at disparate intervals on some radio stations around the time of its release. Typically recouping less than its recording costs, the single and album will not be expected to make a profit for the artist or the label, but rather break even or more likely serve as a 'loss leader' for tours. Writing on the application of economic principles to the music industry at the turn of the century, Laing states 'When demand exceeds supply, prices rise, and where supply is in excess of demand, prices tend to fall' (2003: 311). The saturation of the song release market has led to falling retail prices and lower earnings, whilst the experience economy has led to increasing demand for the live experience and a subsequent recalibration of income streams.

Recorded in March and released in May 1977, *In the City* features a selection of the first of Weller's original compositions, written between 1972 and the date of recording. During this time, as Julie Burchill and Tony Parsons put it in their ungenerous contemporary account of the punk era, the repertoire of The Jam 'gradually replaced mod museum pieces with Weller's own' (1978: 52). As such, viewed through a stylistic lens the songs seem to move in and out of focus. Showcasing songs proven popular through live performance, In the City seeks to meet a number of audiences. 'Art School' and the title track 'In the City' possess the youthful revolutionary urgency of punk, while 'Bricks and Mortar' and 'Time for Truth' offer polemics without targets. In contrast, 'I've Changed My Address' and 'I Got by in Time' are approachable, melodic songs with involved storylines. 'Takin' My Love', 'Non-Stop Dancing' and Larry Williams' 'Slow Down' are 12 bar tunes played with the aggressive intensity of Dr. Feelgood, while stylistic anomalies are 'Sounds from the Street' and 'The Batman Theme', the former an amalgamation of The Who's 'So Sad About Us' and The Ramones 'Blitzkrieg Bop', and the latter an encore form the live set of The Jam. Capturing the evolution of Weller as a songwriter in a single set, the stylistically ambiguous 'In the City' appeals to a number of different crowds.

Projecting a visceral, immediate and unpretentious introduction to The Jam, the record is more of a performance capture than a production. Arrangements are 'as live', and although perhaps earmarked as singles, some songs receive more attention than others; 'In the City' 'Away from the Numbers' and 'Art School' have guitar overdubs that create layers of sound, giving them added sonic dimension and greater listening durability. By comparison other songs are recorded away from concert pitch; 'Sounds from the Street', 'Takin My Love', 'Non-Stop Dancing' and 'Bricks and Mortar' are all captured slightly lower than their intended keys of E, G and A, perhaps indicating the realities of recording with time limitations and perhaps having hastily tuned guitars without the requisite tuning equipment. Alternatively, this effect may relate to the use of a varispeed recording process, in which the tape is slowed down for the purpose of moderating some of the band's live energy in order to translate more effectively to home listening formats.

On post 1977 Jam recordings, guitar capos are used to alter keys and set songs in the optimum key for the vocal. Unwittingly generating sonic continuity, on 'In the City', 11 of the 12 songs begin with an A or G chord; each song is recorded as written without modification. A number of early compositional traits are audible; Weller's voice comes in a third above the root note on six occasions, and throughout the record his vocal range moves between E and the E an octave above. Within these habitual parameters, some of Weller's signature compositional methods are debuted in 'Away from the Numbers' which features a wistful post-chorus that foretells the mood of 'All Mod Cons', and three separate instrumental sections, an unusual structural feature, absent elsewhere on 'In the City' that recurs in later works.

The first single 'In the City' has an immediacy beyond that of any other track on the album. Like the most prominent and memorable lines on debut singles by contemporaries The Damned, The Sex Pistols and The Clash, 'In the City' uses 'I' to personally address the audience. The first of the London bands to emerge from the punk scene to swear on vinyl, The Jam ingratiated themselves within the punk community through their distinctively aggressive and uncompromising energy. That they were the only band within the punk community to play soul covers or wear matching suits should in theory have added to their punk credentials. Polished punks, hard rhythm and blues band, singer songwriter vehicle and emerging voice of youth; on 'In the City' each stylistic projection can be heard. Tight, uncompromising, occasionally flawed and occasionally visionary, 'In the City' is unified by its singular, pulsating energy.

Writing with prescience in 1977, NME journalist Phil McNeill's review of 'In the City' states 'ominously for punk rock, they probably aren't the new Pistols, Clash, Damned or Stranglers ... they might even blow the whole scene apart and make the more 'offensive' stance of punk obsolete' (1977: 33). In competitor weekly Sounds, reviewer Chas De Whalley writes 'The Jam are more widely accessible than just about anybody sheltering under the new wave umbrella.... Aside from three real thrillers, 'In the City', 'Sounds from the Street' and 'Away from the Numbers', the others are dogged with immaturity in the writing, arranging and playing' (1977: 41). Illustrating the fickle and taciturn nature of the UK music press, two months earlier in February 1977 De Whalley had confidently stated The Jam were 'going to be huge', while a contemporary Sounds editorial dismisses The Jam as 'a 60's revivalist band'. Never achieving Platinum or Gold status, 'In the City' reached number 20 in the UK album chart. Released the previous month, 'The Clash' peaked at number 12 and was certified Gold, and The Stranglers 'Rattus Norvegicus' reached number 4 and was certified Platinum, both outselling 'In the City' in the United Kingdom.

In between their first and second albums, The Jam released a single 'All Around the World', which appears on neither album. The culture of the non-album single had been nurtured in the sixties by The Beatles, who used it for a dual purpose; to portray a sense of restless invention and also to persuade album buyers that they were getting value for money. Removed from any long form context, 'Paperback Writer', 'Penny Lane' and 'Hello, Goodbye' each possess a singular identity, a transient aesthetic. As if seeking to update a prior expression, 'All Around the World' revisits the cyclical chord sequence of 'Time for Truth' (itself borrowed from The Kinks' 'Tired of Waiting for You') and features a prominent bass line evocative of the Animals version of Barry Mann and Cynthia Weil's 'We Gotta Get Out of this Place'. To amplify the expressive intent of these reference points, both of which yearn for resolution, call and response verses emphasise a sense of urgency. However, as with 'Time for Truth', the panacea sought in the lyric, which, in a pointed reference to The Sex Pistols urges construction over destruction, is unspecified. Where the Sex Pistols prescribe anarchy and The Clash incite listeners to riot, as arbiters of change The Jam seem relatively unfocused. The lyric speaks of a need for direction, but that direction remains unclear.

Following six months after 'In the City', like its predecessor *This is the Modern World* has a number of competing aesthetics. Where 'In the City' is unified by its resonance with contemporaneous live scenes, 'This is the Modern World' is more distant and disparate. Veering from the irritated angularity of 'The Combine' and 'In the Streets Today' to the pastoral melodicism of 'Life from a Window' and 'Tonight at Noon' and on again to the sloganeering pub rock of 'Here Comes the Weekend' and 'London Girl', The Jam's sophomore album stretches in a number of directions, sometimes achieving and sometimes falling short. As Weller was quoted as saying at the time, 'We've got to forget about the future, forget about the past. At the moment, we've got to think about the present' (Bonello Rutter Giappone, 2019: 74). Starved of time to make informed reference to the past or to speculate with clarity on the future, many of the songs sound like improvised expressions in need of further development or editing. Good ideas are often unsustained and the music is occasionally jarring. A chordal move from F sharp to C sharp minor in the verse of 'In the Street Today' feels calculated to alienate, and any opportunity to sustain an authentically hostile expression is overturned by a leaden and withdrawn solo in G, followed by a subsequent move to a D chord that essentially creates compositional dead space; a sense that nothing is happening, and that the next idea is not yet here but on its way.

Released in the same month as The Sex Pistols' 'Never Mind the Bollocks', an era-defining work 10 months in the making, 'This is the Modern World' pales in comparison. Like a number of later albums recorded by Weller, the tracks seem to have been gathered from separate sessions with different aesthetic moods. Whereas on his most successful records contrasting moods are complimentary, or held together by an overarching narrative thread informed by editorial oversight, on 'This is the Modern World' the sub-grouped aesthetics are often at odds. As a songwriter, Weller seems torn between two personae; the furious polemicist and the sensitive introvert; as such the album has a schizophrenic character. Adding to the limitations on its musical accessibility, lyrics about recent events in Rhodesia and Zaire are likely to have been difficult for any audience not versed in the subtleties of geopolitics to relate to. Elsewhere, 'London Girl' offers unfortunate over-tones of misogyny similar to the type favoured by the 'Aftermath' era Rolling Stones on 'Under My Thumb' and 'Stupid Girl'. Some songs rail against collective apathy, and despite its relatable exhortation to freedom of choice, the title track conveys an impression Weller is settling scores with music critics; again, the choice of theme threatens to alienate members of the audience who don't share such directive bile.

Whilst some of the songs are clearly of lesser quality and as a collection it is ill-fitting, a number of tracks on 'This is the Modern World' are progressive and exploratory, paving the way to more lasting artistic statements. In what subsequently became a Weller trope, 'Standards' borrows from multiple sources, most notably The Who in its approximation of the motif underpinning 'I Can't Explain', and Randy Newman in its use of third person narrative to project the singer, or storyteller as villain. Based on an Adrien Henri poem and using a 12-string guitar to attain a Byrds-like texture, 'Tonight at Noon' is similarly adventurous and indicative of a growing self-confidence in Weller's belief in the efficacy of placing his own compositional voice at the centre of a postmodern collage of influences. Drawing the material away from traditional structure, like The Beatles' 'She Loves You' and 'Can't Buy Me Love' the title track effectively has two chorus hooks and, like the Beatles 'I'll Be Back', 'I Need You (for Someone)' features two middle-eights. Perhaps the most audible link to the following 'All Mod Cons' lies in 'Life from a Window'. Here the acoustic texture, lightly reverbed vocal, limber arrangement, and observational lyric are all leaps away from the rock and soul-centric aesthetics to date. Elsewhere, with its D minor to G repetitions and subsequent transposition of both chords up a tone, the middle eight of 'Here Comes the Weekend' prefigures the later, more complete 'Monday'.

Surprisingly, since Weller had by his own admission been specifically trying to re-write The Who's 'My Generation' while writing material for 'In the City', reviews of 'This is the Modern World' repeatedly draw reference to The Who. In a polemic against new wave and Weller in particular, NME's Mick Farren (1977: 33) reasons 'You can't call someone like Pete Townshend a geriatric scumbag in one breath and then load all his early work onto a supermarket trolley and pass it off as your own'. Conversely, Farren hears a production 'well on the thin side' with 'vocals that lean towards the monotonous' whilst also hearing 'excellent, streamlined rock n' roll'. Published in the same week, Chris Brazier's review for Melody Maker highlights the 'competent and dynamic' playing whilst also addressing perceived limitations created by a lack of development from the first album. As Brazier perceptively notes 'conclusive proof that introspective optimism suits The Jam lies in 'Life from A Window' and 'Tonight at Noon', two really fine songs…. 'Life from a Window' radiates human warmth…. Seeming to transcend life while at the same time remaining healthily rooted within it' (1977: 25).

Writing a year later with trademark vigour, Julie Burchill and Tony Parsons call 'This is the Modern World' 'an artistically miserable failure…. Overstretched, tuneless and bitter' (1978: 52). Released three weeks before 'This is the Modern World', 'Never Mind the Bollocks, Here's the Sex Pistols' reached number 1 in the UK album chart and was certified Double Platinum for sales over 600,000. Although it outsold 'In The City', the highest UK chart position for 'This is the Modern World' was number 22, for which it was certified Silver for sales of over 60,000. Such comparisons are relative; released on the same day as 'This is the Modern World' and similarly dismissed by contemporary critics, the second Damned album 'Music for Pleasure' failed to make the UK Top 100 album chart. Over the following months, following their dismissal of new songs presented by The Jam in the spring of 1978, by the summer Polydor had shifted their promotional attention from The Jam to Sham 69, who were outselling their label mates (Jack, 2015: 60).

In the intervening years, plenty has been written and said about *All Mod Cons*, Weller's third album with The Jam. Whilst bands associated with the movement had splintered and evolved, within British popular culture the punk look initiated by Malcolm McLaren and Vivienne Westwood continued to be pervasive at a cultural consumer level. Like The Jam, during 1978 The Clash released occasional singles, slowly piecing together the album 'Give 'Em Enough Rope', while John Lydon, the prominent Sex Pistol, was embarking on a dub reggae odyssey with Public Image Limited. In terms of artistic progression, evolving post punk subsections were quite distinctive; The Stranglers, Magazine, and latterly Joy Division had adopted a dark, industrial aesthetic that attracted those with a sensibility towards the brooding and intense; Blondie, Elvis Costello, The Police and Squeeze had a brighter, more melodic sound that attracted audiences both in the United Kingdom and across the Atlantic; The Fall and The Slits opted for a DIY mode that held a particularly empowering appeal for those who wanted to make music with limited instrumental skills; Crass appealed to political crowds, notably anarchists; and The Cockney Rejects and The Angelic Upstarts were the southern and northern heirs to the bar chord heavy bombast of the Sex Pistols.

Released in November 1978, 'All Mod Cons' immediately occupied its own strata. Disconcertingly, the title track is entirely atypical of the remainder of the album. Angular and through composed, it revisits the limitations of earlier accusatory lyrics, neglecting to identify a target. Who is the 'you' Weller is singing to? Is it Polydor? Punks? Critics? A curious opening to the record, 'All Mod Cons' mirrors The Beatles 'Sgt. Pepper's Lonely Hearts Club Band' in the way it uses a partly formed idea to usher out an 'old' band and ring in the new. Ultimately, it proves to be a farewell to the ambiguous target; from here on in, any object of lyrical scorn is clearly visible. Introducing the idea that lyric communication might not necessarily be framed from singer to listener, 'To Be Someone (Didn't We Have a Nice Time)' introduces the narrator as dreamer, the conveyor of an implied inner voice. The degree to which any lyric is written in 'inner voice' is debatable, but here, as in many of the Beatles mid-period lyrics the inference is that the words are 'sung to self'. Whilst 'Michelle' is being sung to 'Michelle', a lyric like 'I Am the Walrus' is easier to interpret as relatively insular. Whereas 'In the City' is concise and calibrated to be sung directly to an audience, in 'To Be Someone' many of the phrases are incidental, seemingly unfiltered for third party consumption. As a lyric, it marks a realisation on Weller's behalf that a fleeting observation might be enough, that not every lyric gesture bears the responsibility of moving the listener, or creating change.

Ray Davies recalls how 'The Kinks Are the Village Green Preservation Society' was about documenting people's existence by capturing them in a portrait (Jovanovic, 2013: 151). The first of a number of character portraits written by Weller for 'All Mod Cons', 'Mr. Clean' sets up the first of a series of oppositions integral to the aesthetic of the album. Where in the following song in the sequence 'David Watts' is the character aspired to, 'Mr. Clean' is the character to be avoided. Where vague targets had been alluded to on the first two Jam albums, here none of the venom is dissipated; the object of Weller's distrust is personalised and made visible to the listener. As the lyric narrator, like Paul McCartney in The Beatles 'Penny Lane', Weller is omnipresent. While McCartney wanders freely from the barber shop to the shirt pocket of a fireman to inside a nurse's mind, Weller roams from the breakfast table where 'Mr. Clean' is eating toast, to a bus, a train and then into Mr. Clean's dreams of pretty young girls. Weller can't have actually been there, but as the omnipresent narrator he can paint us an indelible and fully dimensional picture. Like McCartney, Weller draws himself into the drama; Mr. Clean is not in Weller's ears and in his eyes, but should he walk down the same street, Mr. Clean should be careful not to cross him. By using omnipresent narratives, both songwriters convince us that they really are there, that images and feelings beyond their experiential sphere are within their grasp. Equally importantly, in 'Mr. Clean' Weller creates plenty of compositional space for the listener to imagine their own version of Mr. Clean; how he looks, how he dresses, how he acts.

A singularly bold gesture, and one of the most abrupt and unpredictable stylistic detours in popular music history, 'English Rose' introduces genteel folk to side one of 'All Mod Cons'. A ballad of longing, it opens the realms of possibility, bringing gravitas to the album. Creating distance between Weller and his peers, it announces him as a songwriter willing to write irony free love songs, an artist whose next move will never be predictable again. Side one closes with 'In the Crowd', a song that seems to revisit and dramatically improve upon the earlier song 'The Combine'. Like 'English Rose', 'In the Crowd' breaks new compositional ground for Weller. From a lyric perspective it seems to be about nothing; its non-sequitur lyric is incidental and exhibits no expressive ambition. The psychedelic drift of its extended coda evokes a sense that The Jam will now move in their own musical time, that economy of structure and conciseness of expression will no longer be de rigueur. Here, the message is ceded to metaphor; like The Beatles 'A Day in The Life', the piece encapsulates the mundanity and magic of human existence.

Next in a series of thematic oppositions, 'Billy Hunt' is the character who would like to be 'David Watts'. Billy seeks to convince the listener he is going somewhere, and is conveyed as a comical and naïve dreamer made likeable by the words, music and performances used to convey him. To convey satirical and social issues, American songwriters Randy Newman and John Prine had earlier in the seventies sung lyrics very obviously in the voices of others, with Newman's album 'Good Old Boys' frequently inhabiting the voice of fictional deep southerner Johnny Cutler, and Prine's 'Angel from Montgomery' delivered from the perspective of an elderly woman. At the time Weller and The Jam were recording 'All Mod Cons', Tom Waits was recording 'Christmas Card for a Hooker in Minneapolis', a song sung in the voice of a pregnant female protagonist for his album 'Blue Valentine'. Critically, this lyric method allows the narrator to break from the implied responsibilities of personal expression, and instead embrace phrases and attitudes that may be attributed to someone else. As such, it is a liberating technique, used for the first time here by Weller, who would return to it on numerous occasions in the future.

A thematically varied trilogy of love songs, 'It's Too Bad', 'Fly' and 'The Place I Love' exemplify the understated and deft arrangements of producer Vic Smith. Where 1977 recordings had been blocky and live, seeking to capture energy, throughout 'All Mod Cons' Weller's multi-layered Rickenbackers provide distinctive and dynamic colourations, Bruce Foxton's bass wanders into higher registers to add expressive melodic counterparts and Rick Buckler's drums respond intuitively; everything clicks. Another improved revision, this time of 'Sounds from the Street', 'It's Too Bad' borrows an instrumental section from the Beatles 'She Loves You', its juxtaposition of upbeat music and bitter lyric from Holland, Dozier and Holland and it's skilfully crafted summative middle eight from Gerry Goffin and Carole King's 'Will You Love Me Tomorrow'. In the middle eight of 'It's Too Bad', the sullen B minor alters the mood of the lyric expression completely, introducing a temporal intensity that gives the tune gravitas. As if to distract the listener from the reality, the place from which there is no escape, the escapist overtones of 'Fly' and 'The Place I Love' reinforce the dream.

Superseding the two-chord motif of 'Art School', the first part of the violent closing phase of 'All Mod Cons', 'A Bomb in Wardour Street' uses its motif as an immediately recognisable riff. The precision of its location similarly supplants Bruce Foxton's 'London Traffic' and Weller's 'London Girl', both of which seem vague and unfocussed by comparison. Critically, in 'A Bomb in Wardour Street' the narrator places himself at the scene of the incident; he is not removed from the drama, instead he is involved. Again, Vic Smith's attention to arrangement detail is significant. Cowbells are heard at the top end of the sound spectrum in verse 1, giving way to increasingly aggressive toms in verse 2. Later, the guitar solo is written more than improvised, and the feedback underscoring verse 3 is replaced by handclaps in verse 4. Mirroring the lyric, the arrangement suggests restless movement within the overbearing claustrophobia of the music.

Revisiting the fear and desperation of 'A Bomb in Wardour Street' in a minor key setting, 'Down in the Tube Station at Midnight' is a story told over a series of chapters. Overshadowing Rick Buckler's inventive pre-coda drum figure, Bruce Foxton's bass has prominence as the lead instrument, its harmonic movement allowing Weller to deliver a vocal in a relatively condensed range; the lowest sung note is a G and the highest C. This restricted range creates an interesting effect in that it implies the singer is reluctant, or unable to cry for help. On 'A Bomb in Wardour Street' the vocal range is similarly restricted to notes between A and E; in both songs this unwittingly adds narrative claustrophobia and resignation to fate. Previously, partly as a consequence of setting so many songs in the keys of G and A, Weller's vocal melodies had typically traversed the range between E and E (To Be Someone, Away from the Numbers); F sharp to E (I Changed My Address); G to E (In the City); G sharp to E (In the Street Today, Standards, Art School) or A to E (Takin' My Love), with the more recent 'Life from A Window' and 'Here Comes the Weekend' occasionally pushing the voice up to F sharp. At the forefront of many producer's minds, the setting of keys for vocals is integral to the capture of energy. Where on the earlier works Weller's voice leaps expressively from the instrumentation, on 'A Bomb in Wardour Street' and 'Down in the Tube Station at Midnight' he subdues his voice, allowing the music to frame the expression.

Tapping into a universal fear, the lyric themes of 'A Bomb in Wardour Street' and 'Down in the Tube Station at Midnight' convey the hopeless feeling of being stranded and under attack. That the lyrics are frequently elude a rhyming scheme makes them more immediate, less composed and ultimately more conversationally authentic. The visual detail of 'Tube Station' is cinematic and the sensory impressions vivid; smells, sounds and sights are threaded into the lyric, which is delivered at a pace and tempo that allows it to be absorbed in real time. Where 'A Bomb in Wardour Street' flashes past, 'Down in the Tube Station at Midnight' seems to happen in slow motion and lingers in the memory. It is one of many lyric narratives on 'All Mod Cons' borne of Weller's imagination. Where previous albums convey experience, this collection imagines. What would be like to be universally adored? What would it be like to escape? What would be like to be trapped? A seamless montage of the ambiguities that lie within the dream and the awakening, 'All Mod Cons' blurs fiction and reality, and in doing so offers a means of escape for Weller as a songwriter.

Continuing the unfortunate theme of implied plagiarism, the headline of NME journalist Charles Shaar Murray's October 28, 1978 review of 'All Mod Cons' reads 'The Jam Sell Out'; a pun on the album 'The Who Sell Out'. It transpires the reviewer is playing to the gallery, as he writes 'It's not only several light years ahead of anything they've done before, but it's also the album that's going to catapult The Jam right into the front rank of international rock n' roll'. Shaar Murray continues: 'Weller has the almost unique ability to write love songs that convince the listener that the singer is really in love.... Without ever descending to the patented sentimentality that is the stock in trade of the emotionally bankrupt'. Shaar Murray characterises 'English Rose' as 'a musical and emotional finger in the eye for anyone who still clings to the old punk tough guy stereotype' (1978: 43). In the concurrent Melody Maker review of 'All Mod Cons', Frances Lass praises 'Mr. Clean' for its 'vitriolic attack on middle class mediocrity and self-satisfaction that is even more compelling for its understated, not to say lyrical melody line'. Later in the review, in a further expansion of the taciturn nature of the critical eye, readers are warned that 'Weller hasn't suffered any deviation from his time warp mentality ... (and) has got himself into a trap by writing love songs ... he should have caught up with the rest of us by 1990. Can you wait' (1978: 26)? Certified Gold for sales of over 100,000, 'All Mod Cons' highest UK chart position was number 6. Released a week later and selling in similar quantities, 'Give 'Em Enough Rope' by The Clash reached number 2 in the UK charts. Poorly reviewed in Sounds and NME yet later considered a ground-breaking example of post punk, 'First Issue' by ex-Sex Pistol John Lydon's new band Public Image Limited was released a month after 'All Mod Cons'. Like 'In the City', 'First Issue' was uncertified, reaching number 22 on the UK album chart.

In between 'All Mod Cons' and 'Setting Sons', The Jam released two singles not included on either album. Continuing their work with Vic Smith, The Jam recorded 'Strange Town' at the end of 1978 and released it in March 1979, followed by 'When You're Young', released in August 1979. 'Eton Rifles', the first and only single from 'Setting Sons', was released in November 1979. Rather than issue a second single from 'Setting Sons', The Jam chose to release 'Going Underground/Dreams of Children' in March 1980. From the perspective of the listening public, as a songwriter Weller was, at this time, flush with compelling ideas.

Continuing the incidental thread established on 'In the Crowd', the single 'Strange Town' is essentially about wandering around; it has no point to make other than to be someone, somewhere. This thematic ambivalence draws the ear to the music, which moves through a modified, confidently embellished ABABCAB structure similar to that used on 'Billy Hunt'. Transitions of sound are embedded in the arrangement, adding harmonic dimension. A precursor of the more complex structuring used frequently on 'Setting Sons', the C section of 'Strange Town' begins with a written guitar solo before moving into a middle eight that was originally demoed on 'Worlds Apart' a year earlier. This leads into a complex instrumental breakdown using a descending chord sequence from C to G which itself has four different sections of instrumental arrangement. With a new coda section, also in four separately arranged parts closing the track, there is a clear sense that the chord and lyric text of 'Strange Town' is only the beginning of its making as a song; the structure and arrangement are integral to its development and give it much of its momentum. Characterised by lateral experimentation to find combinations of sounds that might 'work', and rigorous in its ambition to sift, collect and perform each combination in its most effective from, its journey from song to record is extensive. Where fine, memorable singles like 'In the City' and 'This is the Modern World' engage and ultimately tie the listener to their meaning, with its lyric ambiguity and sonic sense of adventure, 'Strange Town' liberates with its possibilities.

Conversely, 'Butterfly Collector', the B Side of 'Strange Town' and only Weller's second song to be written in a minor key, pays scant attention to arrangement detail. Rather than disappoint by comparison, 'Butterfly Collector' has an uncomplicated charm, a looseness that compliments the intensity and rigour of its counterpart. Like 'Strange Town', the second standalone single of 1979 'When You're Young' has its own introductory motif, this time a three-note sung part clearly created with crowd response in mind. As Frith writes, 'Pop's history is obviously marked by moments of collective sentimentality where we are involved; not just the singer sings, but we sing from the heart' (Frith, Street and Straw, 2001: 103, 106). In 'When You're Young' a collective motif of this kind recurs after each chorus and doubles as a coda. The attention to recording detail is again evident; voices are doubled on some parts and not on others; drums are used to differentiate the sonic impressions made by verses; electric guitars are overdubbed on choruses to expand the spectrum of sound and the controlled feedback used on 'All Mod Cons' returns as a signature texture.

Dashed by the realities of adulthood, the lyric of 'When You're Young' pre-empts the theme of the fourth Jam album *Setting Sons*. On this album, Weller's songs are further enhanced by basslines that move inventively between the electric guitars and drums. Where the live heaviness and scattergun fury of 'In the City' and 'This is The Modern World' was superseded by the deft economy of touch and controlled energy of 'All Mod Cons', 'Setting Sons' feels entirely settled; as if the band naturally know how to play, how to sound. Perhaps for that reason, it is highly inventive in terms of structure, arrangement and lyric writing, to the extent it seems to test compositional limits. Demo recordings of 'Eton Rifles' and 'Burning Sky' indicate that Weller's initial compositions for 'Setting Sons' were relatively sparse, that the bare bones of his initial songs were used as frameworks around which numerous instrumental parts were eventually built. On 'Eton

Rifles', the only original song on the album to hinge upon an immediately identifiable chorus, the two chords before the chorus (F to G) were added between the demo and the final version. Here, Weller will likely have sensed that the verse was moving to the chorus too rapidly for the verse to be absorbed in real time, and that counter intuitively, some extra, relatively featureless music would be needed to punctuate the sections.

Uniquely within the Weller canon, 'Setting Sons' is an album of unorthodox and adventurous middle sections. Before verse 3, 'Girl on the Phone' moves from its established home key of D to incorporate an angular E flat and G sharp; surprisingly, the effect is dynamic rather than jarring. After verse 3, there is a second middle eight, this time over a descending riff, followed by a repeat of the earlier, first middle eight. Moving to two new sections after its opening verses, 'Thick as Thieves' follows a similarly unconventional structural path. In an imprint of the signature compositional style of 'Setting Sons', neither section is definitively a chorus or pre-chorus, rather both sections are pieces of music that 'work'. Seemingly the result of having played through numerous iterations of the raw song to discover and edit ensemble interpretations that work together, continuing the aesthetic established by 'Strange Town', on 'Thick as Thieves' and 'Private Hell' the band arrangements are intricate. The attention to detail is extreme; on 'Saturday's Kids', the spectrum of sound changes eight times in the middle section alone.

The compositional weight of the album is leavened by songs that orbit at a remove. A concept album about disillusionment, 'Setting Sons' is, tempered by the occasional distraction, or wavering from theme. Like the Beach Boys 'Pet Sounds' and Willie Nelson's 'Red Headed Stranger', both of which call upon covers adjacent to their prevailing theme, The Jam occasionally lighten the mood. Using touches of humour and up-tempo frameworks, 'Girl on the Phone' and 'Saturday's Kids' explore social issues with a relative lightness, and the closing cover of Martha Reeves and the Vandellas 'Heatwave' overturns any notion of conceptual purity. As Frith writes 'From the earliest days of music hall, comic turns would wrap up their act with a directly sentimental song: Forget the cynicism and humiliations of music-hall humour they seemed to say, this is the real me, the real you' (Frith, Street and Straw, 2001: 103). Closing a complex set of original works 'Heatwave' seems to serve a similar purpose. The sub-themes of the original songs on 'Setting Sons' are:

Girl on the Phone: We are all under surveillance
Thick as Thieves: Our youthful ideals fade
Private Hell: We all experience inner turmoil
Little Boy Soldiers: Our destiny is not in our own hands
Wasteland: We are surrounded by worthless matter
Burning Sky: We are conditioned to value finance over friendship
Smithers Jones: Those who control us don't care about us
Saturday's Kids: We don't have much
The Eton Rifles: We are dominated by elites.

Amidst the resignation to fate, many of the lyrics have in-built cracks in the clouds, moments when the darkness is illuminated by fleeting victories; the promise of time to relax on 'Smithers Jones'; a quick capstan wall filter on 'Saturday's Kids'; the promise of returning for more next week in 'Eton Rifles'; even the self-deception of solace in 'Burning Sky'. Using layers of implied meaning, the overbearing nature of these lyric themes is countered by the quick movement of the music; none of the songs are below mid-tempo. Cementing the idea that Weller is involved in the various scenarios or short stories, the lyrics are predominantly written in the first person; as the narrator he is careful not to place himself outside of the action. Paradoxically, this method enables him to circumvent autobiography by using a range of fictional character voices. Moral and ethical judgements are implied; like Bob Dylan before him, in the writing of 'The Lonesome Death of Hattie Carroll', Weller dispassionately reports what he sees around him, leaving us to draw our own conclusions.

Technically, 'Setting Sons' is atypical. 'Saturdays Kids' uses soft rhyme on four disparate stanzas, and 'Eton Rifles' and 'Private Hell' are similarly indiscriminate, allowing some couplets to rhyme and others not to. 'Thick as Thieves' is rhyme free until its repeated first middle eight, while 'Wasteland' and 'Little Boy Soldiers' are entirely free of rhyme scheme. The effect of this deliberately free lyric approach is to project the songs as conversational, unburdened by convention or expectation. Considered in tandem with the unconventional approach to structuring, 'Setting Sons' is an anomaly within the context of mainstream pop artists of the time. Shadowing Bruce Springsteen's progression from 'Born to Run' to 'Darkness on the Edge of Town', where 'All Mod Cons' glides through its dream universe of infinite possibility, here, with freedom closing in and options narrowing, 'Setting Sons' projects a harsh and angular set of realities.

Writing for Melody Maker, Paolo Hewitt (1979: 27) reasons: 'Whereas before he (Weller) railed against the uncertainties and injustices of the modern world, now he's really taking stock of all the evidence, and supplying us with his bleakest picture yet. Two opposing points of view are presented – the conquering and the vanquished' – to present what Hewitt calls 'a reflection of the ideals and values that society foists upon us at an early age, and which ultimately tear us apart as we grow up'. Musically, according to Hewitt, the album portrays 'Screaming guitar work, sardonic orchestrations, military backdrops and fiery chording'. Writing for the New Musical Express, Tony Stewart adopts a similarly reverent tone, noting how 'It took three albums to find their own identity and step out of the warm security of imitation.... Setting Sons is a major development and something of a departure. Its scope has wider connotations but paradoxically, its subjects are narrower and less easy to identify'. Like Hewitt, Stewart notes the breadth of expression, citing 'ragged anger, mellow prettiness, theatrical drama and staccato spiky guitar' (1979: 44). For the first and only time in the chronology of The Jam, UK music media critical reviews were unconditional in their praise for the expansive range and artistic depth of the music. Buoyed by recent hit singles and the bands increasing popularity as a live act, 'Setting Sons' reached number 6 in the UK charts, and was certified Gold for sales of over 100,000. Exemplifying the extent to which many artists considered part of the new wave scene had outgrown punk, as The Jam were recording 'Setting Sons', Elvis Costello and the Attractions were listening to Abba and David Bowie to find inspiration for 'Armed Forces', while The Clash were channelling rockabilly, ska, jazz and New Orleans R'n'B to assemble 'London Calling'. By contrast 'Setting Sons' and the singles released to accompany it overlook external influence and instead build upon previous Jam recordings.

A standalone single released in between 'Setting Sons' and 'Sound Affects', 'Going Underground' was hugely popular in terms of record sales. As might be anticipated of a hit record, from the perspective of the listener it has an unquestioning flow; each progression makes unquestioning sense. From the perspective of the writer, players and producers, however, within its 171 seconds it comprises 21 separate sections, 17 of which are never repeated in their initial form. As if to disprove there is a formula for hit making, Weller references nuclear textbooks, atomic crimes, kidney machines, hatred, brass bands, braying sheep and an exploding head; as a pop song it defies gravity:

000 Intro: guitar and bass (written guitar chord D)
0.07 Verse 1: voice, guitar, bass and occasional drum (written guitar chord D)
0.17 Pre chorus 1: full band, percussive rhythm (written chords B to D sharp)
0.23 Pre chorus 2: full band, straight rhythm (written chords B to D sharp)
0.28 Pre chorus 3: full band (ascending chord sequence)
0.36 Chorus 1
0.48 Turnaround
0.52 Verse 2: voice, guitar, bass, occasional drum and organ – new lyric
1.04 Pre-chorus 4: full band, percussive rhythm – new lyric
1.09 Pre-chorus 5: full band, straight rhythm – new lyric
1.15 Pre-chorus 6: full band (ascending chord sequence, repeated)
1.21 Chorus 2 (as Chorus 1, up a tone)
1.32 middle section 1 (syncopated drums)
1.38 middle section 2 (snare hits)
1.43 middle section 3 (straight rhythm)
1.49 middle section 4 (guitar solo)
1.59 middle section 5 (drum fills)
2.10 middle section 6 (middle section 1 twice)
2.20 Pre-chorus 6 (repeated)
2.26 Chorus 2 (repeated)
2.35 Chorus 2 (repeated and embellished)

Accommodating Weller's angular composition which moves from its home chord of D to an alternating B and E flat, the constant invention and movement of the drum and bass parts effectively blur the lines between sections, creating a rapid succession of pre-choruses and an extended middle section that explores numerous variations on the arrangement of three chords. The impression made is one of a band testing the boundaries of what might be possible in popular song. With its repetitive, circular structure and pastoral feel, 'Dreams of Children', the flip side of 'Going Underground' further amplifies this high level of aesthetic ambition, the two sides conjoining much as the Beatles earlier 'Paperback Writer' and 'Rain' to convey hitherto unheard facets of a sound at its creative zenith.

After the daring originality of 'Going Underground' the lead single from *Sound Affects*, 'Start!' features the most obvious lift in Weller's recorded canon; the bass line from the Beatles 'Taxman'. This is apt, since the aesthetic variety of 'Revolver' is very much reflected in 'Sound Affects' itself. Following the observational and bleak 'Setting Sons', 'Sound Affects' is autobiographical and immersed in love of sound. Where 'Setting Sons' frequently uses complex structure across static arrangement, 'Sound Affects' favours economy of structure and is more preoccupied with texture. Within the overarching production aesthetic, each song has its own sonic identity. Galvanised by their increasingly involved roles, Bruce Foxton and Rick Buckler are often to the fore in 'Sound Affects'. The rumbling bass is a key feature underpinning 'Pretty Green' and provides a McCartneyesque sense of restless melodic adventure on 'But I'm Different Now'. Elsewhere, the drums are integral to the chaptering of 'Dream Time' and the intricate arrangement of 'That's Entertainment'. Where the rhythm section had previously framed Weller's songwriting, here they shape it. Adding a sonic lift and bringing the energy of the music closer to the Beatles, who often used G as the highest sung note, keys are shifted to enable Weller to sing up to G, a transition that helps to make the record sound and feel lighter and more melodically limber than any other Jam album.

Like 'Setting Sons', on 'Sound Affects' it is often unclear which parts are intended to be verses, choruses or bridge sections. Unencumbered by convention, 'Boy About Town' and 'Man in the Corner Shop' are simply presented as a collection of musical ideas. Elsewhere, the most memorable phrase, or hook in 'Pretty Green' is not found in the tense lift of its 'chorus', but in the opening line of its verse. 'Monday', whose verses makes their unorthodox way from F sharp minor to B minor, to C, to B minor, then up to F, and finally resting on E minor, begins with a chorus which is later repeated an octave higher. Akin to the uncomplicated 'But I'm Different Now' and 'Music for the Last Couple', 'That's Entertainment' is a strophic composition with six verses.

A masterclass in sensory projection and highly unusual within the context of popular music, 'That's Entertainment' features a lyric that makes no reference to its narrator, to an 'I' or 'me' figure. As such, it makes no demand on Weller's behalf; his role is to observe and describe what he is seeing without judgment or implied hierarchy. An extended list of observations, it follows in the tradition of Dury, Jankel and Payne's 'Reasons to be Cheerful Part 3', recorded by Ian Dury and the Blockheads and released a year earlier. Where Dury's lyric references musical icons Dimitri Shostakovich, Rico Rodriguez, Buddy Holly, Little Richard, John Coltrane and Smokey Robinson alongside artistic figures The Marx Brothers, Woody Allen, Salvador Dali and such collected ephemera as Scammell Lorries, oatmeal and equal voting rights, Weller's narrative reports more than it curates. Each couplet evokes a sound, an incidental sight or scene, a feeling of sharp discomfort or impatience, a stolen moment of intimacy. In its fleeting attempt to distil the elusive essence of its vast subject matter, 'That's Entertainment' celebrates the joy, wonder, misery and mundanity what it means to be alive.

On side two of 'Sound Affects', the unassuming masterpiece 'Man in a Corner Shop' is sequenced in between the breezy 'Dream Time' and the incidental soundscape 'Music for the Last Couple'. Here, as in the zen refrain of 'Start!', spirituality emerges in sharp relief. In another volte face, where 'Setting Sons' was about inequality, 'Sound Affects' is more concerned with equality. Alternating between the keys of D and B, 'Man in the Corner Shop' reflects on how the grass is always greener on the other side, and how those who appear to have got ahead in life are victims to the same frailties and insecurities that haunt those lower down the rung. In a variety of ways, on 'Sound Affects' Weller portrays himself as unassuming, open to possibility, equal or aspiring to be equal to those around him. Easily surpassing 'In the City' and 'This is the Modern World' in terms of lyric, textural and melodic breadth, 'Sound Affects' warmly confronts the escapist tendencies of 'All Mod Cons' and eclipses the knowing cynicism of 'Setting Sons'. In his November 22, 1980 review for the New Musical Express, Paul Du Noyer writes:

> This album takes the band forward.... More than ever, The Jam's attacking spirit is being allied to melodic invention and to lyrics that are increasingly thoughtful.... The guitar work is evocative of 'Revolver'. The crucial point, though, is that these influences are incorporated only to enrich what's already there, and remain subservient to Weller's own songwriting gifts and to the distinct, powerful identity of The Jam.
>
> (1980: 41)

Published on the same day in 1980, Patrick Humphries' Melody Maker review is more reserved. He asks 'Why am I not convinced? What I hear is a Jam album I respect, but don't necessarily like.... I do not doubt Weller's sincerity – he has proven his ability at articulating the frustrations which form a sad foundation for this society'. Humphries concludes that 'Sound Affects' is flawed and beneath Weller's capabilities (1980: 29). Nevertheless, continuing the upward commercial trajectory of The Jam, the album reached number 2 in the UK charts and was certified Gold, selling over 100,000 copies.

In the aftermath of 'Sound Affects', The Jam released three new original Weller songs; 'Funeral Pyre', 'Absolute Beginners', and 'Tales from the

Riverbank'. A template of sorts for the eclectic final Jam album 'The Gift' released the following year, the percussive and elliptical 'Funeral Pyre' seeks to appeal to an alternative listenership, the brass driven and melodic 'Absolute Beginners' captures the pop face of the band and 'Tales from The Riverbank' exudes a brooding psychedelia. Of Weller's contemporaries, only Madness, who released the dour 'Grey Day' and the refrain free 'Shut Up' in the midst of the hook laden 'Baggy Trousers' and 'Driving in My Car' were equally willing to embrace the accessible and the inaccessible, to openly void any pretentions towards the commercial single. Presaging 'The Gift', there is a sense across these singles that the fabric of the sound, the identity of The Jam is being stretched, that the number of available variations is finite and beginning to narrow.

Like 'Scrape Away', 'Funeral Pyre' is structured to sound unstructured, intricately arranged to sound improvised. Cited in an interview with Adrian Thrills a year earlier, Weller mused 'I think we're getting more and more into rhythm, more into primal music, like African drum music.... England must be the only country in the world with no real ethnic music like that' (1980: 21). He continued 'As things have got so much bigger for the group, people expect a lot more of you, which is something I'm trying to fight against' (ibid.). Weller's response to this commercial and artistic pressure, reflected in the slight 'Pop Art Poem', given away free to readers of the magazine Flexipop, and in the lightweight instrumental 'Music for the Last Couple', is perhaps also reflected in the daring commercial disdain of 'Funeral Pyre'. Ending with a drum solo, like 'Going Underground', 'Funeral Pyre' has an intuitive structure likely unique in the history of popular music. Unlike 'Going Underground' its character is rooted in atmospheric more than in songcraft; there is no hook, its third and sixth verses are extended and the turnaround sections that punctuate the verses alternate between autumnal E minor and A minor chord changes.

Exchanging the abrasive, ringing guitar texture of 'Funeral Pyre for a soft electric guitar sound that allows brass to co-exist within the sound spectrum, vocal continuity aside, the following single 'Absolute Beginners' could easily have been written and recorded by a different band. Neatly structured, with bespoke intro, solo and coda sections added to create compositional balance, it sits comfortably with much of the chart music of its time. The B-side 'Tales from the Riverbank' returns to the theme of youth explored by Weller in 'When You're Young' and 'Saturday's Kids', this time in a more directly autobiographical sense. Emphasising the ongoing appetite of The Jam to revisit and re-examine, the bass line is recycled from 'Scrape Away' and 'Funeral Pyre'. Forefronting an extended coda reminiscent of those appended to 'Down in the Tube Station at Midnight', 'Private Hell' and 'Set the House Ablaze', the guitar textures on 'Tales from the Riverbank' are immersive and foreboding. Like the equally mysterious and impenetrable 'Funeral Pyre', 'Tales from the Riverbank' favours metaphor over meaning.

The final album by The Jam, *The Gift* finds Weller's songwriting having travelled full circle. like in 'In the City' it conveys three distinct styles, each of which correspond to a 'live' aesthetic. Whereas the songs on the debut album might be divided into punk, pub rock and an evolving original sound, 'The Gift' integrates soul, protest and a fully formed original sound. Unlike any of the previous three Jam albums, each of which settles into a distinctive aesthetic, 'The Gift' possesses an overarching impatience. The painstakingly written and edited sections that make 'Setting Sons' so immersive are absent, as are the deft touches of arrangement that give 'Sound Affects' its unique sense of economy. Here, it seems the impetus to build, to add lateral layers has diminished. Rather, the primary aim is to commit a collection of ideas with bespoke energies to tape and to present them unadorned. Like side two of the Beatles 'Abbey Road' – a record made under similarly trying circumstances – many of the compositional ideas that make up 'The Gift' are presented 'as is'.

As overseen by producer Peter Wilson, fortunately many tracks benefit from this approach. Where it lacks structural adventure, 'The Gift' benefits from a surfeit of great tunes and poised lyrics. A Motown homage with a modern social agenda, 'Town Called Malice' reaches an ecstatic sonic altitude. Similar to the unlikely chord sequences used in 'Going Underground', by making the dour shift from F sharp minor to E minor the verses of 'Town Called Malice' defy pop music convention to generate an unmistakable positivity. Melodic and robust, 'Happy Together' is a dimensional love song with intricate guitar lines augmented by a typically inventive and supple bass. On 'Ghosts', which like some tracks on 'In the City' seems to have been varispeeded to acquire the requisite energy, a simple lyric and melody are given ingenious dimension by adding a different number of handclaps to each verse – 4, 7, 6, 3, 5 and then for the final verse none. Typifying Peter Wilson's approach to the capture of songs on the album, 'Ghosts' seems to have been committed to tape quickly and painstakingly embellished at length. Similarly bittersweet and wintry in sentiment, the poetic 'Carnation' evokes and supersedes the earlier foreboding ballad 'The Butterfly Collector'.

The soft guitar settings used on 'Absolute Beginners' are reprised for the brass driven 'Just Who is the Five O' Clock Hero', in which Weller overtly re-establishes the 'us and them' theme. With Weller in the role of narrator, this time 'them' are the privileged classes and 'us' the working classes. Repeated twice, a panoramic vista shaped from a handful of phrases, the middle eight is at once concise and expansive. Revisiting the melodic framework of 'Liza Radley', 'The Planner's Dream Goes Wrong' juxtaposes an exotic musical landscape with a fiercely literal lyric to lacerate the folly of the government. Surreal and extreme, it is a biting counterpart to the more conventionally structured and equally confrontational 'Just Who Is the Five O Clock Hero'. Elsewhere, in 'Running on the Spot' Weller seems to explicitly refer to the condition of The Jam, who he would split later in the same year. With a similar resigned detachment to that shown by Paul McCartney in 'You Never Give Me Your Money', the words convey imminent demise, the knowing acknowledgement of a loss of power. Respectively concerned with protest, love and life, 'Trans Global Express', 'Precious' and 'The Gift' are energetic mood pieces, slight as compositions but welcome as metaphorical counterweights to the extremes of unbridled joy and dark introspection threaded throughout 'The Gift'.

Published on March 6, 1982, Adam Sweeting's Melody Maker review predominantly avoids the music:

> I guess that it's not much fun being Paul Weller, for all his success. I don't just mean the melancholy and introversion which has always run through his music.... Weller, more than anyone is aware of the absurd tensions which his pop star role automatically afflict him with. Specifically, how does he reconcile the inherently selfish nature of stardom with a broader class consciousness?

Writing in the NME, Graham Lock calls the album:

> The Jam's ball of confusion.... Though its purpose is laudable – to stir up a defiant dance step at the heart of the Tory wastelands, it is undermined by a failure to balance questions of style.... The tensions on which their records fed so brilliantly, have, on The Gift been pushed into irreconcilable extremes.... Weller wants to be optimistic, but not escapist, he distrusts politics but is drawn to political affairs.

Calling two tracks 'a fiasco', Lock laments the 'abstract's simplifications' that have replaced the 'complexities and rich social detail that went into All Mod Cons and Setting Sons' (1980: 31). Despite these critical reservations, aided by over 600,000 sales of the January 1982 UK number 1 single 'Town Called Malice', 'The Gift' sold over 100,000 copies and reached number 1 in the UK charts.

Released six and eight months respectively after 'The Gift', the final two Jam singles 'The Bitterest Pill (I Ever Had to Swallow)' and 'Beat Surrender' both use singular line chorus repetition, a technique used on earlier singles 'This is the Modern World', 'That's Entertainment', 'Going Underground' and 'Eton Rifles'. Continuing the sequence of singles that use bespoke instrumentation to evoke different genres beginning with 'Funeral Pyre' and moving through 'Absolute Beginners' and 'Town Called Malice', 'The Bitterest Pill' is a Northern Soul variation on The Jam sound, with lush strings and a richly evocative backing vocal by Jennie Matthias of the Belle Stars. The ongoing submergence of the identity of The Jam as a trio can be seen on the sleeve for the singles, which feature Weller's friend Vaughan Toulouse, and latterly Weller's girlfriend Gill Price. Amidst a wash of textures, in these final band recordings the roles of Bruce Foxton and Rick Buckler are relatively subdued. 'Beat Surrender', a glorious valedictory single performed without bitterness, is dominated by piano, organ and brass. The impression is clear that Weller's vision can no longer be restricted to guitar, bass and drums, that his vista has outgrown the limitations of the trio. Paradoxically, the effect is of an artist retreating into the shadows whilst effortlessly writing number one singles.

Writing about The Beatles in 1969, Cohn (133–137) theorises:

> Between them, the four of them being so complimentary, they managed to appeal to almost everyone.... Painful and obsessive, Lennon trapped the intellectuals and wrote songs as if he was suffocating. A full-blown romantic and vastly sentimental, McCartney was stylish, charming, always elegant. If Lennon was tactless, McCartney was a natural diplomat. Starr was solid where Harrison was mystical. And if Harrison seemed dim, Lennon was very clever. And McCartney was arty, Starr was basic.... Round and round in circles, with no loose ends leftover it all made for a comforting sense of completeness.

Like The Beatles in 1969, in 1982 The Jam were the biggest band in the United Kingdom. Because of the partly natural, partly media-imposed reticence of Foxton and Buckler to adopt similarly charismatic roles, the pressure was continuously on Weller to be all these things. The abrogation of that pressure was inevitable, and during 1982 Weller very publicly drifted away from The Jam and towards his new project The Style Council. Other English bands to split at the peak of their artistic and commercial powers, most notably The Beatles and The Smiths, did so without valedictory appearances, leaving The Jam in the unique position of playing farewell concerts and releasing records announced as their last.

On The Style Council, Polydor A&R man Dennis Munday reflected 'With perhaps the exception of Bob Dylan, David Bowie, Neil Young and Van Morrison, most artists have not been able to indulge themselves as Paul did during the Council years' (Munn, 2014: 23). As Wilson recalls, The Style Council were peerlessly adept at 'confusing even the most ardent fan' (Weller, 2010: 5), and one retrospective review of the career of The Style Council conveys a mood prevalent in the eighties: 'Inscrutably arch.... In the art of pissing people off, The Style Council were grandmasters' (Goddard, 2018: 40). The Style Council made an inauspicious start to their relationship with their label Polydor, who having agreed for the final two contracted Jam albums to be a live record and a compilation, had not anticipated that Weller would only sing on six of the 13 tracks on The Style Council's first album 'Café Bleu' (Munn, 2014: 70).

Perhaps unsurprisingly, some aspects of the initial Style Council releases, particularly those released in 1983, resonate with those of The Jam. 'Money Go Round' in particular extends the single chord groove of 'Precious' and 'A Solid Bond in Your Heart' shares a Motown soul aesthetic with 'Beat Surrender'. The softer guitar setting used on many of the late Jam recordings is a staple, Weller apparently intent on letting his instrumental duties take a background role. Where guitars are heard, they are drawn to jazz colourings, minor sevenths that alter the feel of the music, typically making it more mellow. There is less of an axe to grind. Occasional reversions aside, Weller seeks to dissolve the burden of his unsolicited role as spokesperson for his generation, to present a less definable persona. Where The Jam gave voice to a collective condition, The Style Council is more concerned with the exposition of Weller's individual condition, a search for expression through exploration of identity.

With regard to the establishment of a new sound on early Style Council recordings, Zeke Manyika's drumming is more open and less dynamic than Rick Buckler's, and the slap bass provided by Kevin Miller adds another layer of stylistic separation. Mick Talbot's keyboards and Tracie Young's backing vocals link 'Speak Like a Child' to the sound of the late era Jam, but the lyrics are comparatively more impressionistic, less concerned with thread, meaning or message. The flip side 'Party Chambers' features some extended virtuoso keyboard playing, a departure from the arrangement code established by The Jam and another sign of a loosening of the creative reins. The title 'Speak Like a Child' is lifted from a Herbie Hancock album, and 'Money Go Round', which similarly borrows a title from The Kinks, recontextualises the funk of James Brown, using its groove to frame a polemical lyric. Extending this new eclecticism, 'Headstart to Happiness' overlooks drums and again favours new textures over dominant guitars. Whilst the consummate attention to detail in the two-part bridge echoes a key Weller songwriting feature first used on 'Setting Sons', the minor seventh chords and bright optimism of the lyric is aesthetically far removed from anything Weller wrote for The Jam. Across the first few Style Council recordings there is a sense of reconfiguration. As Frith notes, pop is not bound to any particular culture or market (Frith, Street and Straw, 2001: 95) and free from the trappings of history or the burden of expectation, with each new gesture unconnected to The Jam, Weller creates room to explore his art.

Where the late Jam material presents a number of variations on an established Jam sound, early Style Council recordings present a similar number of variations on an as yet unestablished sound. The Style Council was generally considered a significant stylistic departure from The Jam, yet were the formed at a time when the UK pop scene, as Chris Bostock, double bass player in contemporary band Joboxers observes: 'was so musically diverse. You could do anything and inspire people as long as you did it with full conviction' (Snowball, 2017: 190). On The Style Council's 'Long Hot Summer', arpeggiated synth dominates and an introspective lyric further transgresses the compositional code of The Jam canon. As with the two-part 'Money Go-Round', Weller decided to simultaneously record and release a 'Long Hot Summer Part 2', essentially a series of textural explorations based on the backing track of the initial single version. The implication is that the text itself is not sacrosanct but open to metaphorical re-interpretation. Ultimately, the leap of stylistic faith is rewarding; 'Long Hot Summer' is an effective, idiosyncratic and singular pop record that captures an expressive mood without complication.

Amplifying a sense of evolution through changing personnel, 'Paris Match' features the third female singer to have sung on the first seven tracks recorded by The Style Council. Following supporting roles played by Tracie Young and Dee C. Lee, Tracey Thorn takes centre stage on a winding and elegant tune that takes the first step in integrating a European aesthetic into the sound and image of The Style Council. On both the original female vocal recording and on the later version sung on 'Café Bleu' by Weller, the playing is reserved and the lyric mood melancholic and reflective. Weller's decision to translate one of the verses into French further forms the impression, at least to listeners encultured in the English mother tongue, that the metaphor of the music, it's capacity to transport is being given priority over the lyric message.

Released three months later, 'A Solid Bond in Your Heart' is texturally and stylistically reminiscent of 'The Bitterest Pill (I Ever Had to Swallow)' and 'Beat Surrender'. Going against the trend established by Style Council releases, it seems to temporarily reclaim old ground. Like The Jam's 'Liza Radley' and 'See Saw', 'It Just Came to Pieces in my Hands' has a demo feel that implies Weller may have lost faith or interest in it as an idea worth developing. Occasionally willing to officially release such creative offcuts, in this instance Weller may have heard a developmental charm, or perhaps given unlikely echoes of Jimi Hendrix and The Band, been inclined to release it as a gesture of the further widening of the Style Council sound, a further broadening of expectations and possibilities. The last single to be released prior to The Style Council's first album proper, 'My Ever Changing Moods' was released in three separate versions. It's Bossa Nova rhythm, played with a lightness of touch more indebted to jazz than rock, underpins another finely honed set of melodies and motifs. Using a structure similar to that used for 'Town Called Malice', the song moves briskly, finding yet another way to convey optimistic introspection. Accompanied by a comedy video featuring Weller and Mick Talbot on racing bikes, the creative intention is clearly to put yet more clear water between the focussed intensity, collective responsibility and social concern of The Jam and this new, ever-changing, ever-evolving band. The import only release *Introducing the Style Council* collects these early recordings to present an eclectic overview.

Unconventionally positioning instrumentals at tracks one, three and four, *Café Bleu* is an even more purposive attempt to establish a unique aesthetic. Borrowing from Herbie Hancock and Jelly Roll Morton among others, side one incorporates jazz stylings, while side two roams from rap to funk to soul. Previously released songs are radically reimagined, and the mantle of lead voice is continuously passed around. On 'Café Bleu' Weller is primarily a curator, surrounded by friends whose contributions he is happy to forefront. Where included, lyrics are often incidental; the need to be accountable largely absent. The melodies remain memorable, yet this is the only thread between the two bands; the mode of projection is entirely different. The neatly structured 'The Whole Point of No Return' sits happily alongside a loose New Orleans rag, and after a saxophone led instrumental, Dizzy Hites is free to rap on 'A Gospel' until 'Strength of Your Nature' imposes a house band aesthetic over a repetitive and meditative chant. As a vocalist, on side two Weller emerges on a single occasion to deliver one fully formed pop song, 'You're the Best Thing'. As with 'Ever Changing Moods' this song was clearly identified as a single and as such was subject to the now customary extended remix. Like the unanticipated return to The Jam sound of 'Solid Bond in Your Heart', the sudden appearance of 'You're the Best Thing' as a textural extension of 'Long Hot Summer' serves as a further reminder of Weller's innate capacity to return to, redefine and improve upon previous expressions.

Reviewing Café Bleu in the NME on March 16, 1984, Richard Cook writes that the LP 'is full of a man changing his mind, his shoes his allegiances. It speaks out in the clutching, awkward way of someone who has slippery and protean concepts like 'style' and 'preaching' nagging in his head, and great skill at his fingertips. They never clearly match up'. Elsewhere in his review, Cook describes the album as a 'patchwork' of 'artificial nostalgia' that finds Weller 'reflecting on what he can't do.... I can't fathom what he expects from such faceless music'. Alternatively, the Melody Maker's Lynden Barber (1984: 31) applauds Weller's move to alienate Jam fans still 'in search of the lost power chord'. Sales in the United Kingdom remained buoyant, with 'Café Bleu' reaching number 2 in the UK album chart and achieving Gold certification for sales of over 100,000. These figures were likely assisted by sales of the singles 'My Ever Changing Moods' and 'You're The Best Thing' both of which reached number 5 in the UK singles chart in early 1984.

Released in October 1984, the single 'Shout to the Top!' is an infectious Northern Soul homage set to a lyric blues on the topic of helplessness. The subtext provided by the gulf between the metaphor of the music and the direction of the lyric echoes Holland, Dozier and Holland's 'Stop! In The Name of Love' and The Smiths 'William, it was Really Nothing', released as 'Shout to the Top!' was being recorded. As previously mentioned, the duality of meaning in each recording allows the listener to perceive these songs from a number of perspectives; to engage with the downbeat lyric; to engage with the upbeat music; to imagine the singer conveying, or concealing a hidden or disguised emotion; to wonder if the condition of the singer isn't so bleak after all; to wonder if the music expresses emotions and experiences felt before the words came to the fore; or conversely to imagine all will be fine in the end. Ensuring longevity, 'Shout to The Top!' has enough channels of expression to accommodate the listener across a range of varied moods.

The deliberate use of multiple musical identities between 1983 and 1985 marks The Style Council out as unique at this point in popular music. Around the same time, Simple Minds, U2, The Smiths and Prefab Sprout were establishing relatively monolithic aesthetics, using textures repeatedly to convey trademark sounds. Having established a singular, binding identity as a songwriter in The Jam, Weller seems to have been engaged in an ongoing attempt to imprint a number of other co-existing identities; to display numerous facets of his character apparently submerged by the restraints of The Jam. Two decades earlier, Bob Dylan had felt a similar sense of restriction that led to a dramatic move from folk to electric blues-rock, and similarly, in 1981 Elvis Costello altered his trajectory as a pop artist to embrace country music with 'Almost Blue'. Both artists challenged their respective audiences to be open minded, to make significant leaps of faith. In the first phase of The Style Council, Weller asks his audience to make similar leaps song by song.

Released in 1985, *Our Favourite Shop* sees Weller back front and centre, his presence as a vocalist constant in the exploration of a series of themes, many of which focus on social displacement and injustice. Where much of the early Style Council material looked inwards, 'Our Favourite Shop' looks outwards, recreating variations on the 'us and them' paradigm of Jam compositions 'Mr. Clean', 'Just Who is the Five O' Clock Hero' and 'Going Underground'. Themes of anger, despondency and the need for collective solidarity against the ruling class are framed in funk, neo-classical and pop settings, and in a reflection of the urgency of the writing, the *'la la la'* type extemporisations that underpin some of Weller's most effective pop compositions including 'Town Called Malice' and 'Man in a Corner Shop' are absent; on 'Our Favourite Shop' motif gives way to density of meaning.

None of the lyrics are ambiguous. Reflecting the immediate concern of young workers in the United Kingdom being forced to move away from their homes to be nearer to their place of employment and the devastating effect on local communities, 'Homebreakers', 'All Gone Away' and 'Come to Milton Keynes' are all direct political meditations on displacement. Exploring separate facets of socialism, 'Internationalists' and 'A Stone's Throw Away' convey themes of solidarity, while 'The Lodgers', 'With Everything to Lose' and 'Walls Come Tumbling Down' are all protest songs. This lyric direction had been presaged prior to the release of 'Our Favourite Shop' with the release of 'Soul Deep', a polemic in support of working-class solidarity, released in eight separate recorded iterations and perhaps signifying the height of the mid-Eighties commercial appetite for remixes. Further signifying the sea change from passive introspection to social engagement. 'Soul Deep' had been coupled with the lyrically ferocious 'Blood Sports'.

'Come to Milton Keynes' and 'Walls Come Tumbling Down', the two singles lifted from 'Our Favourite Shop', in some ways echo The Jam singles 'Funeral Pyre' and 'Going Underground'. The former is intense, intricately structured, has no chorus and is at times mildly discordant, while the latter moves briskly through 22 non-repetitive sections in which either the lyric, music or arrangement changes. Both songs resonate with earlier Jam recordings in other ways. The brass section parts on 'Come to Milton Keynes' are similar to those on 'Just Who is the Five O' Clock Hero' and the intuitive rhythmic changes on 'Walls Come Tumbling Down' evoke the restless energy of 'Happy Together'. Unlike the vast majority of Style Council releases of 1983 and 1984, which studiously avoid Jam tropes, the energy and approach are unafraid to embrace elements of the past.

Typically, contemporary reviews for 'Our Favourite Shop' interweave the positive with the negative, with Paul Du Noyer of the NME praising 'an astute resolution of conflicting styles' and The Melody Maker's Adam Sweeting dismissing it as 'awkward ... in the familiar lounge-funk format' (Quantick, 2020: 70). Across the critical spectrum, the album was generally considered more cohesive than 'Café Bleu', and it reached number 1 in the UK charts. Like every Jam or Style Council album since 'All Mod Cons', the album was certified Gold for over 100,000 sales.

The first of Weller's self-produced albums, 1987's *The Cost of Loving* foregoes any focus on politics in favour of a return to the lyric introversion of 'Introducing' and 'Café Bleu'. Unlike those two albums, however, 'The Cost of Loving' has a relatively static musical aesthetic. Indicating a lesser degree of engagement in the expressive, exploratory aspect of songwriting, with the exception of 'Waiting', middle-eights are absent. Lyrically, the songs appear to be about relationship ups and downs, with the listener often excluded by the absence of compositional, arrangement, production or performance conduits to add metaphor to meaning. Perhaps because of the absence of long-time producer Peter Wilson, the music feels less confident, less engaged and less willing to seek frames of stylistic reference; as a consequence, it feels sullen as it looks inwards.

On the 'Cost of Loving', only 'Walking the Night', with its brass arrangement and inner narrative voice, succeeds in capturing a sense of purpose. In a comparative sense, this high point is humble; at the same time contemporaries The Smiths, The Cure and New Order were experiencing artistic and commercial high tides. Throughout 'Cost of Loving' instrumental motifs are infrequent and both Weller and Talbot's roles are frequently sublimated. Stylistic references are grasped for but fail to connect; as a composition 'Heaven's Above' seems to aspire to Andy Fraser's 'Every Kind of People' and Marvin Gaye's 'What's Going On', but as a production it falls short. Bringing to mind the malaise at the heart of some of the lesser material on 'This is the Modern World', switches of rhythm at 4.35 and 5.30 project uncertainty more than adventure. 'Fairy Tales' is a strophic two chord funk work-out with minimal dynamic narrative direction, and elsewhere, when the music doesn't sound 'in-progress' it sounds tentative. On the title track itself, the words and music seem to be at odds. Weller's vocal on the single 'Waiting', released in March 1987, lacks energy and the following single 'Wanted' incorporates a fanciful lyric detour that punctures any sense of coherent expression. Ultimately, recordings from this era are characterised by a lack of conviction; an absence of collective belief in the songwriting reflected in lacklustre arrangements and performances.

Reviews were tepid, as illustrated in the review selection gathered from a range of UK music publications in Ian Munn's Mr. Cool' Dream (2014: 147); 'I've got a lot of time for Weller but I get the impression he doesn't have a lot of time for us. The Cost of Loving is the sound of Weller getting, older, wiser and richer'; 'too lovey-dovey for these lugs'; 'Anaemic, slick Eighties soul as bad as anything else around'; and finally, from Simon Reynolds writing in Melody Maker 'a surprisingly accurate imitation of that most spineless idiom, Brit-Funk' (1987: 29). Despite widespread critical disapproval, 'The Cost of Loving' was certified Gold for 100,000 sales, and reached number 2 in the UK charts.

Confessions of A Pop Group retains the lack of lyric focus of the previous album but returns a sense of musical exploration. Here, an uncontrolled eclecticism creates the impression is that Weller is increasingly focussed on inventing music, more so than shaping or editing music. As on 'The Gift', when Weller was minded to include the vocal free 'Trans Global Unity Express' and 'Circus' and to augment the collective sound by introducing a brass section, there is a sense that the songwriter is departing into the shadows in full view. Leaving the question of who is responsible for the work open amidst an expansive cast of guest musicians, Weller is absent from 'Confessions of A Pop Group' for significant periods.

In an aesthetic sense, the album is infused with surrealness. On the title track, the audience is invited to reconcile the committed socialist and author of 'Town Called Malice' with a vitriolic auteur, railing against an invisible target; to allow for abrupt switches from gleeful humour to bitter anger, to countenance artistic freedom on a cinematic scale. Like Dylan's 'Self Portrait', 'Confessions of a Pop Group' is both wildly adventurous and lacking critical discernment; the creative impetus seems to be driven by a need to allow the audience to view aspects of the artists' musical identity that surprise, or elude even the artist himself. Typical of this multi-layered ambiguity, in 'Life at a Top People's Health Farm' students plot in the stables, a mother plays bingo and a series of other unrelated activities combine. Amidst the hysteria, unsure whether to celebrate or deride, instrumentalists seem at a loss as to where to pitch expression. Where such an approach might, in some instances, allow the listener to make up their own minds, the number of ambiguous lines of expression is often too great for any one line to be reliably interpreted. This overwhelming complexity inevitably creates uncertainty in the quality of the music.

On 'Confessions of a Pop Group' the instrumental inhibition of 'Cost of Loving', which seemed to bind the musicians to an introverted code of sorts, is overturned in favour of uncoded exuberance. 'It's a Very Deep Sea' opens with some delicate jazz piano phrases and progresses to a theatrical refrain, while 'The Story of Someone's Shoe', a comedy title that promises and neglects to deliver comedy, has a bleak performative thread at odds with its borrowed Beach Boys aesthetic. Like 'It's A Very Deep Sea', 'The Story of Someone's Shoe' has no chorus, motif or middle eight. 'Changing of the Guard' and 'The Gardener of Eden (A Three-Piece Suite)' extend the ballad concept, introducing a number of narrative voices, sound effects, and, for Weller, new textures including harp and Cor anglais. Written and played without edge, the compositional and instrumental transitions frequently feel random.

Elsewhere, 'Why I went Missing' meanders musically, 'How She Threw It All Away' meanders structurally and 'Iwasadoledadstoyboy' meanders lyrically. Open to interpretation, 'Confessions 1, 2 and 3' is either a blithe postmodern collage or a psychological journey towards escape, with Weller urging his fellow musicians to 'count me out'. With its randomised themes of anger, incidental observations and reference to an imminent breakdown, in hindsight the title track seems disconcertingly autobiographical. Bewildering and frequently demanding in its thirst for disconnection, 'Confessions of a Pop Group' is a portrait of an artist who knows he wants something else, but has yet to figure out what that something else is. For an artist so closely tied to his musical identity, one so inclined to make music as self-discovery, this uncertainty reflects not only a derailment from a musical journey, but also from a personal one, and as such the album frequently makes for uncomfortable listening.

The UK Top Twenty singles chart in the week 'Confessions of a Pop Group' was released includes singles by Bros, The Fat Boys with Chubby Checker, Sabrina, Glen Madeiros, Matt Bianco and an unlikely collaboration between Wet, Wet, Wet and Billy Bragg. Promotional materials for 'Confessions of a Pop Group' included full page spreads in the music weeklies with the eye-catching wording: 'Original cast: Now in its fifth spectacular year.... The Style Council – New York, Gstaad, Tokyo, Marble Arch: Europe's finest'. Referencing comedic characters from the long running BBC sit-com 'It Aint Half Hot Mum', a contemporary review by Allan Jones in Melody Maker published on June 25, 1988 is scornful, claiming 'Weller and Talbot, the Windsor Davies and Don Estelle of supine albino funk, have only the most lamentable grasp of the ironic mode'. Critiquing what he calls 'lumbering self-regard and bloated aspirations ... ludicrous examples of uninspired craft', Jones labels Weller 'a hod-carrier, not a visionary' (1988: 29). Similarly dismissive, Peter Kane in Sounds hears 'another catalogue of dismal expressions of vexations about life under Mrs. T.... A joyless sequence of songs swimming against life's currents.... A hollow, humourless sham of a record' (1988: 31). Elsewhere, Mark Sinker of NME (1998: 47) writes 'I suspect Weller despises those who once loved him'. 'Confessions of a Pop Group' reached number 15 in the UK album chart, and for the first time in Weller's career since 'This is the Modern World', failed to attain Gold status, achieving Silver certification for sales of over 60,000.

'Modernism (A New Decade)', recorded in 1989, but shelved for release until almost a decade later, is a primarily instrumental album with Weller's vocal presence almost entirely absent. Logically, given the vocal uncertainties on 'Cost of Loving' and 'Confessions of a Pop Group' this makes sense; a singer without much to say as a lyricist may as well hold fire until something comes along. Problematically, however, the absence of Weller's accent as a singer and songwriter renders 'Modernism (A New Decade)'

interchangeable with any number of other artists or bands; its identity as a Style Council record is negligible. As on 'Café Bleu', from Weller's perspective the psychological impetus seems to be to find ways to convey expression whilst removing oneself from the sonic arena. In this instance, the expression conveys a singular facet, an impression of club music, relentlessly extended without innovation or pretence. Along with his voice, Weller's guitar is absent as is Mick Talbot's signature Hammond organ; as such the original sound of The Style Council is erased, the rationale for the existence of the band having been gradually diminished over a series of disconnected steps. The response of the label was to pre-empt the questioning voice of the audience; how much of this music is actually being made by Paul Weller? Because David Munns at Polydor 'didn't think it was good enough' (cited in Munn, 2014: 187), Polydor declined to release 'Modernism: A New Decade' in 1989, and as a consequence there are no contemporary reviews.

Spanning 1989 to 1991, the period before the recording of the debut solo album titled *Paul Weller* is characterised by biographer Paolo Hewitt as one of intense uncertainty for Weller as a songwriter and artist (2007: 240–243). As Weller reflected in 1995:

> The evil curse had ended or the beautiful dream had just begun.... Nothing happened. I went on tour. Nothing happened.... In 91/92 I toured fairly consistently. In the Sheffield Octagon there was a small crowd. In Manchester Academy, a full house. It varied. People were in two minds. So was I.
>
> (Watson and Hewitt, 1995: 6)

Carefully wrought, the songs on 'Paul Weller' seem to rely upon a limited number of creative methods that were found to 'work' as songwriting mechanisms. Compositions are often directed by the instinctive positioning of the fingers on the fretboard: 'Uh Huh, Oh Yeh' and 'I Didn't Mean to Hurt You' use similar B minor descending chord sequences, 'Into Tomorrow' and 'Kosmos' revolve C and D chords around an underpinning A minor, and to counterbalance the minor chordal feel, 'Bull Rush' and 'Fly on the Wall' use similar chord sequences incorporating switches from E to D and A to G. The effect is of a songwriter forging a series of grouped impressions, and the result is a robust set of tunes, made more durable by the skilful addition of occasional unexpected chords. Meyer (1956) writes that music and life are closely connected in the sense that, in both contexts, emotions are evoked by deviations from what we expect to happen. Equivalent moments, in which songs move to unanticipated chords and notes the listener would likely not expect, occur in the unsettling move from D minor to B minor in 'Round and Round'; in the decision to resolve the chorus of 'Into Tomorrow' with a B7 to E that feels angular in the context of its surroundings; in the unexpected progression from G sharp to F sharp in the verse resolution of 'Strange Museum' and in the gravitational pull of G minor following the

D chord in 'Kosmos'. Such moments lift the commonplace into the rare, and in their evocation of nuance play a significant role in making the songs both immediate and lasting. Creating a sense of fragility, arrangement and production touches occasionally portray a lack of confidence in the material; intros are occasionally hesitant, middle-eights sometimes feel short, and saxophone solos arrive where instruments played by Weller might once have been deployed.

Some of the recordings from this era sound like jams; 'Arrival Time', 'That Spiritual Feeling' and 'All Year Round' come across as unreconstructed ensemble efforts to locate a spark, to find a basis for a feel that might later be developed into a more structurally defined work. Elsewhere, 'Round and Round', 'Above the Clouds' and 'The Strange Museum' have verses that sound as if they may have been generated through a conscious move, not for the first time, to distil the feel of Marvin Gaye's (1971) masterwork 'What's Going On'. In summary, like 'In The City' and 'The Gift', the songs on 'Paul Weller' fall into three distinct categories; tightly honed verse-chorus compositions, jams developed into full songs, and jams that remain undeveloped. Providing numerous opportunities for intensity to be released and recaptured, this mixture gives the collection of songs a levity. This realisation, that not every song *has* to be as detailed and immersive as 'Town Called Malice' or as metaphorically freewheeling as some of the material recorded in the latter phases of The Style Council; that the two might not only happily co-exist, but that there might also be a middle ground between the two, seems to have helped Weller ease back into songwriting and record making.

Against this partly tight, partly loose musical backdrop, the lyrics are often autobiographical, with six lyrics featuring 'I' or 'my' in their opening lines. Looking backwards and forwards, these predominantly inward-looking lyrics convey a spectrum of emotional themes connected to regret, rediscovery, reconciliation and the promise of a bright future. Creating a holistic balance, other lyrics project a sense of the collective, ensuring the album both re-introduces the artist and avoids insularity. Predominantly, the album searches for a means of expression, sometimes glimpsing it; as such it evokes an authentic and relatable universal frame of mind.

Citing Van Morrison, Bill Withers and less expectedly Gary Numan as influences on the work, in his 1992 review David Quantick writes 'The Style Council parted company because their records had become so deranged that no-one could comprehend even the tiniest part of them. (This album is) the best thing he has done since he binned those awful black and white golf shoes and invented frothy coffee.... Paul Weller is back. Nearly, anyway' (Quantick, 1992: 32). Extending the UK music media tradition of critical disagreement, writing in the August 29, 1992 publication of NME, Steve Sutherland warns 'Beware, there is nostalgia in the air ... (a) sudden longing for an Englishness.... I've scoured the grooves for a motive but I can't find one.... I think it's time we left him to rest in peace. Paul Weller doesn't exist anymore' (1992: 45). Certified Gold and consequently more popular in the United Kingdom than the final Style Council album, 'Paul Weller' reached number 8 in the UK charts and sold over 100,000 copies.

Unlike 'Paul Weller', which integrates contrasting materials gathered using a limited range of creative methods, *Wild Wood* is a stylistically unified collection. A masterclass in planned spontaneity, the songs seem to have been developed through extensive ensemble workshopping and overdubbing, resulting in a magically coherent, painstakingly assembled musical jumble that feels as if it were conceived instinctively. Both as individual pieces and as a whole, the music and words are confidently written and shaped, and there is a sense that the quality of the ideas have been rewarded with thoughtful arrangements that at times both enhance and degrade the sound, giving the music a ragged flow. This effect can be heard on the master recording of 'Sunflower', which unlike its cleaner sounding demo, uses loosely double tracked vocals to convey a kind of ramshackle liveness. Indicating a return to a willingness to embrace unorthodox structuring, 'Sunflower' contains three melodic guitar motifs, one in the opening riff that descends from D to E, another across the A minor to E minor section that frames the verses, and another on the E chord that arrives mid-way through the track, and later acts as a coda. From a listening perspective, the music seems to follow where its spirit takes it. Within this rich display of creativity, Weller's lyrics sprawl, often hung together by a single predominant, projected lyric line, in each instance acting as an intimate expressive thread, a line which beams from the tune and around which other phrases revolve. A series of orbiting impressions, the lyrics surrounding these directly communicative hooks only have to *sound* right to make the song project with clarity. At around the same time, Crowded House were writing and recording 'Take the Weather with You' and 'Four Seasons in One Day', songs which similarly surround luminous titles with lines of less direct meaning.

Like many other tracks on 'Wild Wood', the song 'Country' is, as MacDonald describes The Beatles 'I'll Be Back' in Revolution in the Head, 'an entirely bewildering construction that rings totally true' (1994: 94). Other structures on the record are likely unique to popular music. In 'Has My Fire Really Gone Out' established verses are halved, established choruses doubled, a new section shaped like a middle-eight is initially presented as an early middle-four and is later repeated and doubled to incorporate a solo, and a disconnected yet wholly effective three-part coda changes its root chord at uneven intervals. Demanding to play, and the result of intense and exhaustive editorial attention on Weller's behalf, 'Has My Fire Really Gone Out'? is structured as follows:

Intro (2 bars)
Verse 1 (8 bars)
Chorus 1 (4 bars)
Turnaround and refrain 1 (2 bars)

Verse 2 (4 bars)
New Section 1 (4 bars)
Diamond/Rest (1 bar)
Turnaround and refrain 2 (4 bars)
Chorus 2 (8 bars)
Verse 3 (8 bars)
New Section 2 (8 bars, part solo)
Diamond/Rest (1 bar)
Single chord section 1 (8 bars)
Single chord section 2 (12 bars)
Single chord section 3 (4 bars)

In another point of historical resonance, around the time of 'Setting Sons' Rick Buckler and Bruce Foxton began to contribute more pronounced instrumental phrases that served to position themselves at the forefront of the expression. A fine balance between the increasing adventurousness of the rhythm section and Weller's guitar and vocal became integral to the most successful work of The Jam. On the song 'Wild Wood', as elsewhere on the record, Steve White contributes a great deal to the dynamic, accentuating the vocal, sometimes pushing the pulse forwards and at other times harnessing it to create an improvised feel. Reminiscent of Foxton's role in The Jam, Marco Nelson's bass notes colour the music, often adding imaginative inversions over guitar chords. Challenging to memorise, single verse lines in 'Hung Up' and 'The Weaver' are reharmonised to generate a loose but tightly plotted aesthetic. MacDonald recalls The Beatles ensemble playing on the metrically challenging 'Happiness is a Warm Gun', particularly how they took 15 hours and 95 takes to get it sounding 'right'. Like Lennon's classic, 'Wild Wood' works on what MacDonald calls 'an emotionally allusive level that draws upon obscurely renewed energy' (1994: 255).

Perhaps reflecting the need for tight quality control, on the previous album the personnel had been limited to Paul (doubling on guitar and bass) and Steve White on drums with a few other players contributing occasional backing vocals, flute and saxophone. On 'Wild Wood' a core ensemble is at work on the initial tracking, but the cast of musicians invited to add overdubs is expansive. Like 'In the City', 'Paul Weller' is more engineered than produced, the sound of songs being cut to tape without a great deal of deliberation or elaboration. Conversely 'Wild Wood' adopts a more expansive approach, with Weller and producer Brendan Lynch both playing a broad range of instruments (in Weller's case 16 in total) and entrusting specific roles to specialists at salient points. Paradoxically, the more creative control is ceded, the more aesthetic effect is acquired.

Creating a sense of immediacy, most vocals on the record arrive quickly and without fanfare. To help the record acquire shape as a continuous listen, extended codas on 'Holy Man', 'Has My Fire Really Gone Out' and

'Shadow of the Sun' create vocal space within the sequence overall. As with the debut solo album 'Paul Weller', there is a lot of movement around chords that will have come naturally to Weller on his guitar, with D, A minor, C, G, E and F sharp minor among the recurring chord shapes used. 'Holy Man' is shifted a semitone from either E or D to E flat to convey the right energy and accommodate its unique feel. The song 'Wild Wood' may also have been lifted a tone from A minor (where it is likely to have been written) to B minor (where it most suits Weller's voice).

To ensure continuity of sound, a number of the more strophic or repetitive compositions are deftly and inventively arranged. Abandoning the conventional pop arrangement method of adding and subtracting textures at the beginnings of new sections, on the title track, mellotron and minimoog textures are added by producer Brendan Lynch and organist Helen Turner mid-section. The effect, as with 'Sunflower' is to introduce threads of the unexpected as a means of creating a more random, organic feel. On the track 'Wild Wood' the arrangement is typically dynamic, with Weller's imaginatively phrased vocal adding contour to a song with a circular structure. Without the subtle yet dynamic colourations provided by Weller's fellow players, the song 'Wild Wood' might have had to reach for dynamic in the form of a new section to shape and extend its expression. As it is, the complex and deft interweaving of sounds around the voice and acoustic guitar create imaginative lines for the ear to follow; as with 'That's Entertainment', no two verses sound the same. With instrumental interjections italicised, the song recording of 'Wild Wood', which consists of 15 verses, illustrates this:

0 – 0.13 Acoustic rhythm guitar, *harmonics from a second 'lead' acoustic on bars three and four*
0.14 – 0.27 Acoustic guitar, bass, drums (constant until 3.20)
0.28 – 0.42 *In bars three and four, lead acoustic adds chords and motif; in bar four, e-bow guitar effect leads into extra bar on root chord*
0.43 – 0.55 *Mellotron introduced in bar two, trailing over into first bar of next verse*
0.56 – 1.08 *Jazz guitar tone plays descending riff in third and fourth bars*
1.09 – 1.21 *lead acoustic guitar solo, moog strings enter in bar four*
1.22 – 1.33 *lead acoustic guitar, flute enters on bars three and four*
1.34 – 1.45 *lead acoustic guitar, jazz guitar tone plays descending riff in third and fourth bars*
1.46 – 1.57 *sudden drum snap, organ enters*
1.58 – 2.10 *organ*
2.11 – 2.22 *lead acoustic guitar and jazz tone guitar play counterparts*
2.23 – 2.35 *e-bow guitar over first two bars, mellotron over second two bars*
2.36 – 2.47 *lead acoustic guitar harmonics over third and fourth bars*
2.48 – 2.59 *drum snap, moog strings and flute*
3.00 – 3.20 *moog strings and flute*

Counterweights to the densely orchestrated and guitar heavy 'Sunflower' and 'Hung Up', 'All the Pictures on My Wall' and 'Country' open up the spectrum of sound, bringing contrast to the sequence. Adding further dimension, 'Moon on Your Pyjamas' and 'Foot of the Mountain' are deliberately under-produced. On his album 'The Impossible Bird', Nick Lowe employed a similar approach, anecdotally including some demo tracks on the album because he liked the hesitant feel of the band coming to terms with the music. Similarly preferring the feel of exploration, a sometimes impossible atmospheric to recapture, on 'Automatic for the People' REM reportedly built overdubs around five demos for the final album sequence.

Although retrospective reviews are universally glowing, music critics at the time of release were relatively ungenerous. Writing in the NME edition of September 4, 1993, Paul Moody complains that 'Wild Wood 'is not the tour de force we might have hoped for', while Melody Maker's Taylor Parkes writes 'this is, after all, a man in his thirties, fusing his perception of now with the ghosts of a past he'll never be able to lose' (1993: 35). Despite the cool critical response, 'Wild Wood' reached number 2 in the UK charts, and was certified platinum for sales of over 300,000, Weller's highest sales figure to date.

Discussing the origination of the concept for 'Kinks are the Village Green Preservation society', Ray Davies reflected that 'the past few years had left him disconnected from the things that had really mattered when he was growing up' (Jovanovic, 2013: 148). Similarly, on *Stanley Road*, Weller seeks to make a series of connections to his youth. In direct contrast to 'Wild Wood', the songs on 'Stanley Road' almost all have traditional structures. Four are verse/chorus, two are verse/pre-chorus/chorus, one is strophic and another AABA, leaving only two to employ the complex structuring techniques used on 'Wild Wood'. This comparative sense of predictability gives the songs a warmth and approachability less evident on its frenetic and elusive predecessor. Evoking the Mick Taylor era Rolling Stones albums 'Sticky Fingers' and 'Exile on Main Street', Weller and fellow guitarist Steve Cradock interweave guitar parts in separate channels; this playing style, which requires virtuosic skill, guarantees a full sound.

Unlike the intricately woven 'Wild Wood', arrangements are typically at set levels, with instruments often playing through entire songs. To make verses and choruses sound and feel different from previous verses and choruses, when new instruments are added or removed, they tend to do so at the beginnings or ends of sections. Perceptively, this traditional approach to arrangement evokes a strong sense of belief in the material, a conviction in its quality. Where 'Paul Weller' and 'Wild Wood' are tentative and cathartic explorations, 'Stanley Road' feels like a realisation, a 'Sargent Pepper' in the wake of 'Rubber Soul' and 'Revolver'. Like 'Sargent Pepper' it is easily absorbed in one listen; in a sonic sense the listener is taken on a narrative journey.

In keeping with the simplicity of the structures and arrangements, on 'Stanley Road' there are two main instrumental settings; full band with

Weller on guitar and full band with Weller on piano. Experimental run throughs using these settings can be heard on pre-album session versions of The Beatles' 'Sexy Sadie' and Etta James' classic 'I'd Rather Go Blind', covers apparently recorded to set the tone. As with both 'Paul Weller' and 'Wild Wood', demo sessions preceded the album recording sessions. As previously mentioned, depending on the project, Weller has recorded demos for some of his albums and not for others. The reasoning for this could be related to limitations on funding, competing touring schedules, the availability of players or instinct on behalf of the artist. The behaviour of labels is also a constant factor, with the music industry traditionally marketing a limited number of 'stars' in order to reduce uncertainty of demand. Falling record sales introduce uncertainty of demand, which in turn can lead to reductions in advances, limited promotional funding and, from the perspective of the artist, sometimes unwanted creative limitations.

With regard to artistic instinct, there is sometimes a sense that material might be better conveyed if not overprepared; that something about it suggests it needs to be captured in its initial state. Emphasising Weller's perfectionist approach during the early to mid-nineties, 'Wild Wood', '5th Season', 'Porcelain Gods' and 'Wings of Speed' were all demoed at least twice, and between 1991 and 1995, Weller recorded demos for most of the tracks that eventually featured on the albums. Usually sketched out with instrument and voice by Weller in advance, secondary demos are band recordings played attentively but loosely by Weller on vocals and guitar with fellow musicians, usually Steve White on drums, a bass player and perhaps one or two others. Essentially works in progress, they often possess the melodies, words and structures of later 'master' versions, but lack the dynamic variation and spark of the recordings we are more familiar with. Occasionally overdubbed, they are primarily 'live in the studio'.

Illustrating a creative trajectory, these demo versions are sometimes markedly different. On the demo for 'Wild Wood' for instance, Steve White moves to a more imposing snare after a minute or so, changing the character of the song definitively. The demo of 'All the Pictures on My Wall' uses a number of brass and slide guitar textures that don't feature on the master take and similarly, 'Broken Stones' is relatively upbeat in its initial demo form. The structure of 'Wings of Speed' is set early on, but on the first demo a space exists where Carleen Anderson's vocals eventually feature. In version 2, Weller repeats the structure but adds a harmony vocal, without words but indicative of the intended sound. On the record itself, Weller's extemporised, wordless vocal is developed into the lyric section sung by Carleen Anderson and heard on the record. The building process is deliberate and gradual, and the outcome settled and assured.

In each instance, the original demo versions fulfil a range of purposes; Weller himself can listen back and make iterative critical changes to words, melodies or structures that may have felt right in the playing, but sound less convincing upon listening. Similarly, other players can use the demos to critique their own approaches, and to examine ways in which alternative approaches might provide a better fit for the music. Significantly, the skeletal demo takes can be heard both individually and placed in potential track sequences by the artist and the producer, who can use the demo outlines to imagine potential arrangement and production embellishments for the album as a sequential whole. Where feels are repetitive across a particular song sequence, this can be identified and alternative approaches planned; as such the collection of demos allows the album to be planned and reimagined prior to final execution. In the case of 'You Do Something to Me', whether it was the songwriter, producer or drummer's decision to bring the drums in earlier, it was an effective choice, and across 'Stanley Road' virtually every decision made to enhance songs works. For the first time since 'Setting Sons', and for only the second time in Weller's recording career to date, contemporary reviews concur, with NME's Ted Kessler (2005: 44) exclaiming it 'feels like the mod recording he's been waiting all these years to make', and Melody Maker's David Stubbs concluding 'Stanley Road rocks, alright' (1995: 27). This critical positivity transferred to the listening public; a commercial high-water mark, Stanley Road was certified 4 x Platinum for sales of over 1,200,000.

Lacking the vivid colour of 'Wild Wood' and the consummate mastery of 'Stanley Road', *Heavy Soul* collects a range of different expressive energies. Whilst overall the mood is more reflective and down tempo, four tracks: 'Brushed', 'Peacock Suit', 'Friday Street' and 'Mermaids' are sonic adventures in pop psychedelia framed by a dense wall of sound. Away from this vibrant quartet, the vocal ranges are frequently compressed and the sometimes unimaginative production values seem to betray a lack of confidence in the material. Where string overdubs appear, they sound tentative, and at other times there are no overdubs at all and this restricts the dimension of the sound. 'As You Lean into the Light' and 'Science' are songs with one or two chord verses that drift, while 'Driving Nowhere' and 'Golden Sands' possess promising verse melodies yet fail to build upon their foundations with effective counterpart sections. As on 'The Gift', in among the fleeting moments of inspiration on 'Heavy Soul' there is a sense of impatience. Opting instead for predictable licks and textures, guitar lines lack the dextrous weaving of those on 'Stanley Road'.

Weller's habit of revisiting song themes is present, yet here the remake often falls short. The tentative 'Up in Suze's Room' feels like a less fleet-footed impression of 'All the Pictures on My Wall', while the formally structured gospel shuffle 'I Should Have Been There to Inspire You' struggles to escape the shadow of 'Wings of Speed'. The title track 'Heavy Soul' references the duelling guitars and scruffy, mistimed vocal overdubs so integral to the previous two albums, but neglects to shift performative gear across its verses, ultimately creating more of a sense of a jam than a direction. It's reprise later in the sequence seems perfunctory. On a more positive note, the winding, wayward structure and percussive vocal of 'Brushed' combine with an intricate arrangement to create a transcendent piece. The same is true of the rolling groove of 'Friday Street'; here the transformative confidence of the band performance is audible. The Beatle-esque 'Mermaids' features autumnal strings and, in a rare moment of exuberance on 'Heavy Soul', the single extemporised vocal on the record. June 1997 reviews of 'Heavy Soul' are reserved, with Everett True of Melody Maker stating 'There's no vitality to Heavy Soul, nothing left of the restless spirit' (1997: 31) and the NME's Stuart Bailie similarly lamenting 'There's no vim' (1997: 53). Emphasising the dip in quality from 'Stanley Road' and indicating the fickle nature level of pop music consumer loyalty in the United Kingdom, peaking at number 2 in the UK album charts, 'Heavy Soul' was certified Gold for sales of over 100,000, a fraction of the sales figure for Stanley Road.

Where 'Heavy Soul' is predominantly leaden and sparse, for the most part *Heliocentric* is compositionally dense and absent of the motifs, riffs and hooks that characterise much of Weller's most immediately likeable work. As if apparently aware that the live take might be the master, the songs are treated with great care by the assembled players, who frequently use performance dynamics to chapter the music. Consequently, the impression is very different to that made by 'Heavy Soul'. By comparison, 'Heliocentric' has fewer moments of melodic inspiration and fewer instances of feeling unfinished. As always, Weller's voice and accent underpin the identity of the music, yet the text itself tends to sound as if written and interpreted without a realistic amount of editing; without the critical perspective previously attained by demoing, or from having a surplus of material to select from.

Much of the material is introspective, written as if in retreat and performed as if the emotional energy that served as its impetus remains elusive. Creating a sense of unevenness, threads of certainty and uncertainty pervade the album. At times, there is a sense that the ensemble, including Weller himself, are looking to make a more upbeat and accessible record than the material will allow. Working against this ambition, 'With Time and Temperance' meanders and 'Back in the Fire' and 'A Whales Tale' tail have sour, George Harrisonesque chord changes that evoke shades of darkness. While 'There is No Drinking When You're Dead' captures a collective mood, for much of the record the compositional meaning is unclear. Within the lyrics there is little signalling of intent, and within the music there is little to either sing along to, or immediately relate to. The absence of space for metaphor, or time for the listener to dream themselves into the narrative ultimately makes Heliocentric an overtly distant set of recordings. Contemporary reviews are underwhelming, with NME journalist John Robinson critical of songs 'very much of one pace and type' (2000: 51). Gavin Martin, writing for Uncut, hears 'an album of gnarled determination and considerable substance … but beneath the surface lies familiar territory' (2000: 70). Reaching number 2 in the UK album charts, Heliocentric was certified Gold for sales of over 100,000.

Presaging the covers album 'Studio 150', *Illumination* leans heavily and transparently on white Folk-Americana references. In particular, 'Now the

Night is Here' is firmly Dylan-esque in its vocal phrasing and the acoustic picking on 'Bag Man' evokes Fred Neil's 'Everybody's Talkin'. 'A Bullet for Everyone' and 'Call Me No. 5' follow a hitherto unlikely southern rock code, leaning towards The Allman Brothers, Buffalo Springfield and Creedence Clearwater Revival. Marking the first time in his career Weller has overtly drawn upon white Americana, as an experiment 'Illumination' is intriguing but, in the absence of memorable melody and accessible lyric, the durability of the concept is limited. Possibly written at different times, lyrics are set at extremes, with some unequivocally direct and others relatively inaccessible.

Evoking the swaggering, warm production aesthetic of Wilco's 'A.M', 'Going Places' sets a lovelorn lyric within an expansive groove; the instrumental textures are bright and the opening verse and chorus consummately written and delivered. Post chorus, however, an unorthodox and uncommitted floating section neither contrasts with, nor enhances the track, and this is followed by an extended instrumental section that meanders, neglecting to add a motif or solo. The aesthetic effect is that the sound is grasping for the regions of 'Wild Wood' but falling short, and ultimately, 'Going Places' projects as a promising, yet insufficiently edited or enhanced idea. Elsewhere, 'One x One' explores a similar feel, and driven by the omnipresent Hammond that gives much of the material on 'Illumination' warmth, the Gospel tinged 'All Good Books' and 'Standing Out in the Universe' coast appealingly without imprinting memorable hooks.

Sequentially, the stylistic wanderlust is distracting. On the later '22 Dreams' a similar trick is performed with wilful ease, but here the quest seems studied and stretched, as if projected in discrete phases rather than captured as one. Strident in its verse and breakdown sections, 'Leafy Mysteries' has the potential to be a minor-masterpiece, yet includes another distracting interjection, this time in the form of a discordant post-verse melodic sequence. The dreamlike and bittersweet chordal swirl of 'Who Brings Joy' ebbs and flows, it's message of love seemingly drawn between rest and restlessness. Like Lennon's 'Julia' it seems to delight in evading a core, making it both immersive and elusive. The textural 'Spring at Last' brings experimental relief and the love song 'Illumination' evokes a similarly spiritual 'White Album' aesthetic. Within all this adventure, the blue-eyed soul of 'Written in the Stars' continues the eclectic trail.

Half Americana, part dark-tinged English Folk, part brass driven pop, 'Illumination' is an uneven patchwork. Where 'In the City' and 'Paul Weller' succeed by combining complimentary styles, the stylistic groupings on 'Illumination' are too distant from each other to form a coherent whole. Contemporary reviews sense the stirrings of a revival, with Jason Fox of NME writing 'The blues rock cul-de-sac that finally reached a dead end with 'Heliocentric' has at last been exited.... Britrock's grumpy uncle has regained his gnarled spirit here and fans will feel the better for it' (2002: 45). Metacritic, a website that aggregates reviews of albums and averages each rating, recorded an average for 'Illumination' of 79, indicating a generally positive critical reception. Reaching number 1 in the UK album charts, Heliocentric was certified Gold for sales of over 100,000.

As an experience, claimed Steve White shortly after its recording, the making of 'As Is Now' was up there with 'Café Bleu' and 'Stanley Road'. *As is Now* opens with the intricately arranged and motif driven 'Blink and You'll Miss It'. Where the songs on 'Illumination' and 'Heliocentric' sound as if they were democratically constructed and embellished in the studio with minimal time devoted to editing, the material here is more idiosyncratic. Structures are deftly constructed, and the ensemble confidence in the music creates a sound that comes across at various times as aggressive, passionate, playful and meditative. An amalgamation of the concise 'Paul Weller', the brawling 'Wild Wood' and the effusive 'Stanley Road', 'As Is Now' regains consistency. Much of the music is unorthodox. Usually an epilogue of sorts, the coda is regularly a core song feature, either revealing the title late on, adding an unexpected discordance courtesy of the sour organ that closes 'Paper Smile', introducing late full-on psychedelia on 'Come on Let's Go' and 'From the Floorboards Up', or announcing an entirely new section on 'Roll Along Summer'. Each time, the intervention of the coda adds an unexpected and welcome layer of exuberance.

Amidst an aesthetic that evokes the approachable meander of 'Between the Buttons' and the sonic adventure of 'Revolver', both released in 1966, the songs on 'As Is Now' are at once untethered and aware of each other, a rare combination achieved in part through reference to earlier originals. The pastoral side two of 'All Mod Cons' can be glimpsed in 'The Start of Forever'; the structural ambiguity and restless aggression of 'Setting Sons' in 'Come on Let's Go'; the balladry of 'It's A Very Deep Sea' in the mystical 'Pan'; and the title track of 'Stanley Road' in the strident 'Here's The Good News'. Where 'Heavy Soul' and 'Heliocentric' are for the most part oblivious to many of the more effective musical traits found in Weller's back catalogue and 'Illumination' is often indiscriminately referential to a disparate range of influences, on 'As Is Now' the main frames of reference come from the work of the artist himself. There is a looseness across the record; 'I Wanna Make It Alright' and 'Savages' are examples of the artist at his most unselfconscious, and even the lesser works 'Bring Back the Funk' and 'The Pebble and the Boy' are made luminous through quirky arrangement flourishes. A contemporary 2005 review by Paul McNamee for NME notes how some tracks channel the energy of The Jam, while Gavin Martin, writing for Uncut, frames Weller as 'an icon reawakened', labelling the album 'a work of rejuvenating power, on which Weller and his long serving band attain a new sense of purpose and focus'. Reaching number 4 in the UK album charts, 'As Is Now' was certified Gold for sales of over 100,000.

Almost twice as long as some other Weller albums, characteristic of its continuous movement, *22 Dreams* uses an array of traditional instrumentation – drums, bass, electric and acoustic guitars, piano, organ, fiddle, brass, strings, while never coming close to using the same arrangement twice. This gives the record an eclectic, virtuosic feel that sustains throughout its relatively lengthy trajectory. Seemingly defiant of musical logic, the wilful absence of continuity of sound on '22 Dreams' creates an internal coherence. This continuity lies in a number of aspects other than arrangement, most notably the 'lean forward' nature of the performances and mixes; the unambiguous nature of the lyrics; and the surfeit of immediately memorable, hook laden melodies. Like The Beatles 'White Album', '22 Dreams' is unshowy, often surprising and exhibits no sign of hesitancy. As on the previous album 'As Is Now', there is a sense that the personnel are finding the making of music easy.

The album is divided into four parts; effusive, meditative, rocking and gentle. Using subtle and carefully realised band arrangements, the opening five songs are effusive variations on the ecstatic nature of being in love. Each track adheres to a pure evocation of the concept, with no metaphorical darkness admitted to induce the doubting, wakeful nature of reality. Punctuated by interludes that add a reflective spirituality, from 'Invisible' to 'Why Walk When You Can Run' the mood is more meditative. Whereas at the turn of the century Weller seemed to have featured a traditional band as a matter of course, here, as on 'Wild Wood', instruments appear only when needed. The cast of players is expansive and their contributions only heard as and when required. Excluding Weller, 22 musicians are involved, with Steve Cradock and Simon Dine both playing over 10 instruments each.

True to Sondheim's previously cited edict, 'Content dictates form' (2010), the compositions on '22 Dreams' sometimes amble, and sometimes observe more conventional pop structure. English folksong is at the root of 'Light Nights', 'Sea Spray' and Where'er Ye Go', yet while grouped together as folk songs, each track is conveyed very differently. 'Light Nights' features bristling acoustic guitars that evoke the magic night of Van Morrison's 'Moondance', 'Sea Spray' adds brushes and mandolins to convey a weary, resigned reverie and 'Where'er Ye Go' uses piano and voice to create a sense of intimacy. The title track '22 Dreams', 'Echoes Around the Sun' and 'Push It Along' are rock n' roll songs with three very different pulses, and in the latter phases of the album, the Cuban son of 'One Bright Star', the spoken word poem 'God' voiced by Aziz Ibrahim, and the extended instrumentals 'Lullabye fur Kinder' and 'Night Lights' are sonic departures, dreamlike in their winding unpredictability.

Writing for Uncut in 2008, John Lewis asserts 'This is his 'White Album', a sprawling song cycle that channels a century of influences into 21 tracks … easily his finest solo album to date'. Also writing at the time of release in 2008, Guardian journalist Amy Raphael praises '22 Dreams', writing 'this collection of songs is way out of the changing man's comfort zone…. Such an eclectic, ambitious record might be expected to sound disparate, desperate even, but instead it's a set of distinctive, strangely addictive songs'. Sustaining sales figures for recent solo albums and reaching number 1 in the UK album charts, 22 Dreams was certified Gold for sales of over 100,000.

In Julien Temple's 2010 film 'Find the Torch', Weller refers to *Wake Up the Nation* as 'a clarion call; I wasn't hearing the music I wanted to hear'. Diverse, playful and profound, 'Wake Up the Nation' is an urban iteration of the bucolic '22 Dreams'. Where its predecessor swoops and glides, it stutters and jolts; where '22 Dreams' celebrates connection, 'Wake Up the Nation' revels in disconnection. Populated by miniature songs (the longest track on side one is 2.24), the sequence moves briskly, often led by heavily effected and unsettling lead guitar lines evocative of those used on David Bowie's Berlin trilogy. Bowie is a consistent presence, from the echoes of 'The Jean Genie' in the title track to the automatic writing style used to sketch some of the lyrics. On 'Moonshine' and '7 and 3 is the Striker's Name', some instruments play a tune while some meander around it as if in search of it; the effect is to project the conscious and unconscious in tandem, to allow the worldly and the other worldly to co-exist. Where '22 Dreams' draws upon complementary textures, 'Wake Up the Nation' is often surreal, combining post punk with Bo Diddley on '7 and 3 is the Striker's Name' and post punk with Dylan's 'Blonde on Blonde' on 'Grasp and Still Connect'. As with all Weller solo albums post '22 Dreams', disparate songwriting styles are given cohesion through a defined, consistent and cohesive production aesthetic; by this means the falsetto soul of 'Aim High' and the relentlessly bleak 'She Speaks' fall within a singular aesthetic code.

On side one of 'Wake Up the Nation', immediately alerted by the chaotic and exuberant 'Moonshine', the listener is shunted and cajoled by the infectious protest of 'Wake Up the Nation', serenaded by the unabashed soul homage 'No Tears to Cry', confronted by the rush hour fury of 'Fast Car/ Slow Traffic', drawn in to the psychedelic haze of 'Andromeda' and eventually given time to catch a breath by the incidental 'In Amsterdam'. As the album progresses, dissonant pianos, organs and guitars appear to add off-centredness, and later tracks appear to be partially obscured reflections of earlier ones. Most remarkable of all is 'Trees', a song written by Weller after visiting his father John in hospital. Shifting back and forth in time, 'Trees' inhabits the voices of the hospitalised elderly in the days of their youth, before age became a burden. Across a four-part structure, Weller adopts the character of a beautiful woman, a mother loved by children, a virile young man and finally an older character who longs to be once more a tree. Ambitious and deeply profound, the gravitas of Trees adds integral flex to the sequence. In her online review, written in 2010, Emily MacKay of the NME concurs: 'It's a collection of ludicrously fresh sounding short and sharp material that confirms he's in the middle of a pretty impressive rebirth', while David Cavanagh's Uncut review of May 2010 notes the eclecticism and breathless pace of the music. Reaching number 2 in the UK album charts, like each of Weller's post 'Stanley Road' albums to date, 'Wake Up the Nation' was certified Gold for sales of over 100,000.

Like 'Wake Up the Nation', *Sonik Kicks* is loaded heavy with instrumental texture yet made fleet of foot by skilful mixing and canny track sequencing.

'Green' opens with a stream of consciousness vocal, its relentless pulse at odds with both the incidental and meandering nature of its lyric and the restless nature of the arrangement, which never repeats for more than two bars. Helping to accentuate a dazzling array of sensory propositions, the headphone mix transports the sound back and forth from left to right ear. Immediately, 'Sonik Kicks' challenges the listener to keep pace with it. Returning to the effect borrowed from Robert Fripp and used frequently in 'Wake Up the Nation', guitars wail quietly in the background of the more formally structured 'Attic', and on 'Kling Klang' disembodied instrumental textures appear and disappear as if being thrust forward and snatched away again. Through this frenetic opening trio and in the slower, regenerative 'Sleep of the Serene', the music has a mysterious and beguiling sense of dislocation.

Switching emphasis, the acoustic guitars and strings of the folk tinged 'By the Water' are more earthed, and underpinned by a chord sequence borrowed from The Who's 'I Can't Explain', 'That Dangerous Age' offers knowing self-referential humour. Providing the integral flex brought by 'Trees' on the previous record, the dub infused 'Study in Blue' brings unhurried space to the mid-point of 'Sonik Kicks'. Here, the record is allowed to stretch and a leavening effect is brought to bear. Like 'Wake Up the Nation', Side two offers refracted, less imposing variations on music presented on side one. 'Dragonfly' revisits the motoric feel of 'Green' and 'Attic'; 'When Your Garden's Overgrown' extends the dry portraiture of 'That Dangerous Age' and, divided by an interlude that again makes entertaining use of headphone separation, the angular and concise 'Around the Lake' and 'Drifters' project as sketches on a shared theme. Closing 'Sonik Kicks', the slow pulse, swirling synths and Eastern classical overtones of 'Paperchase' are joined by the similarly narcotic 'Be Happy Children'. Energetic adventurous and elliptical, 'Sonik Kicks' marks the end of a trilogy of albums that reinvigorate Weller's canon by gathering an eclectic range of ideas, pooling the resources of an extended group of collaborators (again over 20 musicians contribute) and each time honing a collective individuality of character through production.

It is notable how during this phase in Weller's career, the physical sales numbers drop as the critical consensus becomes more positive. This is likely to be related to a number of effects; the global decline in album sales, the emergence of Spotify and other streaming services as listening hubs where consumers can hear music on subscription terms without requirement to purchase and the increasingly diluted nature of reviewer influence. As Rutherford Johnson (2017: 6) writes, 'the birth of the Internet and World Wide Web in the early 1990s, as well as the widespread popularisation of digital technologies, transformed the production and consumption of culture in every sphere'. That there were at least 24 published critical reviews of 'Sonik Kicks' in the United Kingdom alone indicates a saturation of the field. In such an environment, particularly good or particularly bad reviews are increasingly likely to have diminishing effect. In response, with some honourable exceptions, modern music critics tend to write variations on supportive reviews. A 2012 review in the Guardian by Kitty Empire says 'Sonik Kicks' 'barrels along hectically, throwing out ideas like a particularly exuberant Catherine wheel'. Based on an average calculated using the aforementioned 24 critical reviews, Metacritic gives a score of 77, indicating a generally favourable reception. Reaching number 1 in the UK album charts, 'Sonik Kicks' was certified Silver for sales of over 60,000.

Where 'Setting Sons' and 'Wild Wood' are extreme in their exploration of compositional structure, *Saturns Pattern* is their match in terms of arrangement and texture. Built from initial tracks laid down by a skeletal band of bass player Andy Crofts, drummer Ben Gordelier and Weller on a variety of instruments and vocals, Saturns Pattern uses imaginative programming to create a soundscape in permanent evolution. It is hard to tell if the band, or even Weller himself had a clear idea of how the songs might turn out. The amount of sound manipulation indicates that producer Jan Stan Kybert and engineer Charles Rees were central to the discovery of sounds, with Weller exploring and exercising editorial control. With the exception of three songs, 'Long Time' and the closing couplet of 'In the Car' and 'These City Streets', throughout 'Saturns Pattern', the ear is continuously directed away from the vocal. Harmonically, the verses of five of the nine songs settle on one chord, three verses use two chords, and only one, 'Going my way' uses three. The effect of this is to project the songs less as harmonically contoured compositions and more as adventures in sound. Moving through E, G sharp, F, E, B, A, E flat minor, G sharp and E minor, song keys are set to convey the energy of the voice.

Some songs on 'Saturns Pattern' seem to have originated on guitar. Following in the footsteps of John Lee Hooker, many of whose songs divest their forward momentum from a single chord, 'White Sky' is effectively a one chord song. Using extended opening atmospherics and a lengthy coda to imprint its driven aesthetic over five minutes, on 'White Sky' the entire band is channelled through multiple effects, creating a psychedelic wall of sound. More likely written on piano, the title track 'Saturns Pattern' is typical of the strategy employed through the remainder of the album; restless textural switches, atonal motifs, angular inversions, casual re-harmonisations and relentless manipulation of sound. Once the ear has acclimatised to the modus operandi of the producers and ceased to anticipate conventional or expected texture, the music winds along in thrall to its own internal logic. On 'Pick It Up' and 'These City Streets' solo instrumental sections change repeatedly; as with 'Wild Wood' the effect created is not of a band, but rather of a floating orchestra whose players are content to drift in and out of the narrative.

Occasional resonances can be heard in the borrowed stylings of The Beach Boys, Lou Reed and Iggy Pop on 'Going My Way', 'Long Time' and 'In the Car', yet unlike 'Illumination', 'Saturns Pattern' does not have an overarching American aesthetic. As previously mentioned, Weller seems content to cede control to chance during the sound shaping process, and here the contributions of Jan Kybert and Charles Rees appear integral. To cite one of Weller's formative influences, Pete Townshend: 'If you are insecure, you are secure in your insecurity' (Herman, 1971: 94). At the time of release in 2015, a review by Michael Bonner in Uncut explains how Weller is 'making a virtue of cut-ups, sound collages, treated instruments and sound effects' (2015: 78). Reaching number 2 in the UK album charts, 'Saturns Pattern' was certified Silver for sales of over 60,000, and speaking in 2017, Weller himself claimed 'Saturns Pattern' to be the album he is most proud of.

Describing his first and only soundtrack to date as 'more abstract and evolving from tenderness and calm, to violent and disturbing', in 2017, Weller told Steven MacKenzie of The Big Issue that the soundtrack for *Jawbone* had been written without having seen the film in advance, a process Weller admits is 'totally arse about face'. Following a meeting with director Johnny Harris, Weller was convinced of the quality of the project and undertook to write the score 'blind'. Often drone like with subtle variations, 'Jawbone' is atmospheric, underscoring rather than overpowering. The conventional songs on the score, 'The Ballad of Jimmy McCabe' and 'Bottle', are affecting and tender folk ballads featuring Weller alone with an acoustic guitar. Typical of his approach to the soundtrack there is minimal effort to imprint his own aesthetic or celebrity, rather the songs are delivered by the performer-as-vessel. The second part of the score integrates film dialogue with a variety of electric psychedelic guitar and drum and string-based combinations, each of which studiously avoids thematic repetition in favour of shadowy colouration. Writing on a similar affect achieved by Brian Eno on 'Music for Airports', Moorefield (2010: 56) writes how it:

> Explores combining and recombining various sound sources in the studio, presenting the listener with variety of possible levels of listening: one can listen casually, while doing the dishes or reading the paper, or one can focus on the content of the music to the exclusion of all else. Thus, the aim of this music is to function on different levels.

Like many of Weller's albums, *A Kind Revolution* is very different from its predecessor. Where 'Saturns Patterns' is highly inventive in its application of sound, 'A Kind Revolution' is conventional, a return to a more settled structural and arrangement mode. In keeping with 'In the City' and 'Paul Weller', the songs seem to have originated from three sources; in this instance Weller with guitar, Weller with piano and band jam session. Seemingly written to tour, the instrumentation on 'A Kind Revolution' features the live band set up of drums, bass, guitars, organ and piano, with occasional moog added. 'One Tear', 'Impossible Idea', and 'Satellite Kid' are verse-chorus structures, while 'New York', 'Long, Long Road' and 'The Cranes are Back' begin with double verse-chorus, and later revert to verse chorus. Within a narrow instrumental setting, the songs are stylistically wide ranging and varied in feel and tempo. The New Wave aesthetic of 'Nova' follows the New Orleans groove of 'Woo Se Mama', yet as a consequence of the continuity of sound provided by instrumentation, the progression is not as incongruous as it might sound. As the record progresses, the predominant aesthetic that emerges is Soul, as borrowed from Philadelphia, New Orleans, New York and Memphis. In each instance, Weller's voice and accent make the music very much his own. On 'The Cranes Are Back' in particular, the audible quality of what Hawkins (2009: 188) calls 'energetic, aggressive, sublime unbridled passion – the emotive qualities of Weller's performance' can be heard.

Another comparative difference is the lyric approach; where 'Saturns Pattern' is predominantly non-sequitur, the songs on A Kind Revolution have immediately traceable themes. There are lyrics about wariness and suspicion of his contemporaries, family, devotion, revelation, the overdue return of hope, individuality, a meditation on religion, a daydream about the ghost of an American painter and finally, borrowed from the poetry of Noel Gallagher, a closing homage to 'The Impossible Idea' that love might change the world. An transparently open and upbeat celebration of the here and now, and of perpetual change, 'A Kind Revolution' possesses a sustained lightness of mood. Evidently pleased with the feel of the music, the makers of 'A Kind Revolution' included an instrumental version of the album and a full set of remixes with its initial release. Writing for Uncut online in 2017, reviewer John Lewis cites the presence of angular funk, New Orleans gumbo, jerky Nigerian afrobeat and dreamy symphonic soul. Reaching number 5 in the UK album charts, A Kind Revolution is as yet uncertified by the British Phonographic Industry, indicating sales of under 60,000.

In yet another aesthetic about turn, *True Meanings* is entirely folk orchestral. Each song arrangement employs a similar dynamic use of instrumentation and structural form, typically moving quickly from brief acoustic introductions to verses and on to other sections that often don't sound entirely like pre-choruses, choruses or middle-eights and consequently elude classification. On 'True Meanings' these unquantifiable sections, familiar from earlier Jam compositions and singularly unusual amongst songwriters, can be found in the connected run of songs that form the main body of the record: 'Mayfly', 'Gravity', 'Old Castles', 'What Would He Say', 'Aspects', 'Bowie', 'Wishing Well' and 'Come Along'. This repeated incidence of 'floating' sections amplifies a sense consistently alluded to in the lyric that the overarching expression is one of air; of how we drift in and out of existence. To paraphrase the track 'Bowie', we are always arriving, always departing.

The playful atonal flecks integral to the character of the previous run of albums are absent here. Trading exploration for reflection, there is a sense that the expression is one of humility and gratitude, the sincerity of which would not be well served by surprise. Temporally assuming the role from Jan Kybert, Weller oversees production. As a consequence, the songs seem to have been initially tracked solo and later subject to tasteful instrumental adornment. Moving away from the metaphorical 'Saturns Pattern' and the stylistically ambitious 'A Kind Revolution', on 'True Meanings' the gentle arc of the melodies and the uniformity of the textures draw the listener towards the words. Moving through a discrete series of lyric phases, the thematic sequence is as follows:

> 'Soul Searchers': The integral and perpetual need to explore;
> 'Glide', 'Mayfly' and 'Gravity': a trilogy of meditations on morality, beginning with an ode to the certainties of youth, progressing to a mystical evocation of equivalence between youth and death and finally to a celebration of the gift of life. Wittingly or unwittingly, the concept of 'air', of being between states, is evident in the titles;
> 'Old Castles' and 'What Would He Say'?: One song of distrust in those entrusted with positions of power who allow the world to degenerate, and one about how he himself is complicit;
> 'Aspects', 'Bowie': The elusive nature of existence and its inevitable temporality;
> 'Wishing Well' and 'Come Along': The unknowable essence of who we are as lovers, and the shifting boundaries of desire and longing;
> 'Books': a brief reprise of an earlier theme visited on 'Old Castles' and 'What Would He Say'? centred upon how we misinterpret spiritual teaching;
> 'Movin' On' and 'May Love Travel with You': contentment with existence and an equivalent wish for others to experience something similar;
> 'White Horses': A full circle realisation of the promise of 'Soul Searchers'; a search for the soul.

Conceptual in scope, the songs encircle a notion that 'True Meanings' are only found in transient settings; all truth and meaning is being sought, elliptically glimpsed and never possessed. The sleeve notes and sleeve design portray a sense that Weller seems to have been thinking of his family, present and past, during the making of the record, and perhaps that this set of songs is intended as a message to them. Unlike the temporal impressions created by previous albums and singles, 'True Meanings' might be viewed as a relatively permanent musical impression of how he sees himself. Perhaps this is why Steve Pilgrim, interviewed in 2019 for the film 'May Love Travel with You' considers it Weller's best solo album. A 2018 online Uncut review by Peter Watts emphasises the inventive use of the use of sitar and harmonium to create soul, country and folk flavours. Reaching number 2 in the UK album charts, 'True Meanings' was certified Silver for sales of over 60,000.

Released in January 2020, the 'In Another Room' EP indulges Weller's interest in experimental tape music and early electronics. A long-time admirer of the Ghost Box label, the EP contributes to the label's ethos to re-imagine a misremembered Olde England, at once warm and comforting, yet off-kilter. A 2019 press release by the label Ghost Box describes Weller's music as 'more than just experiments; tape manipulation, field recordings and instrumental passages are artfully arranged to create a gently uncanny and psychedelic atmosphere'. The track 'In Another Room' is a found sound collage, while 'Submerge' uses a disembodied piano with assorted tuned and untuned sounds to create a spectral aesthetic. On side two of the EP, 'Embarkation' combines birdsong with radio frequency effects and 'Rejoice' samples 'Walkin' from the forthcoming 'On Sunset' collection. Like 'Jawbone', there is an impression that Weller wanted to be associated with the project, that the idea of engaging in a particular spirit of collaboration appealed.

In keeping with Weller's inclination to present collections in very different styles, *On Sunset* moves from the folk of True Meanings to a west coast aesthetic that seems to have, as one of its focal points of reference, the lush textures of Roy Ayers Ubiquity 1975 album 'Vibration'. Here, the instrumental textures combine to create a light, limber and unhurried sound. Evoking a sun-drenched landscape, the mix is spacious, allowing all instruments to be heard with clarity. Predominantly mid-tempo, On Sunset begins with 'Mirrorball', a conventionally structured and arranged song made to sound unconventional through the insertion of a surprising, yet apt Stockhausen influenced section after the first chorus. Following 'Mirrorball', the laid back 'Baptiste' is a Hammond driven gospel-soul tune featuring warm electric guitars, and on 'Old Father Tyme' the turnarounds between verse and chorus sections groove with a similar unassuming simplicity that further projects the impression that the work has no axe to grind.

Continuing the reflective lyric mode of 'True Meanings', in the middle phase of the record, lyric themes glide from acceptance of one's lot in life in 'Village', to the value of experience in 'More', to an acceptance that the past is in the past in 'On Sunset'. Arriving after the recorded sound of waves gently rolling in, percussion adds Californian warmth, and with a sage wisdom prevailing, contentment with living in the moment pervades, palm trees sway and the sun is high. Reminiscent of the planned improvisation that characterises the arrangements on 'Wild Wood', in the extended coda of 'More', flute, acoustic guitar, string, woodwind, brass and piano textures are interwoven with delicacy, and the vocal, shared with Julie Gros, along with the appearance of Mick Talbot evokes the spirit of The Style Council. Seemingly cut at separate sessions, the stylistically removed yet equally fine 'Equanimity' and 'Rockets' are outliers that interrupt the relentlessly laid-back tempo. Resolved in its covenant to keep searching, 'On Sunset' avoids extremes, preferring instead to glide. Based on 16 critic reviews, the Metacritic score of 82 for 'On Sunset' is 5 higher than Weller's career Metacritic average of 77. Selling 24,000 in its first week of release and reaching number 1 in the UK album charts, On Sunset is, as yet uncertified by the British Phonographic Industry, indicating sales of under 60,000.

Written and recorded during the UK pandemic lockdowns of 2020, *Fat Pop (Volume 1)* trades the extended codas and broad structural vistas of On Sunset for more concise, classic single structures. Weller explains 'I wanted to make an album where every song could be released as a single. If that sort of thing still existed' (Kessler, 2021: 69). As such, like 'Wake Up the Nation', 'Fat Pop (Volume 1)' moves quickly. As if it would be frivolous or disrespectful to experiment and convey a sense of self-absorption while others around the globe were suffering in so many ways, most of the lyrics avoid introspection and project outwards. The disarmingly short opener 'Cosmic Fringes' is motoric in the krautrock style, using synths, bass and guitar sparingly to create arrangement space. In 'Cosmic Fringes' Weller is the keyboard warrior who disseminates his unsolicited worldview from his bedroom. The only lyric on the album written 'in character' in the style of 'Billy Hunt' and 'Little Boy Soldiers', it is the first of a number of tracks that, like 'Our Favourite Shop' seek to reflect contemporary social issues. Using similar instrumental settings for continuity of sound, and featuring a duet vocal with co-writer and The Mysterines vocalist Lia Metcalfe, the second track 'True' is similarly brisk. The only track on the album to briefly introduce musical dissonance, the title track 'Fat Pop' introduces a questioning lyric emphasis that is accentuated by a repetitive melody line. Like Bob Dylan's 'All Along the Watchtower', once the melody has been absorbed, the ear is inclined to stay with the words.

The remainder of 'Fat Pop (Volume 1)' continues to explore classic single structures and to integrate themes of loss and emptiness reflective of the times. The effect is to remind the listener of the past, to emphasise the healing power of music in the present and to look forward to its return. Co-written and performed with his daughter Leah, 'Shades of Blue' extends the theme explored in the previous year on 'Village', while 'Glad Times' uses string-laden soul to convey its blues. As if to avoid confronting the listener, the textures are never aggressive, and the meaning of the words and music never elusive. Whilst 'That Pleasure' has glimpses of the glide and grit of Marvin Gaye's 'What's Going On', 'Failed' expresses its author's frustration at the scale of the world's ills and his lack of capacity to intervene. As is the case on 'Wake Up the Nation', 'Sonik Kicks' and 'Saturns Pattern' and 'A Kind Revolution', the closing tracks are less imposing impressions of earlier tracks. As with Weller albums since '22 Dreams', the consensus among reviewers was favourable, with the NME calling it 'a generous collection of expertly crafted pop … masterful with flashes of magic'. 'Fat Pop (Volume One)' went to number 1 on the UK album charts, making Weller the only artist apart from The Beatles to have topped the UK album chart in five separate decades.

3.2 Typology

The multiplicity of levels attributable to Weller's songwriting over the past five decades inevitably render any typology incomplete. As his songs adhere to Sondheim's dictum 'Content dictates form', the raw materials are assembled and shaped according the nature of the materials themselves. Consequently, song structures, lyric themes and modes of instrumentation are widely varied. Some elements recur, however, and these combine to create a sense of an artistic signature. Depending on the date of authorship, some themes are relatively temporal while others echo over time. As discussed earlier, to add to the complexity when it comes to applying typological labels, songs often have textures that colour the core text with metaphorical undercurrents. In shaping tracks, songwriters and producers seek to balance words, music, arrangement, performance, and production to enable listeners to absorb some elements of the song in real time, and to like what they hear enough to want to listen again for what may have been missed. This happens on a spectrum; the busy arrangement and dense structuring of The Beatles 'Got to Get You into My Life' would require numerous listens for the listener to be cognizant of the full extent of what is happening across the multiple threads of sound, whereas the vocal and string arrangement of 'Eleanor Rigby' can be absorbed by alternating the focus of the ear between two threads of sound, strings and vocal.

Songs are often grasped through their words, and exist to convey the meaning of the song (Frith, 1996: 163, 166). Like many Lucinda Williams songs including 'Sweet Old World' and 'Can't Let Go', title repetition of the type found in 'This the Modern World', 'Shout to The Top' and 'Have You Ever Had It Blue', seeks to amplify core expressions. At odds with regular conversation, which tends to be non-repetitive, the repetition of lines demarcates an expression of significance, a line that demands prominence. Music and lyric do not, however, necessarily pull in the same expressive direction and the apparent meaning of words can be modified, or given new meaning by music. In the field of communication studies, Hills (1986) notes how non-verbal behaviour can support or deny verbal communication, and writing on music philosophy, Langer (1957: 218, 222, 244) argues that music is a metaphor for human feeling in the broadest sense; that its ambivalence gives it a greater power then words. Griffiths (2003: 39, 43) adds that the inherent meaning of lyric cannot be identified away from its music. Performance adds a further layer of complexity; performing 'Where Did Our Love Go', Diana Ross sings a blues lyric over bright swinging major key music in a voice that sounds neither happy nor sad, at what might be considered an ambiguous emotional pitch. For the listener, this opens up a range of interpretive possibilities; to let the soul go with the music, let the body go with the swing; let the mind go with the words or to set the imagination free to draw conclusions about what it all means. Similarly, a vast range of inferences, conventions and dissonances can be found in Weller's music. As a rule of thumb, the following typology is based on instances that recur within the recorded catalogue; as such, it seeks to forefront ideas valued effective enough by Weller to revisit.

Griffiths (2003: 50, 51, 55) identifies a range of possible rhyming schemes in popular song, including full-rhyme (fight, right), half-rhyme (mittens, sickens) and non-rhyme (back, speech). He observes how some lyrics conform to non-rhyme in that that they move away from the rectitude of rhyme towards conversational plain statement. Weller's lyric writing spans each of these schemes, but, somewhat unconventionally, he often alternates schemes within songs. In The Style Council songbook, 'Paris Match', 'Money Go Round' and 'Have You Ever Had It Blue' adhere to full-rhyme, but in The Jam, and as a solo artist, Weller tends to be less formal. 'Pretty Green' rhymes 'green' with 'machine' and then drifts away from full-rhyme. Similarly, after establishing half-rhyme, 'He's the Keeper', 'Come On/Let's Go', 'The Pebble and the Boy', 'To Be Someone' and 'Black River' gravitate towards non-rhyme. Often, rhyming schemes are overlooked from the beginning. The closing words in each of the four lines of verse one of 'Man in the Corner Shop' are 'shop', 'him', 'life' and 'really'. Initially written as a letter in the format of Brian Patten's prose poem 'Towards A Definition of Itself' (Henri et al., 2017: 101) and later set to music, 'Burning Sky' is an example of anti-rhyme, while 'Running on The Spot', 'Invisible' and 'Start!' are among dozens of kindred compositions that similarly evade rhyme entirely. Ultimately, and perhaps uniquely in popular music, Weller's phrasing frequently renders the types inseparable; rarely is it obvious that rhyming or non-rhyming schemes are being used.

On the subject of effective communication, Moffatt (1978: 10, 47) writes of a 'spectrum of discourse' that covers what happened, what *is* happening and what *may* happen. The implications for lyric writing are significant; if one or more of the three elements of communication is missing, the sharing of communicative meaning may be compromised. In 'Bewitched, Bothered and Bewildered' by Rodgers and Hart, the first verse is written and sung in the present tense, the second verse in the past and the third verse in the future. An unusually precise example, in this song, Moffatt's 'Spectrum of Discourse' is achieved in three equal chapters. Similarly, the lyric of 'The Suburbs' by Arcade Fire begins in the past tense, moves to the present and later dwells on the future before moving back to the present. Arcade Fire's Win Butler, who we have likely never met, has told us something about where he has been, where he is now and where he is going. As listeners, we are engaging with communicative meaning.

During the writing process itself, it is unlikely that many songwriters are aware of a need to consider tenses within their lyric writing, or that a lyricist would deliberately set out with the intention of balancing past, present and future. Analysis, however, supports the notion that popular songs perhaps knowingly or more likely unwittingly comply to a 'spectrum of discourse', and it is likely that, during the editorial process, a lyricist is aware, instinctively if not forensically, if a lyric that contains elements of past, present and future is 'working', and of one that is missing one or more elements is not. In 'Town Called Malice' the opening verse is focussed on the future, on how things will be. Verse two moves the imagery to the present tense before threading past tense in to the narrative. As listeners, we have a sense of what things have been like, what they are like and what they could be like; we are placed within a 'spectrum of discourse'. In a variety of ways, the vast majority of Weller's lyrics drift across tenses in a way that conveys a sense of context, currency and agency. Analysis of the lyric text for the LP 'All Mod Cons' reveals how Weller, likely unknowingly, interweaves the past, present and future across the record to communicate his transient identities to a vast, unknown audience:

All Mod Cons: Past; Future; Present
To Be Someone: Future; Present; Past
Mr. Clean: Present; Future; Past
English Rose: Future; Past
In the Crowd: Present
Billy Hunt: Present; Past; Future
It's Too Bad: Present; Past; Future
Fly: Present; Future; Past
The Place I Love: Present
'A' Bomb in Wardour Street: Present
Down in the Tube Station at Midnight: Present; Future

Many of the above uses of lyric tense are interchangeable and could have been altered by Weller without compromising the syllable count, word-sound or meaning. Ultimately the lyric tenses chosen by Weller are the ones that encircle the listener in communicative language, that persuade us to believe in his places, motives and characters.

In terms of mode of communication, the relationship between the song and its audience is mediated by the framing of the position of the narrator. An 'I to You' song can be interpreted in three ways; as a song sung by the narrator to us the listener; as a song sung by the narrator to someone other than us; or as a song being sung by us to someone else. An example of an 'I to You' song is 'How Deep Is Your Love' by The Bee Gees. Here, the words 'I' and 'You' are almost continuously interwoven into the lyric text, creating a sense that anything extraneous to the intensity of the one-to-one dynamic is non-existent. Weller's 'I Should Have Been There to Inspire You', 'All on A Misty Morning' 'Fly' and 'Start!' all share this lyric mode. As listeners, we are invited to dream ourselves into these lyric texts. We can regret not having been there to inspire, or perhaps regret that someone wasn't there to inspire us. Alternatively, we can watch, as if viewing a film, the dynamic as played out by Weller and his other character.

Had Paul McCartney named his famous song 'And I Love *You*' it would have a similar dynamic. The narrator of a song titled 'And I Love *Her*', however, narrows the scope for interpretation. As listeners, we can either love her too, or listen as the singer tells us of his love for her. On 'English Rose' and 'Time Passes', Weller sings to us of a specific loved one, who, like the object of McCartney's romantic attention, remains unidentified. In 'Private

Hell', 'Butterfly Collector', and 'Eton Rifles' the lyric infers Weller is singing to specific characters. Weller is singing to 'them' and we listen from the outside. In a slight variation, Elvis Costello's 'Alison' involves the singer singing to a named other, as Weller does in 'Up in Suze's Room'. Unless our name happens to be Alison or Suze, once again we are on the outside looking in. Similarly placing us at a remove from the narrative, some of Weller's lyrics are sung to his family; 'Sweet Pea, My Sweet Pea' and 'Moon on your Pyjamas' are written and sung to his children, and 'Going My Way' to his wife Hannah. Relatively universal, 'Wild Wood', 'Empty Ring', and 'Ghosts' are written and sung to a collective 'you'; effectively to 'Us'.

Conversely, Sheryl Crow's 'Home' refers only to the singer herself; as such its discourse is introspective and could be perceived as 'inner voice'. A number of Weller's songs are introspective, or are written as if sung to self. 'Shopping', 'Friday Street', 'Pretty Green', 'Absolute Beginners', 'Brand New Start', 'It's A Very Deep Sea' and 'It Just Came to Pieces in My Hands' are all lyrics in which we are invited to overhear Weller's inner dialogue. Autobiographical songs such as 'The Changingman' and 'God' are intensely personal and explore the inner workings of Weller's emotional and philosophical core. Lennon's 'Lucy in the Sky with Diamonds' (1967) was inspired by a drawing by his son Julian, and 'The Changingman' was similarly sparked by Weller's daughter Leah's description of a toy doll (Weller, 2010: 136). As Weller clarifies: 'Some of my songs are definitely biographical, but probably a very small percentage of them to be honest' (Rachel, 2013: 193). On a related note, 'Science', 'As You Lean Into the Light' Hung Up', 'Empty Ring', 'Bull Rush', 'Andromeda' and 'Brand New Start' fall into the category of philosophical sense-making. Here, Weller explores the inexplicability of the cosmos; the healing power of optimism; the need to accept change; learning how to move on; taking notice of signs and new beginnings.

Writing on the authorship of narrative, Barthes (1977: 105–115) asks: Who is the subject? Are there a privileged class of actors? What is the code which signifies narrator and listener? Who is the donor of the narrative? If not actually the author, the narrator may appear omniscient; at once inside and outside the featured characters. Either way, the narrative and the characters are essentially what Barthes calls 'paper beings', meaning that the author of the narrative, the storyteller, is in no way to be confused with the narrator. However, as Frith notes in 'Performing Rites', the pop singer has to enact both their own image and the personality of the song at the same time (1998: 212). Speaking in 1995, Weller explained 'I'm wary of songs that are autobiographical. They might start off being about me, but the rest of the song is about something else' (Heatley, 1996: 80). Evidently, the narrator of 'Billy Hunt' or 'Little Boy Soldiers' is not Weller himself, but is instead the author in a refracted, or transposed sense. This approach enables Weller to adopt personae that may or may not share his worldview or reflect his experience; as such it opens up a range of engaging characters and perspectives. Where

'Billy Hunt' is a rookie with dreams of world domination, the narrator of 'Little Boy Soldiers' is a pawn in a military game. In 'Ghosts of Dachau' Weller adopts the perspective of a character from Tadeusz Borowski's 'This Way for the Gas, Ladies and Gentlemen' and in 'Just Who is the 5 O' Clock Hero' he enacts the voice of his father John returning home exhausted from a building site. Ultimately, Weller is all, and none of these characters.

Frith writes (1996: 171) 'popular music has always featured the 'character' song.... The lyrical and narrative convention here is to portray a character while simultaneously drawing attention to the art of the portrayal'. Written in 1978, 'Standards' is the first example of such a lyric in Weller's catalogue, and in the intervening years, a multitude of satirical character voices are drawn into his songs. As mentioned in the sub-chapter on modernism, on 'Sunny Afternoon' Ray Davies adopts the voice of a wealthy individual to bemoan the fact that some of his wealth is inaccessible to him. To convey his incredulity at the willingness of the electorate to vote as they have, on 'Going Underground' Weller cordially invites the leader of the day to embark on an apocalyptic manifesto. Continuing the satirical dynamic, in 'Life at a Top People's Health Farm' Weller sardonically thanks Margaret Thatcher by adopting the voice of a gullible Tory supporter. Written to highlight the inanity of keyboard warriors who use social media to express their unsolicited worldview, 'Cosmic Fringes' is another song written 'in character'. In each case, the finger is not pointed from the outside by Weller, rather he inhabits personae to enact the folly itself, leaving us to make our own judgement.

In the absence of reference to self, as discussed in the analysis of 'Sound Affects', Weller's lyric for 'That's Entertainment' is unusual in that it solely observes. Writing on Patti Smith's 'Land', Sheila Whiteley (2006: 83) says: 'its effectiveness as a sound-poem lies primarily in and the fragmentation and manipulation of words which juxtapose the mundane ... with the poetic'. In 'That's Entertainment', Weller removes himself from the action entirely to convey an observational lyric in which violence, romance and the mundane living, breathing sounds of human existence are interwoven. Similar to the way Adrien Henri's poems integrate the ghost of Wilfred Owen, soldiers, feathers and wild strawberries, in 'That's Entertainment' the permanent and the incidental co-exist. Unusually in popular song, nothing is at stake for the narrator, who stands aside from the scene. Elsewhere, Weller's observational lyrics tell us about himself and the way he views society. In 'Saturdays Kids' he looks back to observe the characteristics of teenagers he grew up with. At each juncture, Weller lays out scenes without overt judgment; the images imply the conditions and conclusions are left to the listener. Similarly removing the narrator from the discourse, Richard Thompson's 'Vincent Black Lightning 1952' is a story about characters other than Richard Thompson. Weller's 'Man in the Corner Shop', has a similar dynamic. Like Paul McCartney in 'Eleanor Rigby', Weller assumes omnipresence to effectively read the minds of the corner shop owner, the customer and the boss from the factory. As discussed in the analysis of 'All Mod Cons', McCartney initiated a similar lyric approach in 'Penny Lane', drifting from the barber's shop, to the fireman's pocket and into the feelings of the nurse. As listeners we experience the characters not as they *look* but as they really *are*.

A number of Weller's songs might be considered clarion calls, and these are divided into lyrics that *address* the collective, and lyrics that locate the singer as *part of* a collective. In the former category, 'In the City', 'Beat Surrender' and 'Ghosts', the latter labelled by Weller as 'A rallying call in the name of inspiration and fulfilment' (2010: 149) place the singer outside of the collective. More typically, with its inclusive refrain 'Absolute Beginners', described by Weller (2010: 173) as 'an attempt to rabble rouse my generation' places him at the centre of the action. Similarly, 'Into Tomorrow', 'Find the Torch, Burn the Plans' and 'Wake Up the Nation' are among lyrics that call the audience to move with Weller as a collective. Machin (2010: 87) discusses how the lyric of Public Enemy's 'Fight the Power' locates the singer as part of a collective. In doing so, as Machin observes, the singer points out it that is not just *his* voice in the lyric, but *ours*. In 'What's Going On' Marvin Gaye places himself within the collective, and establishing a similar sense of solidarity, in 'A Stone's Throw Away' (1985) Weller does likewise.

In their youths, both Ray Davies and Paul Weller were swiftly transported from working class backgrounds to the upper-class world of the music industry, the transposition acting as the catalyst for a number of sharply observed class-based songs. Inevitably, once a career in music is established, immersion in showbusiness and its trappings and rewards threaten to dilute the potency of class as a credible song theme. During The Jam and The Style Council eras the enemies are real; the privileged classes in Eton Rifles; Neo-Nazis in 'Set the House Ablaze'; architects in 'The Planner's Dream Goes Wrong'; the establishment in 'Saturday's Kids'. Casting aspiration as a universal malaise, perhaps the ultimate meditation on class division, 'Man in the Corner Shop', acknowledges that someone is always further up the ladder. As Wilson writes in his introduction to 'Suburban 100', when writing on the subject of class division, Weller's lyrics are always imbued with empathy (Weller, 2010: 5).

For the purpose of analysis, popular music love song lyrics can be divided into four types. Firstly, worship from afar; secondly in love; third experiencing turbulence and finally post-love. In order, examples of each type are Roy Orbison's 'Oh, Pretty Woman', Smokey Robinson's 'My Girl', Barry Gibb's questioning and agitated 'Heartbreaker' and Lily Allen's vengeful 'Smile'. Songs including 'Aim High', 'Up in Suze's Room' and 'All on A Misty Morning' are blissful evocations of love in the tradition of 'My Girl', yet the majority of Weller's love songs are indelibly tinged with darkness. Engaged with the phase involving turbulence, a number of Weller's love songs, including 'English Rose', 'Monday', 'Paris Match' and 'Wings of Speed' are about yearning for separation to end, for the loved one to once again be near. Like the protagonist in Adrien Henri's 'Love is what's there when you're away from me' (2017: 12), the narrator is in love, but tortured. 'You Do Something to Me' is about unattainable love (Weller, 2010: 114), while 'It's Too Bad' and 'The Bitterest Pill' convey a sense of post-love regret. Across most of Weller's love songs, evoking a sense of reverie beneath the often taciturn surfaces of the lyric narrative, the music exudes warmth.

Songs with lyrics about dreams that revolve around an identical chord sequence include The Chords 'Sh-Boom' and The Everly Brothers' 'All I Have to Do Is Dream'. Something about the synergy between the chord sequence and lyric theme seems to click in the public imagination. Dreams are a recurring theme in Weller's songwriting, which uses a number of chordal frameworks and structures to convey good and bad dreams. On 'All Mod Cons' a number of characters are dreamers; the aspiring musician (To Be Someone), the tawdry businessman (Mr. Clean), the rookie employee (Billy Hunt) and the daydreamer (In the Crowd). 'When You're Young' and 'Thick as Thieves' explore the realisation that dreams will be broken, while 'The Dreams of Children' captures the dream as nightmare. Conceptually broad, the brisk and energetic '22 Dreams' explores multiple facets of a waking dream.

Frith (1996: 158–159) discusses how song meaning is not only in the lyric, and some of Weller's lyrics are knowingly minimal, placing the music at the forefront. Commenting on 'Start!' Weller acknowledges how, at the time of writing he was drawn to using the bare minimum of words (2010: 67). The Beatles 'Hello Goodbye' and 'I Want You (She's So Heavy)' are historical templates for a similar mode of expression; in each instance the music speaks on behalf of the words. Pauses in speech relate to emotional activity and help the listener to organise the meaning of sentences (Goldman-Eisler, 1961), and where lyrics have a minimal effect, listeners can draw upon their own experiences and feelings to immerse themselves in the metaphor. Beginning with 'Saturdays Kids', and perhaps inspired by the live response to covers of 'David Watts' and 'So Sad About Us', a number of Weller's songs feature phonetic vocal motifs that emphasise tunes without involving lyric meaning. Largely absent from early and late recordings, the high watermark for the writing of such sections coincides with Weller's decision to sing in a higher vocal register between 1979 and 1982. 'But I'm Different Now', 'Man in the Corner Shop', 'Set the House Ablaze', 'That's Entertainment', 'Running on The Spot', 'Town Called Malice', 'Whirlpool's End' and 'Mermaids' all use *'la, la, la'* or similar phonetic variations to allow lyrics to emerge in relief on recordings, and allow audiences to sing back to the band at live shows. Acknowledging that some lyrics do not seem to make any sense or have a coherent message, Machin (2010: 77–85) perceptively argues that even seemingly nonsensical lyrics can communicate idiolect and tell us something of how an artist wants us to hear it. In 'Suburban 100', Weller asks 'Do all songs have to mean something? Sometimes a meaning springs from the sheer pleasure of simply putting words together on a page' (2010: 175).

Elsewhere in the same text, 'Moonshine' and '7 and 3 is the Striker's Name' are described as 'streams of consciousness stuff … fleeting thoughts, but a type of expression nonetheless' (Weller, 2010: 78, 135).

Within the apparatus of song, structure is a significant factor, the form that frames the content. Musical materials provide templates for elaborating self-identity, 'for identity's identification' as De Nora (2006) puts it. Weller's pre-choruses, or sections that bridge verses and choruses, fulfil a number of such roles. Holland, Dozier Holland's 'How Sweet It Is to Be Loved You' and Stevie Wonder and Ivy Jo Hunter's 'Loving You is Sweeter Than Ever' use horizontal repetitive chord sequences to contrast with and accentuate the melodicism of their respective verses and choruses. Without the addition of these relatively undynamic pre-choruses, the flowing sections on either side would struggle to emerge in relief. In a musical sense these pre-choruses are counterintuitive, since they make the music revolve rather than evolve; their purpose, however, is to create a tension that ultimately gets resolved by the chorus. In this way, 'The Changingman', 'In the Crowd' and 'Billy Hunt' all use pre-choruses to break the melodic and harmonic drift of their surrounding sections. Other Weller pre-choruses alter the expressive mood. In 'This Is the Modern World', 'All Around the World' and 'The Bitterest Pill (I Ever Had to Swallow)' minor chordal sections temporarily change the prevailing mood from upbeat major to relatively downbeat minor. Musical conduits, these sections 'earth' the expression; without them gravitas and authenticity are compromised.

Pre-choruses are almost entirely absent from songs written around the time of 'The Cost of Loving' and 'True Meanings', while 'Setting Sons' has a significant number of customised middle-eights that help to create winding, unpredictable sections within the main compositional body. Elsewhere, like The Beatles unusually structured 'I'll Be Back', Weller compositions 'I Need You (for someone)', 'To Be Someone' 'Girl on the Phone' and 'Country' each have two middle eight sections. In these instances, the songwriter generates more material than is needed, and discovers that the additional sections can co-exist. Double verse structures are common in Weller's songs; 'Butterfly Collector', 'Absolute Beginners', 'Paris Match', 'You Do Something to Me', 'Soul Searchers', 'Gravity', 'White Horses', 'Woo Se Mama' and the majority of songs on 'A Kind Revolution' use double verses to delay the arrival of the chorus. The reason for this structuring technique usually relates to a need to arrange the materials in relative proportion. At other times, more needs to be said in the lyric before the chorus makes sense, or has full impact.

Within Weller's catalogue, songs with verse-chorus structures considered conventional in popular music like 'Fat Pop', 'Pink on White Walls', 'Bull-Rush', 'Fly on The Wall' and 'When Your Garden's Overgrown' are unusual. The decision to turn convention upside down, perhaps by reversing verse-chorus to chorus-verse on 'Monday' is more typical. Similarly, in the Weller songbook, conventional verse, pre-chorus, chorus songs like 'Happy

Together', and 'The Changingman' are in the minority, outnumbered by unorthodox structures of the type used on 'Roll Along Summer', 'Has My Fire Really Gone Out'?, 'The Bitterest Pill (I Ever Had to Swallow)' and 'Funeral Pyre'. An AABA or verse/verse/bridge/verse structure like 'Just Who is the 5 O' Clock Hero' or 'Broken Stones', familiar from the catalogues of Tin Pan Alley songwriters including Cole Porter and George and Ira Gershwin, is less likely than a song that plays with that form. Some of Weller's songs are strophic, meaning they use only verses. 'Aspects', English Rose', 'Ghosts', 'Rockets' and 'Wild Wood' are in this category, familiar to folk song. Fittingly, Weller's strophic songs often tell stories; once the listener is familiar with the music, the intention is to move the listener's ear towards the words.

Song recordings, particularly those made after 1977, are set in keys that enable Weller to sing in his preferred range. On 'In the City' the songs are in A or G, with Weller's voice set between G sharp and E (Art School, Bricks and Mortar), F sharp and E (I've Changed My Address), E and E (Away from The Numbers, Sounds from The Street), G and E (In the City), and A and E (Takin My Love). The condensed and repetitive nature of the keys and sung notes is part of what gives the record its focussed intensity. As The Jam progressed, and Vic Smith became more involved, vocal keys began to flex to accommodate less compressed sonic energies. In each instance, a balance is to be struck between the energy of the song as played in a specific key, the capacity of the singer to sing the song in any particular key and how the energies of the voice and the music combine. Often, because of the way instruments are designed, a song played in F sharp can sound very different from the same song played a step higher in G; depending on the chord changes involved, it might require musicians to concentrate to the extent the *feel* becomes elusive. Sometimes vocal and key combinations are immediately obvious, and at other times more elusive, and subject to trial and error. Post 1977, with the aid of a capo, Weller has been able to try out options for different variations, and this creates the possibility for recordings to be more variable and sonically adventurous than 'In the City'. By 'Sound Affects', Weller was inclined to sing in a higher register, and the keys of songs were calibrated to accommodate this. On 'Sound Affects' song keys include F, F sharp, G, B, B minor, C, D and D minor; the use of capos and the increased dexterity of the musicians enables the keys to be set at optimum ranges, the keys that make the vocal sound 'right'. While the vocals of 'Boy about Town', 'Pretty Green' and Scrape Away' peak on E, 'But I'm Different Now', 'Start!' and 'Set the House Ablaze' push the vocal to F sharp, and 'Monday', 'Dream Time' and 'Man in the Corner Shop' to G. This significant heightening of vocal keys is tempered by 'That's Entertainment', 'Down in the Tube Station at Midnight', Butterfly Collector', 'Absolute Beginners' and 'Funeral Pyre', on which in each instance the highest sung note is the lower C. A similar blueprint is used on 'Fat Pop (Volume One)' in which Weller hits E on True, but sings mostly in a range that peaks at C.

Three of Weller's songs that feature prominent instrumental motifs are 'In the City', 'My Ever Changing Moods' and 'Attic'. Like The Rolling Stones 'I Can't Get No Satisfaction', 'Jumpin' Jack Flash and 'Brown Sugar', these are instrumentally driven music phrases that may not have worked as vocal patterns, but that contrast with the vocal melody. Providing somewhere for the ear to go in between lyric sections, these motifs facilitate recognition. Without them, songs can be over-condensed, and challenging to absorb in real time. As if propelled by muscle memory, a number of different songs in Weller's catalogue repeat chord sequences, adding new lyric themes and varied melodies to disguise the repetition. The G-C-D combination used in 'Sounds of the Street' is echoed on 'It's Too Bad' and 'Saturdays Kids' and the C-Am-F-G sequence used in the turnaround of 'Strange Town' recurs in 'It's Too Bad', These durable sequences may have been familiar to Weller from 'She Loves You' by The Beatles and 'Blitzkrieg Bop' by The Ramones, both of which he will have been cognizant of as a player and as an attentive listener.

3.3 Visual

Intended to attract viewers to concerts and to buy records, early films of The Jam are representations of stage performances. The promotional video for 'In the City' features the band on stage, shot from front and side with metropolitan imagery as a backdrop. Similarly, 'Art School', one of a number of planned but never released Jam singles, is a simulation of a live performance with painters at work behind the band. Introduced by Tony Wilson on his show 'So It Goes' as 'a band who a lot of people say are not avant-garde enough', 1977 performances of 'In the City' and 'Slow Down' at Manchester Circus very much reflect the ones made for the debut album, albeit at an adrenalised tempo. In a stage formation The Jam used until their split in 1982, Weller is stage right, Foxton stage left and Buckler is between them at the back. Weller's left leg pumps in line with the beat and, craning over the microphone in a way that emphasises his height, should he drop a plectrum he has several more taped to his microphone stand. Everything about the communion between band and audience is physical and visceral. The crowd 'pogo', the band sweat profusely and conveying a frenetic energy, Weller and Foxton alternate between moving and singing roles. Coordinated to convey the songs, this movement is continuous and frenzied. Unsmiling, they never look at each other, and in this sense, with reference to Cohn's earlier observation (1969: 175–176), it is a very 'mod' presentation.

On the TV show Marc, filmed shortly before the singer's tragic death in 1977, The Jam appear in trademark black suits, white shirts and black ties, playing red Rickenbackers and even wearing the same shoes. Whilst also reminiscent of the early Beatles, the sense of uniform evokes their contemporaries The Ramones, who similarly adhered to a strict dress code to project a tribal band identity. In the absence of an audience, the band play at the same tempo as the recording; this is also the case in their contemporary appearance on The Old Grey Whistle Test. Intricate and played at high speed, the performances require Weller and Foxton to constantly reference the fretboards of their guitars, to ensure the right notes are being played by the left hand. Introduced by Peter Cook on 'Revolver', a show presented in 1978 as the antithesis to the family show inclusivity of 'Top of the Pops', the Jam appear in matching light blue suits. Here, the audience pogo as they did at Manchester Circus.

In a visual statement that helped to imprint their identity as a London band, to promote the release of 'News of the World' in late 1977, The Jam simulated a live performance on the roof of the Battersea Power Station. Similarly, the promotional video of 'Strange Town' begins with the band consulting an A-Z guide book at the entrance of a tube stop. This tentative foray into the world of acting is repeated in the promotional video for 'When You're Young', which takes place on a bandstand in Queen's Park, North West London and is enlivened by the enthusiastic presence of a group of schoolchildren. Possibly influenced by the financial consideration of not having to transport a film crew outside of London, the visual thread throughout this phase conveys urban identity, of a band 'among the people'. By the time of their performance of 'When You're Young' on the BBC programme 'Something Else' in September 1979, like the Beatles before them, The Jam have moved away from uniform to regular clothing. Also like The Beatles circa 1966, the limitations of live projection are evident in Weller being physically unable to play the signature double tracked guitars featured on the record.

Away from the United Kingdom, and in less familiar surroundings, the intensity of The Jam live experience appears dissipated. For the Swedish TV show 'Mandagsborsen' the setting is relatively surreal. An older audience are seated at tables, while a small, seemingly segregated group of youthful fans wave scarves on the balcony. Situated on a velvet carpet, the band and the audience are separated by a lit staircase. Perhaps sensing the low stakes, exhibiting a camaraderie prohibited during UK live appearances, Weller frequently smiles at Foxton and Buckler and waves to the youths on the balcony, pointedly ignoring the VIP guests seated at tables. For the cameras, the band try out an extended, ill-fitting arrangement of 'Tales of the Riverbank'. As if to reflect the draw of The Netherlands as a more viable commercial territory, filmed at Amsterdam Paradiso for the Dutch TV show 'Popkrant', the performance is more formal and the playing more technically accurate.

Promotional videos for the late-period Jam continue to use simulated live performance as the focal medium. On 'Going Underground' a 1980 in-studio performance is interspersed with images evoking war that appear fleetingly as the band plays. Mirroring the lyric, at one point the band watches an image of itself on a TV screen. Elsewhere, Bruce Foxton sings along, seated. The impression is that the mode of operation for video directors of the time is to film a performance, film some random footage of the band, acquire some stock images and edit the three together. Promotional films for 'Dreams of Children' and 'Funeral Pyre' follow a similar editorial code, this time with the band outdoors and the latter featuring fans carrying lit torches and laughing exaggeratedly into the camera. Like 'When You're Young', the effect indicates the integral nature of the fan community to the aesthetic. Using light and shade to create agnostic settings that allow for psychedelic colorations to illuminate the footage, 'Start!' and 'That's Entertainment' are more stylised. Moving the impression away from the live experience, here the direction moves closer to the faces of the band.

Like the personal relationships between band members, the final Jam videos, for 'Absolute Beginners', 'Town Called Malice' and 'The Bitterest Pill' are increasingly ragged. 'Absolute Beginners' juxtaposes the band sprinting down a suburban street with footage of them playing in the studio. The intended contrast is unclear, as if a concept was initiated but never fully realised. In a further unexplained non-sequitur, in 'Town Called Malice', an unidentified character scowls at the camera. The first and only time The Jam used a storyboard for a promotional video, 'The Bitterest Pill' is a bizarre visual tale, seemingly unrelated to the song text, that features a female actor in a variety of romantic settings with Weller and Foxton. Perhaps allegorical, scenes of cobwebbed rooms feature.

In sharp contrast, evoking the joyous visual mode established by Madness in the early eighties, the first Style Council promotional video 'Speak Like a Child' accentuates the stylistic departure from The Jam. In a frozen field landscape, Weller sits in a rocking chair as three female brass players dressed in pink dance and play brass instruments. Perhaps symbolically, the location is rural, and there is much smiling as Weller dances with the assembled troupe on an open top bus as it travels through the winter countryside. At one point in the video Weller tries to make a performative gesture with his arms that doesn't quite come off, and collapses with laughter; tellingly, the out-take is included. The overt joy and surrealism of the video add a bright aesthetic to an already ebullient track. Performing 'Speak Like a Child' without an instrument was initially challenging; on Top of The Pops in March 1983, 'Weller lurked uncomfortably guitar-less at the back of the stage, jiving stiffly like a dad at a wedding' (Trousse, 2020: 58).

Further imprinting the move away from the urban aesthetic of The Jam, for 'Long Hot Summer', director Tim Pope uses the River Cam as a second bucolic setting in which to frame The Style Council. Here, in a hierarchical in-joke echoed in the video for 'The Boy Who Cried Wolf' in which Mick Talbot plays Weller's butler, Weller reclines in a punting boat while Talbot plays the role of the punter, extolling much energy to propel the boat through the waters. In another gesture far removed from the visual aesthetic of The Jam, at the start of verse two, a smiling and reclining Weller's shirt is open to reveal his bare chest. He then waves at a bongo player, in actuality a heavily disguised Steve White, on the riverbank wearing a mariniere, or

French striped sweater. Continuing the French theme given emphasis by contemporary Style Council releases 'Café Bleu' and 'A Paris', in a visual evocation of Edouard Manet's 'Le dejeuner sur l'herbe', Weller and Talbot are shown relaxing by the riverside. In the second half of the video, Talbot appears upset when the bongo player catches up with him and Weller, falling to the ground distraught before recovering to engage in a genteel dance with Weller. Happily, Weller and Talbot serenade each other in silhouette for the finale. As Weller later remarked on ear rubbing with Talbot: 'Miss that. Tender moments' (Kessler, 2006: 60).

Initially written as the final Jam single before being relegated in favour of 'Beat Surrender', the promotional video for 'A Solid Bond in Your Heart' also features Weller and Talbot, this time as friends nostalgically arranging a dance at a social club to which no one arrives. In this storyline, the pair imagine a scene from their youths, and depart vowing to make a similar arrangement the following year. Like the sound and feel of the track itself, the mod aesthetic of the video harks back to The Jam, but with an element of camaraderie. Returning to the visual surrealness of 'Speak Like a Child', 'My Ever Changing Moods' finds Weller and Talbot again enjoying the English countryside, this time in full racing gear on racing bikes. A mystery character appears with a starting pistol and the two set off, occasionally waving to imaginary figures out of camera shot. A number of dramatic gestures are elliptical or obtuse; Talbot applies gel to his lower leg, Weller gestures to the viewer to be silent, and both appear to be startled by the sudden appearance of three angelic figures. Completely at odds with the aesthetic, echoing the video for 'Going Underground', occasional images of war flash onto the screen before the cast gather together at the end to drink champagne. Much is provided for the viewer to engage with and question. Why cycles? Why the war imagery? Why the application of gel?

Traditionally structured and balladic, 'You're the Best Thing' uses long single shots and the shaded lighting of late Jam videos to convey the song without complexity. In just over a year The Style Council audience have enjoyed consistently inspired pop music, visually accompanied by surreal comedy, roleplay, light nostalgia, genericism, and juxta-positional allegory; the apparent effortlessness of the music placed against an ever-evolving and increasingly unpredictable appetite for aesthetic eclecticism. Featuring an inexplicably furious Mick Talbot making a gallery of angst-filled facial expressions and bookended by mayoral officials arguing and then posing in front of a mural of miners and policemen, 'Shout to The Top' further evades definition, eliciting more questions. Are The Style Council making light of the issue? If so, is their political stance intended to ridicule? To add to the growing ambiguity, the promotional video for 'Walls Come Tumbling Down', shot in a particularly austere looking Poland, includes a live audience. Despite the distraction of a half-realised storyline in which the band arrives late for the show, as with the earlier Jam videos for 'When You're Young' and 'Funeral Pyre', the effect is of band and audience solidarity.

Whilst the 1985 album 'Our Favourite Shop' was critically lauded for its clear-eyed political focus, the videos released to accompany singles from it are frequently disorienting. For 'Come to Milton Keynes', Weller and Talbot take to the stage dressed as music hall entertainers while an older man salutes a Union Jack bed of roses. Watching from a window above, a blank-faced character quickly closes a pair of curtains. Children made up to look like extras in a horror movie are brandishing knives. Having apparently raided the theatre prop box, Weller and Talbot appear in a variety of costumes, including cricket gear and shirtless braces. Wearing a lapel with 'Big Chopper' emblazoned on it, Talbot serves a little girl a 'Greed Burger'. A spangle jacketed game show host appears, revealing a rocket as a prize, ice creams cover a female model's nipples and a statue of liberty figure uses an American Excess card to slash its wrists. Weller and Talbot reappear wearing tennis gear and strumming harps. Overtly dystopian, the video projects as heavy with allegory, little of which is delivered with any subtlety. Veering between random improvisation and meticulous planning, the mixture of comedy and political comment is bold, yet uneasy.

Later in 1985, The Style Council made videos for 'The Lodgers' and 'Boy Who Cried Wolf' with horse racing and artistocratic themes respectively. In 'The Lodgers', Dee C Lee features as an usherette serving strawberries to race-going types, Mick Talbot is rosy cheeked and Steve White made up with a head injury. Weller joins them to cheer on the horses, who are given comedy names. In 'The Lodgers' Weller plays indoor croquet and has his butler Talbot carry his bags for him. In both 'The Lodgers' and 'Boy Who Cried Wolf', the rationale for choice of setting in which the films are based is oblique. Repeatedly, the capacity of the Style Council audience to share in an increasingly impenetrable humour is tested. As if to emphasise a loss of energy, towards the end of The Style Council, promotional videos for 'It Didn't Matter' and 'Promised Land' return to the straight-ahead video performances of The Jam, with disengaged members facing straight ahead. The effect is of the adventure having grown weary; the capacity for experimentation irretrievably undermined by the dull pressure of making hit music.

With reference to the Style Council videos Weller later reflected: 'Me and Mick Talbot were the same age and we shared all these reference points from Galton and Simpson and Hancock, to Kenneth Williams and 'Carry On' films.... It felt like being free again, being young again. It was like stepping out into a summer's day. There were no rules, and that infuriated people' (Gilbert, 2008: 76). However innocent the intention, the regular tendency to juxtapose politics and comedy, to ironically feign wealth whilst actually having acquired it, may have led to some audiences questioning the value and authenticity of the music. Promotional metanarratives became increasingly eccentric, with one press release in 1988 stating: 'The Style Council embarked upon a new course of treatment for the world ... one of the finest musical forces to come from this continent ... you will not be able to ignore them any longer'. This communique was accompanied by advert in the NME promoting 'Life at a Top People's Health Farm' with Weller wearing NHS 80's style specs held together with Elastoplast, hair slicked back, sports jacket and a polka dot tie. As Munn (2014: 169) later reflected 'You have to look twice (or more) to convince yourself its him'. Made in 1987, the inscrutable feature film 'Jerusalem' echoed the camp psychedelia of the 1975 Granada TV drama 'Starmaker' starring the Kinks and The Beatles 'Magical Mystery Tour' aired on the BBC several years earlier, neither of which were high water marks for either band.

Promotional videos for Paul Weller solo singles follow a loose pattern intended to simultaneously convey him as a stand-alone artist, and as a band member. Seeking to forefront the music, promotional videos for early singles 'Into Tomorrow' and 'Above the Clouds' are filmed with a shaded effect evocative of the videos for 'Start!' and 'You're the Best Thing'. Uncomplicated and free from thematic distraction, the films allow the songs to emerge. In his notes for 'Country' in 'Suburban 100', Weller recalls a field near Woking he would visit in the early nineties to reconnect to his youth (2010: 85). The first of a series of songs written to explore this reconnection, 'Uh Huh, Oh Yeah', features Weller walking around Woking. 'Porcelain Gods' extends the theme, and in director Douglas Hart's 'Friday Street', Weller rides a Lambretta around suburban Woking. Other videos from this era encircle this concept; shot in the fabled field, Sonja Phillips' video for 'You Do Something to Me' brings a family home movie aesthetic that enhances the mellowness of the track. Elsewhere, videos for 'Broken Stones', 'Brand New Start' and 'Hung Up' feature band members set up and playing in outdoor locations; in each instance, the films convey a visual sense of music that is not hemmed in.

Particularly in the late nineties, a number of directors including Andy Hylton, Terry Hall and Pedro Romhanyi apply a set of primary green, red, yellows and blues that add a youthful, child-like effervescence. Band performances intermingle with solo performances and actors occasionally join Weller. At other times Weller is absent. The inclination to use an alternating variety of approaches continues through promotional videos made in the 21st century through 'Come On, Let's Go', 'Wake Up the Nation' and 'Cosmic Fringes' (band performance), 'Gravity' and 'Echoes Around The Sun' (Weller performing seated solo, integrated with footage of dancers), 'Dragonfly' and 'These City Streets' (featuring female actors), 'Pick It Up' and 'Movin' On' (featuring male actors), 'Have You Made Up Your Mind Yet' (animation with stills) and 'On Sunset' (Weller driving around Los Angeles). The visual effect is of an artist moving, sometimes in shadow and sometimes in light.

A counterpart to video films, Weller's stage performances, and those of his band members reflect their temporal frame of mind and their surrounding environments. Working at his Black Barn recording and rehearsal complex, Weller writes set lists and leads tour rehearsals. Once on tour, the initial set list sometimes evolves, but tends to keep to songs rehearsed prior to the tour. Clearly in thrall to the experience of being on stage, in Joe Connor's 2019 documentary film 'May Love Travel with You', Weller describes playing live as 'the closest thing to flying'. From adaptation through rehearsal and finally to stage, live music performance is a complex undertaking, as Theberge (2001: 24) writes: 'The live performance of popular music is dependent upon the technologies of audio production and reception.... Technology must be understood as both an enabling and they constraining factor that acts in complex and contradictory ways'. While some performers prioritise live performance, for others the staged representation can only approximate the care and attention to detail of studio practice (Moore, 2012: 14). As a trio, The Jam sometimes found it technically challenging to replicate the double tracked guitars that characterise their seminal recordings. As acknowledged by Weller in a 1979 interview, some of the early Jam songs, like the progressively textured 'Life from A Window' are impossible for a three-piece band to do live (Heatley, 1996: 18). Consequently, Jam recordings were often transformed to meet the live environment. Live performances of 'Slow Down' are consistently much faster than the recorded version, while performances of 'Man in the Corner Shop' and 'Carnation' in the early eighties are also significantly quickened. By this means, the songs closest to ballads can, like their upbeat recorded counterparts, be played with a beat audiences can move to.

Surveying the history of English music, Ackroyd discusses how:

> The English have always excelled at popular song ... dance songs, ballads and processional chants were as much part of communal life as the social and religious ceremonies which decorated existence in a more formal way.... The interest is in shared and common feeling ... with eliciting a popular voice.
>
> (2004: 143–148)

Reinforced by the ritual of gathering at live performances, audiences in the late seventies grew to perceive themselves as a part of the experience of The Jam. Contemporary recordings emphasise how much of the mid-period Jam material lent itself to the kind of collective singing discussed by Frith (2001: 106); songs of shared ownership that the audience felt moved to perform as one with the band. Alongside the warmth of this shared communality, Jam concerts were characterised by violence both inside and outside the venue. Two separate 1979 Jam concert reviews by Sounds staff writer Garry Bushell, one in Paris in February, and one in London in November, report scuffles between French and English fans and latterly 'a vicious sea of fists and bottles.... A security man wielding a piece of wood with nails jutting out of it.... A bunch of skinheads who had come looking for trouble' (2012: 25, 106–107). Writing in 2012, Weller gives his perspective: 'I'm glad I was on stage and not in the audience, as most nights it was fucking scary!.... It was also very tribal.... Every night would kick off and the sea would part in the middle and blood and beer would fly. Scary but always exciting' (Snowball and Deabill, 2012: ix). Writing in 2020, Danny Eccleston reminded Weller that a fist fight broke out at his seated orchestral Royal Festival Hall concert in 2018, and Weller responded 'Yeah, I heard about that. I mean, you'd think they'd have grown out of that kind of thing. On the other hand, there's something sweet about it. There's still some life in 'em!' (Eccleston, 2020: 70).

For a variety of reasons, touring with The Jam became increasingly challenging for Weller, who recalled an atmosphere of constant complaint, even under privileged circumstances (Munn, 2014: 34). Despite this inner turmoil, even as they became the most successful band in the United Kingdom, The Jam retained a close bond with their fans. Presaging the 21st century marketing trend for music artists to offer exclusive access as exemplified by Patreon and similar social media platforms, The Jam continued to play secret, more intimate and exclusive gigs (Peart, 2019: 45). The democratic ethos remained, as Weller reflected in the film 'About the Young Idea' in 2015: 'I didn't have to put myself in their shoes. I was already in their fucking shoes'. The sense of communion wavered at times during the Style Council years. Speaking about the 1989 Royal Albert Hall concert, which was poorly received by fans and critics alike, bass player Dr Robert blames the negative reception on the increasing insularity and defensiveness of The Style Council (Munn, 2014: 19). Weller's re-emergence in 1991 was characterised by a revised approach to live performance that replaced the introversion of The Style Council and re-emphasised communion. In his vivid notes on the Paul Weller live experience circa 1993, photographer Lawrence Watson writes:

> Paul's shows followed a distinct pattern. Little was said on stage. It was implied that the music would do all the communicating.... Music was their language and the means of communication was mostly in their hands....... They so obviously belonged. And because of that, because of this commitment, this was the point where the music would take on a life of its own, where it would charge you and take over, where it would dip and change colours, rushing upwards and then swerve sideways for a brief resting place.
>
> (Watson and Hewitt, 1995: 10–11)

Live performances and recordings are two different media (Grayck, 1996: 80) and as a guest on the online show 'Records in My Life' in 2017, Weller notes how 'As most songs do live, they take on their own life and become something else'. Some records connect with live audiences and inexplicably, some don't. As Weller observed, many of his live audiences reacted to songs from 'Wake Up the Nation' with indifference, leading him to consider touring it a 'disaster' (Eccleston, 2020: 70). Conversely, Weller says of the song 'Wild Wood': 'I tried to write a folk song, or at least my interpretation of one.... When we played it in Glasgow last year, the crowd started to sing with us, the whole crowd. It then felt like 'Wild Wood' was a real folk song and that touched me' (Watson and Hewitt, 1995: 21).

Particularly in the 21st century, the promotion of albums often involves an accompanying metanarrative, or story around the recording. A successful example, Julien Temple's film 'Find the Torch' is based on a focal concept of Weller as Londoner. More typically, 'The making of' films feature images of musicians looking at mixing boards in contemplation; a slow-moving collage of largely impenetrable and mildly industrious scenes. As Ackroyd (2004: 444–447) quotes Vaughan Williams on his fourth symphony: 'I don't know whether I like it, but it's what I meant'. In short films made to provide album metanarratives, Weller is happy to comment on his music without necessarily reaching a point of enlightenment. An example transcript from the 2019 film 'May Love Travel with You' reads: 'There is never a rhyme or reason for creativity. It's something that I think just happens really. I don't put myself in any special place or do anything different. It's just there, or not there really'. This relatively circular thought process never comes across as evasive, rather it reflects the difficulty in self-analysing and making sense of creative works from a close distance.

In 'Suburban 100', Weller describes the concert experience:

> Playing live on a good night you can feel the energy rising through your body to the ceiling, from the floorboards up. That energy is not just about swinging an arm or smashing a stick on a drum, it's more fundamental and grounded than that. On a great night, it's a beautiful and inspiring feeling. I look out into the hall and like to think of all the reverberations and vibrations that have soaked into the walls and chairs from all the great bands that have played there over the years.

Returning to the quote cited in the introduction (Watson and Hewitt, 1995: 52), Weller says: 'I don't want to do the same things in life. I don't want to play the same sort of music all the time. I want to change. I need to change and find something different along the way'. This philosophy is borne out in seven setlists: for The Jam at Hammersmith Odeon, London in 1977, at Brighton Centre in 1982; for The Style Council on tour in 1984 and 1989, for Paul Weller at the Royal Albert Hall in 1993, Brighton Centre in 2010 and the Royal Festival Hall in 2018. Across these performances, of 141 songs played, only nine are played more than once.

Interviewing Weller at Black Barn in February 2021, Ted Kessler (2021: 66–71) writes: 'Unusually in the orbit of an international rock star, everyone is on equal footing'. In the interview, Weller is in philosophical mode, musing:

> Music has been my most reliable friend, and I am blessed with many great friends. Music's a spiritual force, it covers so much ground: as a way of informing us, making us question things. It's been my whole

> life. Everything has been governed by it.... It's important to be humble, to say thank you to the power of prayer. Not to a Christian God, necessarily, but to the universe. To recognise your place in it all.... All you really need is love. John was right. Whether it's love for what you're doing, love for your fellow human. Through love comes positivity. You look forward to things when you're in love.... My gratitude to music is boundless.... Music's forever giving, it's a living thing ... it's information, education, entertainment. And generally, it tells the truth!

At the start of his career, Weller once famously wore a placard around his neck onstage that asked: 'How can I be a revivalist when I'm only fucking 18'? Moving through multiple contexts characterised by extremes, a similar duality has followed him throughout his career; a need to revisit to shape his present and future. 'When I was a kid, I remember asking my dad how long a mile was', says Weller in the 2015 GQ feature:

> He took me out into our street, Stanley Road, and pointed down to the far end, towards the heat haze in the distance. To me there was a magical kingdom through that shimmering haze, the rest of the world, all life's possibilities. I always return to where I came from, to get a sense of my journey and where I'm heading next.

References

Ackroyd, P. (2001) *London: The Biography*, London: Vintage.

Ackroyd, P. (2004) *Albion: The Origins of the English Imagination*, London: Vintage.

Adelt, U. (2016) *Krautrock: German Music in the Seventies*, Ann Arbor: University of Michigan Press.

Agawu, K. (2004) 'How We Got Out of Analysis, and How to Get Back in Again', *Music Analysis* 23(2/3), 267–86.

Amabile, T. (1996) *Creativity in Context: Update to The Social Psychology of Creativity*, Boulder, CO: Westview Press.

Anderson, P. (2013) *Mods: The New Religion*, London: Omnibus Press.

Ashe, G. (1975) *Camelot and the Vision of Albion*, Portsmouth, NH: Heinemann.

Bailie, S. (1997) 'Review of Heavy Soul', *New Musical Express*, 53, 21 June.

Bakhtin, M.M. (1981) *The Dialogic Imagination: Four Essays*, M. Holmquist, ed., C. Emerson and M. Holmquist, Trans., Austin: University of Texas Press.

Barnett, A. (2012) *Iron Britannia: Time to Take the Great Out of Britain*, London: Faber and Faber.

Barthes, R. (1977) *Image Music Text*, London: Fontana Press.

Becker, H.S. (1982) *Art Worlds*, Berkeley and Los Angeles: University of California Press.

Bennett, A. (2000) *Popular Music and Youth Culture*, Basingstoke: Palgrave.

Bennett, A. and Stratton, J. (eds.) (2011) *Britpop and the English Music Tradition*, Farnham: Ashgate.

Bennett, A. and Strong, C. (2018) 'Popular Music Heritage, Grass-Roots Activism and Web 2.0: The Case of the 'Save the Palace' Campaign', *Cultural Sociology* 12 (3), 368–83.

Birchall, J. and Parsons, T. (1978) *The Boy Looked at Johnny: The Obituary of Rock 'n' Roll*, London: Pluto Press.

Blaney, J. (2007) *Lennon and McCartney: Together Alone*, London: Jawbone.

Bonello Rutter Giappone, K. (2019) *The Punk Turn in Comedy: Masks of Anarchy*, London: Palgrave MacMillan.

Bonner, M. (2015) 'Review of Saturns Pattern', *Uncut Magazine* 216, 78.

Borowski, T. (1946) *This Way for the Gas, Ladies and Gentlemen*, New York: Viking Penguin.

Boyd, J. (2005) *White Bicycles: Making Music in the 1960s*, London: Serpent's Tail.

Brackett, D. (2016) *Categorising Sound*, Oakland, CA: California University Press.

Bradley, L. (2013) *Sounds Like London: 100 Years of Black Music in the Capital*, London: Serpent's Tail.

Brake, M. (1985) *Comparative Youth Culture: The Sociology of Youth Subcultures in America, Britain and Canada*, London: Routledge and Kegan Paul.
Brazier, C. (1977) 'Review of This Is the Modern World', *Melody Maker*, 25, 12 November.
Bricheno, T. (2003) '1990s', in J. Winterson (ed.), *Pop Music: The Text Book, revised* edition, London: Edition Peters.
Bricheno, T., Kaye, B. and Winterson, J. (2003) '2000s', in J. Winterson (ed.), *Pop Music: The Text Book, revised edn*, London: Edition Peters.
Burns, L. (2010) 'Vocal Authority and Listener Engagement: Musical and Narrative Expressive Strategies in Alternative Female Artists (1993-95)', in M. Spicer and J. Covach (eds.), *Sounding Out Pop: Analytical Essays in Popular Music*, Ann Arbor: University of Michigan Press.
Burrell, I. (2015) The Man Who Dresses Britain's Style Tribes Celebrates 60 Years in Retail, Interview with John Simons, *The Independent*, 8 August.
Bushell, G. (2012) *Time for Action: The Mod Revival 1978-1981*, London: Countdown Books.
Cain, B. (2016) *77 Sulphate Strip: An Eyewitness Account of the Year That Changed Everything, second* edition, Falmouth: Red Planet Books. Cambridge Dictionary [online] https://dictionary.cambridge.orgviewed 5 May 2020.
Carr, P. (2017) *Sting: From Northern Skies to Fields of Gold*, London: Reaktion Books.
Cavanagh, D. (1994) 'What Do You Know About Music?', Interview with Paul Weller, reprinted in *Q Magazine*, 395, 26–30.
Cavanagh, D. (2010) Paul Weller - Wake Up the Nation, *Uncut* [online], 30 April, https://www.uncut.co.uk/reviews/paul-weller-wake-up-the-nation-4927/viewed 10 August 2021.
Cavanagh, D. (2018) 'Heart of the Country', Interview with Paul Weller, *Mojo Magazine*, 298, 70–82.
Chambers, I. (2002) *Popular Culture: The Metropolitan Experience*, New York: Routledge.
Clements, P. (2009) 'Cultural Legitimacy or "Outsider Hip"? Representational Ambiguity and the Significance of Steely Dan', *Journal of Leisure Studies* 28(2), 189–206.
Cohen, S. (1991) *Rock Culture in Liverpool: Popular Music in the Making*, Oxford: Clarendon Press.
Cohen, S. (2019) Racing off the Cliff – What Comes Next after Streaming? 18 January, Eurosonic, Groningen.
Cohn, N. (1969) *WopBopaLooBopLopBamBoom*, London: Wiedenfeld and Nicholson.
Conrad, P. (1998) *Modern Times, Modern Places: Life and Art in the 20th Century*, London: Thames and Hudson.
Cook, N. (2003) 'Music as Performance', in M. Clayton, T. Herbert and R. Middleton (eds.), *The Cultural Study of Music: A Critical Introduction*, New York: Routledge, 204–214.
Cook, R. (1984) 'Bleu'd Visionary', Review of *Café Bleu, New Musical Express*, 16 March, 31.
Copland, A. (1949) A Modernist Defends Modern Music, The New York Times, 25 December.
Costello, E. (2016) *Unfaithful Music and Disappearing Ink*, London: Penguin/ Random House.

Cote, J.E. (2006) 'Identity Studies: How Close Are We to Developing a Social Science of Identity? An Appraisal of the Field', *Identity* 6(1), 3–25.
Csikszentmihalyi, M. (1990) *Flow: The Psychology of Optimal Experience*, New York: Harper and Row.
D'Souza, D. (2017) *In Echoed Steps: The Jam and a Vision of Albion*, Studio Skellett.
Davies, R. (2013) *Americana: The Kinks, The Road and The Perfect Riff*, London: Virgin Books.
Davis, S. (2013) *This Wheel's on Fire: Levon Helm and the Story of the Band*, Chicago, IL: Chicago Review Press.
De Bono, E. (1970) *Lateral Thinking: A Textbook of Creativity*, London: Ward Lock Education.
De Nora, T. (2006) 'Music and Self-Identity', in A. Bennett, B. Shank and J. Toynbee (eds.), *The Popular Music Studies Reader*, New York: Routledge.
De Whalley, C. (1977) 'Review of the Jam at the Nashville', *Sounds*, 19 February, 43.
Dibben, N. (2003) 'Musical Materials, Perception and Listening', In M. Clayton, T. Herbert and R. Middleton (eds.), *The Cultural Study of Music: A Critical Introduction*, New York: Routledge, 193–203.
Doyle, T. (2015) 'There Is No Drinking', *Mojo Magazine*, reprinted in P. Gilbert (ed.) *Mojo: The Collectors' Series: Modern Classics 1991-2019.*
Du Noyer, P. (1980) '"Beatle Riflers", Review of Sound Affects', *New Musical Express*, 22 November, 41.
Du Noyer, P. (1985) 'Review of Our Favourite Shop', *New Musical Express*, 11 December, 39.
Du Noyer, P. (1995) 'Has My Fire Really Gone Out', Mojo Magazine, reprinted in P. Gilbert, (ed.) (2019) *Mojo: The Collectors' Series: Modern Classics 1991-2019*, 22–34.
Duckworth, W. (1999) *Talking Music*, New York: Da Capo.
Duffy, R. (2015) Paul Weller - Modernist with a Capital M, Concert Review, *San Diego Reader*, 16 October.
Eccleston, D. (2020) 'Move on Up!', *Mojo Magazine*, 321, 70–80.
Edmondson, J. (2010) *John Lennon: A Biography*, Santa Barbara, CA: Greenwood.
Elborough, T. (2008) *The Long Player Goodbye: The Album from Vinyl to iPod and Back Again*, London: Hodder and Stoughton.
Empire, K. (2012) Sonik Kicks Review, *The Guardian* [online], 18 March, https://www.theguardian.com/music/2012/mar/18/paul-weller-sonik-kicks-review viewed 10 August 2021.
Eno, B. (2005) 'The Studio as Compositional Tool', in C. Cox and D. Warner (eds.), *Audio Culture: Readings in Modern Music*, New York: Continuum.
Farren, M. (1977) 'Review of This Is the Modern World', *New Musical Express*, 12 November, 33.
Fowles, J. (1963) *The Collector*, London: Johnathan Cape.
Fox, J. (2002) 'Review of Illumination', *New Musical Express*, 45, 13 September.
Frith, S. (1983) *Sound Effects: Youth, Leisure and the Politics of Rock n Roll*, London: Constable.
Frith, S. (1987) 'Why Do Songs Have Words?, in A.L. White (ed.), *Lost in Music*, London: Routledge and Kegan Paul.
Frith, S. (1996) *Performing Rites: Evaluating Popular Music*, Oxford: Oxford University Press.
Frith, S. (1998) *Performing Rites: On the Value of Popular Music, reprint* edition, Harvard University Press.

Frith, S. (2001) 'Pop Music', in S. Frith, W. Straw and J. Street (eds.), *Cambridge Companion to Pop and Rock*, Cambridge: Cambridge University Press.

Geldner, S. (2017) 'The German Music Business', *Associated European Conservatoires Pop and Jazz Platform Meeting: Crossing the Bar Line*, 18 February, London: Trinity Laban Conservatoire of Music and Dance.

Gilbert, M. (1989) *On Social Facts*, London: Routledge.

Gilbert, P., (2008) Interview with Paul Weller, *Mojo Magazine*, 175, 65–76.

Gilbert, P. (2018a) 'To Be Someone', in T. Kessler (ed.), *Q Legends: Paul Weller*, 10–11.

Gilbert, P. (2018b) 'Burning Bright', in T. Kessler (ed.), *Q Legends: Paul Weller*, 12–14.

Gioia, T. (2019) 'The History of Song Is All about Outsiders', *The Wall Street Journal* [online] 16 October, https://www.wsj.com/articles/the-history-of-song-is-all-about-outsiders-11571457661 Viewed 24 June 2020.

Goddard, S. (2018) 'We Were Like a Moving Youth Club on Wheels', in T. Kessler (ed.), *Q Legends: Paul Weller*, 6–9.

Goldman-Eisler (1961) 'Hesitation and Information', in C. Cherry (ed.), *Information Theory*, London: Butterworth.

Grayck, T. (1996) *Rhythm and Noise: An Aesthetics of Rock*, Durham, NC: Duke University Press.

Green, L. (1990) 'The Assessment of Composition: Style and Experience', *British Journal of Music Education* 7(3), 191–196.

Green, L. (2002) *How Popular Musicians Learn: A Way Ahead for Music Education*, London: Ashgate.

Griffiths, D. (2002) 'Cover Versions and the Sound of Identity in Motion', in D. Hesmondhalgh and K. Negus (eds.), *Popular Music Studies*, London: Bloomsbury Academic.

Griffiths, D. (2003) 'From Lyric to Anti-Lyric: Analysing the Words in Pop Song', in A. Moore *Analysing Popular Music*, Cambridge: Cambridge University Press, 39–59.

Hall, S. and Du Gay, P. (eds.) (1996) *Questions of Cultural Identity*, London: Sage.

Hamblett, J. (1978) 'All Dressed Up and Somewhere to Go', Interview with the Jam, *New Musical Express*, 4 November, 31.

Harris, J. (2018a) 'The Young Idea', in T. Kessler (ed.), *Q Legends: Paul Weller*, 6–9.

Harris, J. (2018b) 'What You Give Is What You Get', in T. Kessler (ed.), *Q Legends: Paul Weller*, 16–19.

Hawkins, S. (2009) *The British Pop Dandy: Masculinity, Popular Music and Culture*, Abingdon: Ashgate.

Heatley, M. (1996) *Paul Weller: In His Own Words*, London: Omnibus Press.

Hecken, T. (2016) 'Popular Culture', in J.G. Papenburg and H. Schulze (eds.), *Sound as Popular Culture: A Research Companion*, Cambridge, MA: MIT Press.

Henri, A., McGough, R. and Patten, B. (2017) *The Mersey Sound, Restored 50th Anniversary Edition*, London: Penguin.

Hentoff, N. (1968) Liner Notes for Herbie Hancock, *Speak Like a Child*, LP, Blue Note.

Herman, G. (1971) *The Who*, London: Studio Vista.

Herndon, M. (1993) 'Insiders, Outsiders: Knowing Our Limits, Limiting Our Knowing', *The World of Music* 35(1), 63–80.

Hesse, H. (1922) *Siddhartha*, New York: New Directions.

Hewitt, P. (1979) '"Taking Stock", Review of Setting Sons', *Melody Maker*, 17 November, 27.

Hewitt, P. (2006) *The Soul Stylists: Six Decades of Modernism - From Mods to Casuals*, Edinburgh: Mainstream.

Hewitt, P. (2007) *Paul Weller: The Changingman*, London: Bantam Press.

Heylin, C. (2004) *Can You Feel the Silence? Van Morrison: A New Biography*, Chicago, IL: Chicago Review Press.

Heylin, C. (2010) *Revolution in the Air: The Songs of Bob Dylan Vol 1: 1957-1973*, London: Constable.

Hills, J. (1986) *Teaching, Learning and Communication*, London: Croom Helm.

Hodgkinson, T. (2016) *Music and the Myth of Wholeness: Towards a New Aesthetic Paradigm*, Cambridge, MA: MIT Press.

Hoffman, S. (2012) My Interview with Peter Wilson, Jam and Style Council producer, [online] 15 August, https://forums.stevehoffman.tv/threads/my-interview-with-peter-wilson-jam-and-style-council-producer.294101/ viewed 24 August 2021.

Holmes, T. (2002) *Electronic and Experimental Music, second* edition, New York: Routledge.

Hoskyns, J. (1992) 'Music Education and a European Dimension', *British Journal of Music Education* 9(2), 97–102.

Huffman, E. (2017) *John Prine: In Spite of Himself*, Austin, TX: University of Texas Press.

Humphries, P. (1980) '"Weller's Bleakest Vision", Review of Sound Affects', *Melody Maker*, 22 November, 42.

Huron (2006) *Sweet Anticipation: Music and the Psychology of Expectation*, Cambridge, MA: MIT Press.

Ingham, C. (1998) 'Reflections', Mojo Magazine, reprinted in P. Gilbert (ed.), *Mojo: The Collectors' Series: Modern Classics 1991-2019*, 39–45.

Inwood, S. (1998) *A History of London*, Basingstoke: Macmillan.

Jack, A. (2015) *The Jam: Sounds from the Street, Revised and Updated Edition*, Richmond: Reynolds and Hearn/Albert Jack Publishing.

Jones, A. (1988) 'The Gripes of Wrath', Review of Confessions of a Pop Group, *Melody Maker*, 25 June, 38.

Jones, D. (2015) GQ Icon: Paul Weller, Interview in British GQ, 7 June.

Jovanovic, R. (2013) *God Save the Kinks*, London: Aurum.

Kassabian, A. (2016) 'Listening and Digital Technologies', in J.G. Papenburg and H. Schulze (eds.), *Sound as Popular Culture: A Research Companion*, Cambridge, MA: MIT Press.

Kawakami, A., Furukawa, K., Katahira, K., Kamiyama, K. and Okanoya, K. (2013), Relations between Musical Structures and Perceived and Felt Emotion, *Music Perception*, 30, 407–418.

Kessler, T. (2005) 'Review of Stanley Road', *New Musical Express*, 20 May, 44.

Kessler, T. (2006) 'Got My Mojo Working', Mojo Magazine, reprinted in P. Gilbert (ed.), *Mojo: The Collectors' Series: Modern Classics 1991-2019*, 56–63.

Kessler, T. (2021) 'Paid the Cost to Be the Boss', Interview With Paul Weller, *Mojo Magazine*, 66–71.

King, J. (2019) Activism, Identity Politics, and Pop's Great Awokening, *Pitchfork* [online] 11 October, https://pitchfork.com/features/article/2010s-pops-great-awokening-black-lives-matter-beyonce-kendrick-lamar-solange/ viewed 23 April, 2021.

Klandermans, B. (2014) 'Identity Politics and Politicised Identities: Identity Processes and the Dynamics of protest', *Political Psychology* 35(1), 1–22.

Korsyn, K. (2002) *Decentering Music: A Critique of Contemporary Musical Research*, New York: Oxford University Press.

Kramer, J. and Carl, R. (eds.) (2016) *Postmodern Music, Postmodern Listening*, London: Bloomsbury Academic.

Laing, D. (2003) 'Music and the Market: The Economics of Music in the Modern World', in M. Clayton, T. Herbert and R. Middleton (eds.), *The Cultural Study of Music: A Critical Introduction*, New York: Routledge, 309–320.

Langer, S.K. (1957), *Philosophy in a New Key: A Study in the Symbolism of Reason, Rite and Art, third* edition, Cambridge, MA: Harvard University Press.

Lass, F. (1978) Review of *All Mod Cons*, *Melody Maker*, 4 November, 42.

Laukkanen, J. (2020) Developing a Lexicon for Texture, Ghent Conservatorium, 6 February.

Lewis, J. (2008) Paul Weller - 22 Dreams, *Uncut* [online], 28 May, https://www.uncut.co.uk/reviews/paul-weller-22-dreams-7839/ viewed 10 August 2021.

Lewis, J. (2017) Paul Weller - A Kind Revolution, *Uncut* [online], 2 June,https://www.uncut.co.uk/reviews/paul-weller-kind-revolution-100502/ viewed 10 August 2021.

Lewis, J. (2020) *As Is Now*, in J. Robinson (ed.), *The Uncut Ultimate Music Guide: Paul Weller*, 112–113.

Lewis, J. (2020) *Confessions of a Pop Group*, in J. Robinson (ed.), *The Uncut Ultimate Music Guide: Paul Weller*, 74–75.

Lines, D. (2007) *The Modfather: My Life With Paul Weller*, New York: Arrow.

Little, S. (2014) *... Isms: Understanding Art*, London: Bloomsbury Visual Arts.

Lock, G. (1982) 'Weller: Where There's a Will but No Way', Review of *The Gift*, *New Musical Express*, 6 March, 31.

Longhurst, B. (2011) *Popular Music and Society*, Cambridge: Polity Press.

Lydon, J., Zimmerman, K. and Zimmerman, K. (1993) *No Irish, No Blacks, No Dogs*, London: Hodder and Stoughton.

MacDonald, I. (1994) *Revolution in the Head*, London: Pimlico.

Machin, D. (2010) *Analysing Popular Music: Image, Sound and Text*, Thousand Oaks, CA: Sage.

MacKay, E. (2010) Album Review: *Wake up the Nation*, *New Musical Express* [online], 19 April, https://www.nme.com/reviews/reviews-paul-weller-11232-311014 viewed 10 August 2021.

MacKenzie, S. (2017) Paul Weller: Why I Picked Jawbone as My First Film Score, *Big Issue* [online], 10 May, https://www.bigissue.com/interviews/paul-weller-i-picked-jawbone-first-film-score/ viewed 21 May 2021.

Malins, S. (1997) *Paul Weller: The Unauthorised Biography*, London: Virgin Books.

Martin, G. (2000) Review of *Heliocentric*, *Uncut*, 164, 70.

Martin, G. (2005) Paul Weller - As Is Now, *Uncut* [online], 28 October, https://www.uncut.co.uk/reviews/paul-weller-as-is-now-10906/ viewed 10 August 2021.

Maultsby, P.K. (1985) 'West African Influences and Retentions in U.S. Black Music: A Sociocultural Study', in I.V. Jackson (ed.), *More than Dancing: Essays on Afro-American Music and Musicians*, Westport, CT: Greenwood Press.

McNamee, P. (2005) Paul Weller: As Is Now, *New Musical Express* [online], 7 October, https://www.nme.com/reviews/reviews-paul-weller-7796-312523 viewed 10 August 2021.

McNeill Whalley, P. (1977) 'Album Review of in the City', *New Musical Express*, 14 May, 33.
Merriam, S.B., Johnson-Bailey, J., Lee, M., Key, Y., Ntseane, G. and Muhamad, M. (2001) 'Power and Positionality: Negotiating Insider/Outsider Status within and across Cultures', *International Journal of Lifelong Education* 20, (5), 405–416.
Meyer, L.B. (1956) *Emotion and Meaning in Music*, Chicago: University of Chicago Press.
Middleton, R. (1990) *Studying Popular Music*, Maidenhead: Open University Press.
Miles, B. (1997) *Paul McCartney: Many Years from Now*, London: Secker and Warburg.
Mills, J. (2020) 'It's A Happening Thing', Interview with Paul Weller, *Shindig!*, 103, 12–13.
Moffatt, J. (1978) *Teaching the Universe of Discourse*, Boston, NH: Houghton Miflin Co.
Mongredien, P. (2021) Fat Pop (Volume One) Review, *The Guardian* [online] 16 May, https://www.theguardian.com/music/2021/may/16/paul-weller-fat-pop-volume-1-one-review viewed 22 May 2021.
Moody, P. (2020) 'A Kind Revolution', in J. Robinson (ed.), *The Uncut Ultimate Music Guide: Paul Weller*, 126–127.
Moore, A. (2012) *Song Means: Analysing and Interpreting Popular Song*, Abingdon: Routledge.
Moorefield, V. (2010) *The Producer as Composer: Shaping the Sounds of Popular Music*, Cambridge, MA: MIT Press.
Morley, P. (1979) 'O Lucky Man!', Interview with John Peel, *New Musical Express*, 18 August, 26–27.
Munn, I. (2016) *Mr. Cool's Dream, third* edition, St. Andrews: Wholepoint Publications.
Negus, K. (1996) *Popular Music in Theory: An Introduction*, Cambridge: Polity Press.
Nettl, B. (2005) *The Study of Ethnomusicology: Thirty-One Issues and Concepts, second* edition, Champaign, IL: University of Illinois Press.
New Musical Express (NME) (1983) *The Big Wind Up*, 24 December, 22–34.
Ogg, A., Foxton, B. and Buckler, R. (1993) *The Jam: Our Story*, Chessington: Castle Communications.
Orwell, G. (1945) *Animal Farm*, London: Secker and Warburg.
Osborne, R. (2015) *'Pop Modernism'*, blog posted [online], 1 June, http://richardosbornevinyl.blogspot.com viewed 1 May 2018.
Paphides, P. (2021) 'Fat Pop (Volume 1)', Review and Interview, *Uncut*, 331, 16–19.
Parkes, T. (1993) 'Review of Wild Wood', *Melody Maker*, 4 September, 35.
Peart, A. (2019) 'Saturday's Kids', Interviews with Bruce Foxton and Rick Buckler, *Vive Le Rock!* 68, 44–49.
Perone, J. (2007) *The Words and Music of David Bowie*, Westport, CT: Praeger.
Petruisch, A. (2019) 'The Survival of Iggy Pop', *New Yorker* [online] 2 September, https://www.newyorker.com/magazine/2019/09/02/the-survival-of-iggy-pop viewed 21 November 2020.
Porter, R. (2000) *London: A Social History*, London: Penguin.
Poulsen, H.B. (2005) *77 The Year of Punk and New Wave*, London: Helter Skelter.
Quantick, D. (1992) 'If the Capuccino Fits', Review of Paul Weller LP, *New Musical Express*, 25 August, 32.

Quantick, D. (2020) 'Sonik Kicks', in J. Robinson, (ed.), *The Uncut Ultimate Music Guide: Paul Weller*, 122–123.

Rachel, D. (2013) *Isle of Noise: Conversations With Great British Songwriters*, London: Picador.

Rachel, D. (2016) *Walls Come Tumbling Down: The Music and Politics of Rock against Racism, 2 Tone and Red Wedge*, London: Picador.

Raphael, A. (2008) Paul Weller, 22 Dreams. *The Guardian* [online], 18 May, https://www.theguardian.com/music/2008/may/18/popandrock.shopping2 viewed 10 August 2020.

Records in My Life (2017) Paul Weller, RIML TV [online], 23 October, https://www.youtube.com/watch?v=-Mw2POG0Fks viewed 27 August 2019.

Regelski, T.A. (2009) 'Conclusion: An End Is a Beginning', in T. A. Regelski (ed.) *Music Education for Changing Times*, Dordrecht: Springer, 187–194.

Reynolds, S. (1987) 'Review of the Cost of Loving', *Melody Maker*, 7 February, 37.

Reynolds, S. (2000) 'Kosmic Dance: Krautrock and Its Legacy', in P. Shapiro (ed.), *Modulations: A History of Electronic Music/Throbbing Words on Sound*, New York: Distributed Art Publishers Inc.

Reynolds, S. (2005) 'Noises', in C. Cox and D. Warner (eds.), *Audio Culture: Readings in Modern Music*, New York: Continuum.

Roads, C. (2015) *Composing Electronic Music: A New Aesthetic*, Oxford University Press.

Robinson, J. (2000) 'Review of Heliocentric', *New Musical Express*, 15 April, 51.

Rogan, J. (2001) *Neil Young: Zero to Sixty, second* edition, London: Calidore.

Russell, D. (1997) *Popular Music in England 1840-1914: A Social History, second* edition, Manchester University Press.

Russolo, L. (1913) 'The Art of Noises: Futurist Manifesto', in C. Cox and D. Warner (eds.), *Audio Culture: Readings in Modern Music*, New York: Continuum.

Rutherford-Johnson, T. (2017) *Music after the Fall: Modern Composition and Culture Since 1989*, Oakland, CA: University of California Press.

Sawyer, M. (2010) 'Paul Weller: I Am Aware of the Words "national treasure" Being Attached to me', Interview in *The Guardian*, 28 March, 12.

Sawyer, M. (2021) Interview With Paul Weller, *The Guardian*, 2 May, 8–13.

Schechner, R. (1998) *Performance Theory, revised* edition, New York: Routledge.

Schleifer, R. (2011) *Modernism and Popular Music*, Cambridge: Cambridge University Press.

Scott, M. (2012) *Adventures of a Waterboy*, London: Jawbone Press.

Shaar Murray, C. (1978) 'The Jam Sell Out', Review of All Mod Cons, *New Musical Express*, 28 October, 43.

Shank, B. (2001) 'From Rice to Ice: the Face of Race in Rock and pop', in S. Frith, W. Straw and J. Street (eds.), *Cambridge Companion to Pop and Rock*, Cambridge: CUP.

Shuker, R. (2008) *Understanding Popular Music Culture, third* edition, Abingdon: Routledge.

Shuker, R. (2017) *Popular Music: The Key Concepts, second* edition, Abingdon: Routledge.

Siebert, V. (2014) 'Modernism vs. Classicism: Paul Weller Interviewed', *The Quietus* [online], 30 June, http://thequietus.com/articles/15640-paul-weller-interview viewed 1 May 2018.

Simon, H.A. (1971) 'Designing Organisations for an Information-Rich World', in M. Greenburger (ed.), *Computers, Communications and the Public Interest*, Baltimore, MD: John Hopkins Press.

Simonelli, D. (2013) *Working Class Heroes: Rock Music and British Society in the 1960s and 1970s*, Lanham, MD: Lexington Books.

Simpson, D. (2014) 'The Byrds: How We Made Eight Miles High', Interview in *The Guardian*, 16 September, 28.

Sinker, M. (1988) 'Review of Confessions of a Pop Group', *New Musical Express*, 25 June, 41.

Sloboda, J.A. (1985) *The Musical Mind*, London: Oxford University Press.

Snaider Lanser, S. (1981) *The Narrative Act: A Point of View in Prose Fiction*, Princeton, NJ: Princeton University Press.

Snapes, L. (2020) 'Lucinda Williams: I don't Mind Pushing People's Buttons', Interview in *The Guardian* [online], 24 April, https://www.theguardian.com/music/2020/apr/24/lucinda-williams-i-dont-mind-pushing-peoples-buttons viewed 21 November 2020.

Snowball, I. (2017) *Sounds from the Studio*, Penryn: Red Planet.

Snowball, I. and Deabill, S. (2012) *Thick as Thieves: Personal Situations with the Jam*, Tarrytown, NY: Marshall Cavendish Editions.

Solt, A. and Egan, S. (eds.) (1989) *Imagine: John Lennon*, London: Virgin Books.

Sondheim, S. (2010) *Finishing the Hat*, London: Virgin Books.

Spicer, M. (2010) 'Regatta De Blanc: Analysing Style in the Music of the Police', in M. Spicer and J. Covach (eds.), *Sounding Out Pop: Analytical Essays in Popular Music*, Ann Arbor, MI: University of Michigan Press.

Stets, J.E. and Burke, P.J. (2000) 'Identity Theory and Social Identity Theory', *Social Psychology Quarterly* 63(3), 224–237.

Stewart, T. (1979) 'Aloneagainorwhat?', Review of Setting Sons, *New Musical Express*, 10 November, 43.

Stokes, M. (2003) 'Talk and Text: Popular Music and ethnomusicology', in A. Moore *Analysing Popular Music*, Cambridge: Cambridge University Press, 218–239.

Street, J. (2006) 'The Pop Star as Politician: From Belafonte to Bono, from Creativity to Conscience', in I. Peddie (ed.), *The Resisting Muse: Popular Music and Social Protest*, Farnham: Ashgate.

Stubbs, D. (1995) 'Review of Stanley Road', *Melody Maker*, 13 May, 27.

Sutherland, S. (1992) 'Review of Paul Weller LP', *Melody Maker*, 29 August, 38.

Sweeting, A. (1982) 'Get Weller Soon', Review of The Gift, *Melody Maker*, 6 March, 17.

Tajfel, H., Turner, J.C., Austin, W.G. and Worchel, S. (1979) 'An Integrative Theory of Intergroup conflict', in W.G. Austin and S. Worchel (eds.), *The Social Psychology of Inter-Group Relations*, Monterey, CA: Brooks/Cole, 33–47.

Theberge, P. (2001) 'Plugged in: Technology and Popular Music', in S. Frith, W. Straw and J. Street (eds.), *Cambridge Companion to Pop and Rock*, Cambridge: Cambridge University Press.

Thrills, A. (1980) 'Down in the Polling Station at Midnight', *New Musical Express*, 19 January, 21

Tingen, P. (2012) Jan 'Stan' Kybert: Producing Paul Weller's Sonik Kicks, *Sound on Sound* [online], June https://www.soundonsound.com/techniques/jan-stan-kybert-producing-paul-wellers-sonik-kicks viewed 25 March 2019.

Townshend, P. (2012) *Who I Am*, London: Harper Collins.

Toynbee, J. (2003) 'Music, Culture and Creativity', in M. Clayton, T. Herbert and R. Middleton (eds.), *The Cultural Study of Music: A Critical Introduction*, New York: Routledge, 102–112.

Trousse, S. (2020) 'Café Bleu', in J. Robinson (ed.), *The Uncut Ultimate Music Guide: Paul Weller*, 58–59.

True, E. (1997) 'Review of Heavy Soul', *Melody Maker*, 21 June, 31.

Trynka, P. (2010) *Starman: David Bowie: The Definitive Biography*, London: Sphere.

Verlinde, J. (2011) Inside Wilco's Loft, *Fretboard Journal* [online], April, https://www.fretboardjournal.com/features/inside-wilcos-loft/ viewed 19 May 2021.

Vygotsky, L.S. (2004) 'Imagination and Creativity in Childhood', *Journal of Russian and East European Psychology* 42 (1), 7–97.

Warner, T. (2016) 'Approaches to Analysing Recordings of Popular Music', in D. Scott (ed.), *The Ashgate Research Companion to Popular Musicology*, Aldershot: Ashgate.

Watson, L. and Hewitt, P. (1995) *Paul Weller: Days Lose Their Names and Time Slips Away 1992-1995*, London: Boxtree.

Watts, P. (2018) Paul Weller - True Meanings, *Uncut* [Online] 18 September, https://www.uncut.co.uk/reviews/paul-weller-true-meanings-107340/ viewed 10 August 2021.

Weight, R. (2013) 'How Mod Became the Mainstream', *The Telegraph*, 26 March, 19.

Weisberg, R.W. (1986) *Creativity*, New York: Freeman.

Weller, P. (1978) 'Singles Review', *Melody Maker*, 4 November, 18.

Weller, P. (1982) Trans-Global Unity Express Tour Programme Notes.

Weller, P. (2005) 'Mod Anthems', Playlist Curated for Q Magazine, in T. Kessler (ed.), *Q Legends: Paul Weller*, 57.

Weller, P. (2010) *Suburban 100*, London: Arrow Books.

Welsh, I. (2010) Sleeve notes for Wake up the Nation, *deluxe* edition, Island Records Group.

West, A. (2016) *The Art of Songwriting*, London: Bloomsbury.

West, D. (2007) 'The Rhythm Interview: Steve White', *Rhythm Magazine*, 139, 46–49.

Westcott Grant, K. (2020) Political Activism and Music in 2020, *Forbes* [online], 16 January https://www.forbes.com/sites/kristinwestcottgrant/2020/01/16/political-activism-and-music-in-2019/?sh=3c240abf7200 viewed 23 April 2021.

Whaley, R. (1976) 'Review of the Damned at Liverpool Erics', *Sounds*, 4 December, 44.

What's in my Bag? (2013) Paul Weller goes shopping at Amoeba Records, Hollywood, Episode 274, [online] 5 March, https://www.youtube.com/watch?v=-Mw2POG0Fks viewed 27 August 2019.

White, J. (2008) *London in the 20th Century*, London: Vintage.

White, S. (2020) MA Music Interview, Leeds Conservatoire, 20 October.

Whiteley, S. (2006) 'Patti Smith: The Old Grey Whistle Test', in BBC-2 TV, May 11, 1976, in I. Inglis (ed.), *Performance and Popular Music: History, Place and Time*, Aldershot: Ashgate.

Whyton, T. (2013) *Beyond a Love Supreme: John Coltrane and the Legacy of an Album*, Oxford: Oxford University Press.

Wilderom, R. and Van Venrooij, A. (2019) 'Intersecting Fields: The Influence of Proximate Field Dynamics on the Development of electronic/dance Music in the US and UK', *Poetics*, 77, 1 September.

Wilson, J. (2008) Chasing the Blues Away, *The New Statesman*, [online] 15 May, https://www.newstatesman.com/music/2008/05/paul-weller-jam-album-song viewed 20 March 2021.

Wilson, L. (2018) It's A Mod, Mod, Mod, Mod World: The Rise of The Jam', *Record Collector*, 290, 74–84.
Wilson, L. (2019a) 'The Paul Weller Movement', in Gilbert, P. (ed.), *Mojo: The Collectors' Series: Modern Classics 1991-2019*, 12.
Wilson, L. (2019b) 'Time for Truth', in Gilbert, P. (ed.) *Mojo: The Collectors' Series: Modern Classics 1991-2019*, 14–22.
Winterson, J., Bricheno, T. and Nickol, P. (2003) 'Style and Structure', in J. Winterson (ed.), *Pop Music: The Text Book*, *revised* edition, London: Edition Peters.
Wiseman-Trowse, N. (2014) 'You Should Try Lying More: The Nomadic Impermanence of Sound and Text in the Work of Bill Drummond', in R. Carroll and A. Hansen (eds.), *Lit-Pop: Writing and Popular Music*, London: Routledge.

Recorded sources

1975, The (2020) Notes on a Conditional Form (CD) Dirty Hit/Polydor.
Adam and the Ants (1978) Young Parisians (Vinyl) Decca.
Allen, L., (2006) LDN (CD) Regal.
Allen, L. (2006) Smile (CD) Regal.
Allison, M. (1957) Back Country Suite (LP Vinyl) Prestige.
Animals, The (1965) We Gotta Get Out of This Place (Vinyl) Columbia Graphophone.
Arcade Fire (2010) The Suburbs (CD) Merge/City Slang/Mercury.
Avalanches, The (2016) Wildflower (CD) Modular/XL/Astralwerks.
Baker, A. (1983) The Songstress (CD) Elektra.
Banton, B. (1995) 'Til Shiloh (CD) Loose Cannon/Island.
Beach Boys, The (1966) Pet Sounds (LP Vinyl) Capitol.
Beatles, The (1963) She Loves You (Vinyl), Parlophone.
Beatles, The (1963) I Want To Hold Your Hand (Vinyl), Parlophone.
Beatles, The (1964) A Hard Day's Night (LP Vinyl) Parlophone.
Beatles, The (1965) Rubber Soul (LP Vinyl), Parlophone.
Beatles, The (1966) Paperback Writer (Vinyl) Parlophone.
Beatles, The (1966) Revolver (LP Vinyl) Parlophone.
Beatles, The (1967) Penny Lane (Vinyl) Parlophone.
Beatles, The (1967) Strawberry Fields Forever (Vinyl) Parlophone.
Beatles, The (1967) Sargent Pepper's Lonely Hearts Club Band (LP Vinyl) Parlophone.
Beatles, The (1968) Lady Madonna (Vinyl) Parlophone.
Beatles, The (1968) Magical Mystery Tour (LP Vinyl) Parlophone.
Beatles, The (1968) The White Album (LP Vinyl) Apple.
Beatles, The (1969) Abbey Road (LP Vinyl) Apple.
Bee Gees, The (1977) How Deep is Your Love (Vinyl) RSO.
Bowie, D. (1972) The Jean Genie (Vinyl) RCA.
Bragg, B. (1983) A New England (Vinyl) Utility.
Bragg, B. (1985) Between the Wars (Vinyl) Go! Discs.
Brown, J. (1965) I Feel Good (Vinyl) King.
Brown, J. (1970) Get Up (I Feel Like Being a) Sex Machine (vinyl), King.
Byrds, The (1966) Eight Miles High (Vinyl) Columbia.
Chairman of the Board (1970) In Session (LP vinyl) Invictus.
Charles, R. (1961) Hit the Road Jack (Vinyl) ABC-Paramount.
Charles, R. (1962) Modern Sounds in Country and Western Music (LP Vinyl) ABC-Paramount.

Chi-lites, The (1973) Stoned Out of My Mind (Vinyl) Brunswick.
Chords, The (1954) Sh-boom (Vinyl) Cat Records.
Clash, The (1977) The Clash (LP Vinyl), CBS.
Clash, The (1977) Complete Control (Vinyl), CBS.
Clash, The (1978) White Man in Hammersmith Palais (Vinyl) CBS.
Clash, The (1978) Give Em Enough Rope (LP Vinyl) CBS.
Clash, The (1979) London Calling (LP Vinyl) CBS.
Clayton, W. (1985) Love Pain (Vinyl) Kirstee.
Coltrane, J. (1963) India (Vinyl) Impulse!
Coltrane, J. (1965) A Love Supreme (LP Vinyl) Impulse!
Conley, A. (1967) Sweet Soul Music (Vinyl) Atco.
Corea, C. (1976) The Leprechaun (LP Vinyl) Polydor.
Cooke, S. (1964) A Change is Gonna Come (Vinyl) RCA Victor.
Cooke, S. (1965) Shake (LP Vinyl) RCA Victor.
Cream (1967) Sunshine of Your Love (Vinyl) Reaction/Polydor.
Crow, S. (1997) Home (CD) A&M.
Crowded House (1991) Woodface (CD) Capitol.
Culture Club, The (1984) War Song (Vinyl) Virgin Records.
Damned, The (1976) New Rose (Vinyl) Stiff Records.
Doctor Feelgood (1975) Down by the Jetty (LP Vinyl) United Artists.
Doctor John (1968) Gris-Gris (LP Vinyl) Atco.
Drake, N. (1969) Five Leaves Left (LP Vinyl) Island.
Drake, N. (1972) Pink Moon (LP Vinyl) Island.
Dury, Ian and the Blockheads (1979) Reasons to be Cheerful Pt.3 (Vinyl) Stiff Records.
Dylan, B. (1963) The Times They Are a-Changin' (LP Vinyl) Columbia.
Dylan, B. (1964) Another Side of Bob Dylan (LP Vinyl) Columbia.
Dylan, B. (1967) John Wesley Harding (LP Vinyl) Columbia.
Dylan, B. (1970) Self Portrait (LP Vinyl) Columbia.
Elvis Costello and the Attractions (1979) Oliver's Army (Vinyl) Radar.
Elvis Costello and the Attractions (1979) What's So Funny 'bout Peace, Love and Understanding (Vinyl) Columbia.
Elvis Costello and the Attractions (1981) Good Year for the Roses (Vinyl) F-Beat.
Elvis Costello and the Attractions (1983) Punch the Clock (LP Vinyl), F-Beat.
Eno, B. (1975) Discreet Music (LP Vinyl) Obscure.
Eno, B. (1978) Ambient 1: Music for Airports (LP Vinyl) EG/Polydor/PVC.
Eno, B. (1978) Music for Films (LP Vinyl) EG.
Everly Brothers, The (1958) All I Have to Do is Dream (Vinyl) Cadence.
Fall, The (1980) Fiery Jack (Vinyl) Step-Forward.
Fitzgerald, E. (1956) Anything Goes (Vinyl) Verve.
Fitzgerald, E. (1956) Love for Sale (Vinyl) Verve.
Floyd, E. (1967) Big Bird (Vinyl) Stax.
Four Tops, The (1966) Loving You is Sweeter Than Ever (Vinyl) Motown.
Frankie Goes to Hollywood (1984) Two Tribes (Vinyl) ZTT.
Free (1970) Fire and Water (LP Vinyl) Island.
Funkadelic (1978) One Nation Under a Groove (Vinyl) Warner Bros.
Gaye, M. (1964) How Sweet it is to be Loved by You (Vinyl) Tamla.
Gaye, M. and Terrell, T. (1967) Ain't No Mountain High Enough (Vinyl) Tamla.
Gaye, M. (1971) What's Going On (LP Vinyl) Motown.

Hancock, H. (1968) Speak Like a Child (LP Vinyl) Blue Note.
Hardin, T. (1967) Tim Hardin 2 (LP Vinyl) Verve Forecast.
Hefti, N. (1966) Batman Theme (Vinyl) RCA Victor.
Holloway, B. (1964) Every Little Bit Hurts (Vinyl) Tamla.
Howlin' Wolf (1964) Killing Floor (Vinyl) Chess.
Impressions, The (1965) Meeting Over Yonder (Vinyl) ABC-Paramount.
Isley Brothers (1976) Harvest for the World (Vinyl) T-Neck.
Jackson, M. (1979) Off the Wall (Vinyl) Epic/CBS.
Jam, The (1977) In the City (LP Vinyl) Polydor.
Jam, The (1977) All Around the World (Vinyl) Polydor.
Jam, The (1977) Back in My Arms Again (Vinyl) Polydor.
Jam, The (1977) This is the Modern World (LP Vinyl) Polydor.
Jam, The (1978) All Mod Cons (LP Vinyl) Polydor.
Jam, The (1978) Strange Town (Vinyl) Polydor.
Jam, The (1979) When You're Young (Vinyl) Polydor.
Jam, The (1979) Setting Sons (LP Vinyl) Polydor.
Jam, The (1980) Sound Affects (LP Vinyl) Polydor.
Jam, The (1980) Going Underground (Vinyl) Polydor.
Jam, The (1980) Start! (Vinyl) Polydor.
Jam, The (1980) That's Entertainment (Vinyl) Polydor.
Jam, The (1981) Pop Art Poem (Flexidisc) Flexipop issue 002.
Jam, The (1981) Funeral Pyre (Vinyl) Polydor.
Jam, The (1981) Absolute Beginners (Vinyl) Polydor.
Jam, The (1982) The Bitterest Pill (I Ever Had to Swallow) (Vinyl) Polydor.
Jam, The (1982) Move On Up (Vinyl) Polydor.
Jam, The (1982) The Gift (LP Vinyl) Polydor.
Jam, The (1982) Beat Surrender (Vinyl) Polydor.
Jam, The (1997) Direction Reaction Creation (CD) Polydor.
James, E. (1967) I'd Rather Go Blind (Vinyl) Cadet.
Joy Division (1979) Transmission (Vinyl) Factory.
Johnson, L.K. (1984) Making History (LP Vinyl) Island.
Kinks, The (1964) You Really Got Me (Vinyl), Pye.
Kinks, The (1965) Tired of Waiting For You (Vinyl) Pye.
Kinks, The (1966) Dedicated Follower of Fashion (Vinyl) Pye.
Kinks, The (1966) Sunny Afternoon (Vinyl) Pye.
Kinks, The (1967) Waterloo Sunset (Vinyl) Pye.
Kinks, The (1967) Something Else (LP Vinyl) Pye.
Kinks, The (1968) The Kinks Are the Village Green Preservation Society (LP Vinyl) Pye.
Lennon, J. (1970) Instant Karma! (Vinyl) Apple.
Libertines, The (2002) Up the Bracket (CD) Rough Trade.
Little Richard (1957) Here's Little Richard (LP Vinyl) Specialty.
Lowe, N. (1994) The Impossible Bird (CD) Demon/Upstart.
Madness (1979) My Girl (Vinyl) Stiff Records.
Madness (1980) Baggy Trousers (Vinyl) Stiff Records.
Madness (1981) Grey Day (Vinyl) Stiff Records.
Madness (1981) Shut Up (Vinyl) Stiff Records.
Madness (1982) Driving in my Car (Vinyl) Stiff Records.
Martha and the Vandellas (1963) Heatwave (Vinyl) Gordy.

Martyn, John and Beverley (1970) Road to Ruin (LP Vinyl) Island.
Mayfield, C. (1971) Move on Up (Vinyl) Curtom.
Murvin, J. (1976) Police and Thieves (Vinyl) Wildflower/Island.
Neil, F. (1966) Fred Neil (LP Vinyl) Capitol.
Neu! (1972) Neu! (LP Vinyl) Brain Records.
Nelson, W. (1975) Red Headed Stranger (LP Vinyl) Columbia.
New Order (1983) Blue Monday (Vinyl) Factory.
Newman, R. (1970) Old Kentucky Home (Vinyl) Reprise.
Newman, R. (1974) Good Old Boys (LP Vinyl) Reprise.
Niles, J.J. (1941) Black is the Color, Trad.
Orbison, R. (1964) Oh, Pretty Woman (Vinyl) Monument.
Palmer, R. (1978) Every Kinda People (Vinyl) Island.
Pickett, W. (1965) In the Midnight Hour (Vinyl) Atlantic.
Pogues, The (1984) Dark Streets of London (Vinyl) Stiff Records.
Pogues, The (1985) Rum, Sodomy and the Lash (LP Vinyl), Stiff Records.
Pogues, The (1986) Poguetry in Motion (Vinyl), Stiff Records.
Pogues, The (1989) Peace and Love (CD), Island.
Porter, C. (1930) Love for Sale, first performed by Kathryn Crawford in The New Yorkers.
Porter, C. (1934) Anything Goes, first performed by Ethel Merman in Anything Goes.
Pretenders, The (1981) Thin Line between Love and Hate (Vinyl) Sire.
Prine, J. (1971) Angel from Montgomery (Vinyl) Atlantic.
Public Enemy (1989) Fight the Power (CD) Motown.
Public Image Limited (1978) First Issue (LP Vinyl) Virgin.
Public Image Limited (1980) Metal Box (LP Vinyl) Virgin.
Radiohead (1995) Fake Plastic Trees (CD) Parlophone/Capitol.
Radiohead (1997) Paranoid Android (CD) Parlophone/Capitol.
Ramones (1976) Blitzkrieg Bop (Vinyl) Sire/ABC.
Rodgers, R. and Hart, L. (1940) Bewitched, Bothered and Bewildered, first performed by Vivienne Segal in the musical Pal Joey.
Rodriguez (1970) Sugar Man (Vinyl) Sussex.
Rolling Stones, The (1966) I Can't Get No Satisfaction (Vinyl) Decca.
Rolling Stones, The (1966) Aftermath (LP Vinyl) Decca.
Rolling Stones, The (1967) Between the Buttons (LP Vinyl) Decca.
Rolling Stones, The (1968) Jumpin' Jack Flash (Vinyl) Decca.
Rolling Stones, The (1971) Sticky Fingers (LP Vinyl) Rolling Stones.
Rolling Stones, The (1969) Exile on Main Street (LP Vinyl) Rolling Stones.
Saint Etienne (1993) So Tough (CD) Heavenly.
Savoy Motel (2016) Savoy Motel (CD) Whats Yr Rupture?
Siouxsie and the Banshees (1978) Hong Kong Garden (Vinyl) Polydor.
Sea, D. (1984) Night after Night (Vinyl) Crown Limited Records.
Sex Pistols, The (1976) Anarchy in the UK (Vinyl) EMI.
Sex Pistols, The (1977) God Save the Queen (Vinyl) Virgin, A&M.
Shirelles, The (1960) Will You Love Me Tomorrow (Vinyl) Scepter.
Simon and Garfunkel (1966) The Sounds of Silence (LP Vinyl) Columbia.
Simone, N. (1958) My Baby Just Cares for Me (Vinyl) Bethlehem.
Small Faces (1966) Small Faces (LP Vinyl) Immediate.
Small Faces (1967) Itchycoo Park (Vinyl) Immediate.

Smith, P. (2002) Land (CD) Arista.
Smiths, The (1984) William, It Was Really Nothing (Vinyl), Rough Trade.
Smiths, The (1986) Panic (Vinyl) Rough Trade.
Smokey Robinson and the Miracles (1964) My Girl (Vinyl) Gordy.
Smooth, J. (1987) Promised Land (Vinyl) DJ International.
Specials, The (1979) Gangsters (Vinyl) 2 Tone.
Springsteen, B. (1975) Born to Run (Vinyl) Columbia.
Springsteen, B. (1978) Darkness on the Edge of Town (LP Vinyl) Columbia.
Springsteen, B. (1984) Born in the USA (Vinyl) Columbia.
Squeeze (1981) Labelled with Love (Vinyl) A&M.
Squeeze (1981) Tempted (Vinyl) A&M.
Squeeze (1982) Black Coffee in Bed (Vinyl) A&M.
Starr, E. (1970) War (Vinyl) Gordy.
Sting (1985) Russians (Vinyl) A&M.
Stockhausen, K.H. (1954) Klavierstuck V, first performed in Darmstadt by Marcelle Mercenier.
Stockhausen, K.H. (1967) Hymnen (LP Vinyl) Deutsche Grammophon.
Stravinsky, I. (1913) The Rite of Spring, first performed by Ballets Russes in Paris, 29 May.
Style Council, The (1983) Money Go Round (Vinyl) Polydor.
Style Council, The (1983) A Solid Bond in Your Heart (Vinyl) Polydor.
Style Council, The (1983) Introducing the Style Council (LP Vinyl) Polydor.
Style Council, The (1984) Café Bleu (LP Vinyl) Polydor.
Style Council, The (1984) Groovin' (Vinyl) Polydor.
Style Council, The (1985) Soul Deep (Vinyl) Polydor.
Style Council, The (1985) Our Favourite Shop (LP Vinyl) Polydor.
Style Council, The (1986) Have You Ever Had It Blue (Vinyl) Polydor.
Style Council, The (1987) The Cost of Loving (LP Vinyl) Polydor.
Style Council, The (1987) Wanted (Vinyl) Polydor.
Style Council, The (1988) Confessions of a Pop Group (LP Vinyl) Polydor.
Style Council, The (1989) Promised Land (Vinyl) Polydor.
Style Council, The (1989) Long Hot Summer '89 (Vinyl) Polydor.
Style Council, The (1998) Modernism: A New Decade (LP Vinyl) Polydor.
Suede (1992) The Drowners (Vinyl) Nude.
Suede (1993) So Young (Vinyl) Nude.
Supremes, The (1964) Where Did Our Love Go (Vinyl) Motown.
Supremes, The (1965) Back in My Arms Again (Vinyl) Motown.
Supremes, The (1966) You Can't Hurry Love (Vinyl) Motown.
T Rex (1972) The Slider (LP Vinyl) T Rex Wax Co.
Tame Impala (2012) Lonerism (CD) Modular.
Thomas dgx yhl (2020) Glory to Hong Kong, online forum LIHKG.
Thompson, R. (1991) Rumor and Sigh (CD) Capitol.
Traffic (1967) Mr. Fantasy (LP Vinyl) Island.
Traffic (1968) Traffic (LP Vinyl) Island.
Undertones, The (1978) Teenage Kicks (Vinyl) Sire.
Various Artists (2006) Tropicalia: A Brazilian Revolution in Sound (Vinyl) Soul Jazz.
Verdi, G. (1853) La Traviata, first performed at Teatro La Fenice, Venice, 6 March.
Waits, T. (1978) Blue Valentine (LP Vinyl) Asylum.

Waits, T. (1983) Swordfishtrombones (LP Vinyl) Island.
Warwick, D. (1982) Heartbreaker (Vinyl) Arista.
Weaver, J. (2017) Modern Kosmology (CD) Fire Records.
Weller, P. (1992) Paul Weller (CD) Go! Discs.
Weller, P. (1993) Wild Wood (CD) Go! Discs.
Weller, P. (1995) Stanley Road (CD) Go! Discs.
Weller, P. (1997) Heavy Soul (CD) Island.
Weller, P. (2000) Heliocentric (CD) Island.
Weller, P. (2002) Illumination (CD) Independiente Records.
Weller, P. (2004) Studio 150 (CD) V2.
Weller, P. (2005) As Is Now (CD) Yep Roc.
Weller, P. (2008) 22 Dreams (CD) Island.
Weller, P. (2010) Wake Up the Nation (CD) Island.
Weller, P. (2012) Sonik Kicks (CD) Island.
Weller, P. (2015) Saturns Pattern (CD) Parlophone.
Weller, P. (2017) A Kind Revolution (CD) Parlophone.
Weller, P. (2018) True Meanings (CD) Parlophone.
Weller, P. (2020) On Sunset (CD) Polydor.
Weller, P. (2020) In Another Room (Vinyl) Ghost Box.
Weller, P. (2021) Fat Pop (Volume One) (CD) Polydor/Solid Bond.
Who, The (1965) My Generation (Vinyl) Brunswick.
Who, The (1965) I Can't Explain (Vinyl) Brunswick.
Who, The (1967) Pictures of Lily (Vinyl) Track.
Who, The (1966) A Quick One (LP Vinyl) Reaction/Polydor.
Who, The (1969) Tommy (LP Vinyl) Track.
Who, The (1970) Live at Leeds (LP Vinyl) Decca/MCA.
Why? (2004) Elephant Eyelash (CD) Anticon.
Wilco (1995) AM (CD) Sire/Reprise.
Williams, L. (1958) Slow Down (Vinyl) Specialty.
Williams, L. (1992) Sweet Old World (CD) Chameleon.
Williams, L. (1998) Car Wheels on a Gravel Road (CD) Mercury.
X Ray Spex (1978) Germ Free Adolescents (Vinyl) EMI.
Young, N. (1992) Harvest Moon (CD) Reprise.
Zombies, The (1968) Odyssey and Oracle (LP Vinyl) CBS.

Film sources

Beatles, The (1968) Magical Mystery Tour, Dir. Dennis O'Dell, Apple Corps/BBC.
Jam, The (2002) The Complete Jam (2xDVD), Universal.
Jam, The (2015) About the Young Idea, Dir. Bob Smeaton, Channel X.
Kinks, The (1975) Starmaker, Dir. Peter Plummer, Granada TV.
Style Council, The (1987) Jerusalem, Dir. Robert Llewelyn, Fulcrum/Polydor/Solid Bond Productions.
Weller, P. (2003) Paul Weller: Live at Braehead (DVD), Independiente/Sanctuary Records Group.
Quadrophenia (1979) (DVD) Dir. Franc Roddam, Universal Pictures.
Weller, P. (2004) Paul Weller: Modern Classics on Film 90-01 (2xDVD), Go! Discs/Universal Island Records.

Weller, P. (2006) As Is Now (DVD), Liberation Entertainment/V2 Music.
Weller, P. (2008) Just a Dream: 22 Dreams – Live (DVD/CD), Universal-Island Records.
Weller, P. (2010) Find the Torch. Dir. Julien Temple, Mrs Grey Productions.
Weller, P. (2019) May Love Travel with You: Live at the Royal Festival Hall, Dir. Joe Connor, Solid Bond Productions Ltd.

Index

Made in the USA
Las Vegas, NV
31 October 2024

c8e590b3-71a8-42db-9932-af3c5c5f111dR01